INDIA CALLING

INDIA
CALLING

AN INTIMATE PORTRAIT OF
A NATION'S REMAKING

ANAND GIRIDHARADAS

TIMES BOOKS
HENRY HOLT AND COMPANY   NEW YORK

Times Books
Henry Holt and Company, LLC
Publishers since 1866
175 Fifth Avenue
New York, New York 10010

Henry Holt® is a registered trademark of
Henry Holt and Company, LLC.

Library of Congress Cataloging-in-Publication Data
Giridharadas, Anand.
    India calling : an intimate portrait of a nation's remaking / Anand Giridharadas.—1st ed.
       p. cm.
    Includes index.
    ISBN 978-0-8050-9177-9
  1. India—Civilization—1947– 2. National characteristics, East Indian.   3. India—
Social life and customs.   4. India—Social conditions—1947–   5. Social change—India.
6. Families—India.   7. Giridharadas, Anand—Family.   8. Giridharadas, Anand—
Travel—India.   9. India—Description and travel.   I. Title.
    DS428.2.G46 2011
    954.05'3—dc22   2010018447

Henry Holt books are available for special promotions and
premiums. For details contact: Director, Special Markets.

First Edition 2011

Designed by Kelly S. Too

Printed in the United States of America
10 9 8 7 6 5 4 3 2 1

To

Mama and Papa and Rukmini,

for

roots and stories, laughter and love

CONTENTS

INDIA CALLING

Dreams

As my flight swooped down toward Bombay, an elderly Indian man leaned over and asked for help with his landing card. We started talking, and he asked why I was visiting India. Actually, I'm moving to India, I told him. His eyes bulged. They darted to my American passport on the tray table and then back up at me.

"We're all trying to go that way," he said after a moment, gesturing toward the plane's tail and, beyond it, the paradisiacal West. "You," he added, as if seeking to alert me to a ticketing error, "you're going this way?"

And so it began.

I was twenty-one and fresh out of college. My parents had left India in the 1970s, when the West seemed paved with possibility and India seemed paved with potholes. And now, a quarter century after my father first arrived as a student in America, I was flying east to make a new beginning in the land they had left.

The first thing I ever learned about India was that my parents had chosen to leave it. They had begun their American lives in a suburb of Cleveland, Ohio, called Shaker Heights. It was a sprawling neighborhood of brick and Tudor houses, set on vast yards, with the duck-strewn ponds, meandering lanes, and ample sidewalks that had lured millions of Americans into suburbia.

In Shaker Heights the rituals of my parents' youth quickly confronted new ones. Suburban Cleveland was not a place where one could easily cling to the Old Country or take refuge in multiculturalism. So they dug in, assimilated, gave my sister and me childhoods with all the American fixin's. Making snowmen with carrot noses. Washing our Toyota Cressida on Sundays, me in diapers working with a watering can. Playing catch with a vinyl baseball mitt. Trying in vain to build a tree house. Catching possums in baited cages. Meandering through summer block parties, where the rules of normal life seemed suspended: the roads were emptied of cars; fire engines rode up and down and could be boarded at will; there were more bubbles and balloons than your cheeks could blow.

Shaker Heights was a warm and generous place. Family was the only community that had mattered in India; in America, my parents discovered the community itself: the people who shared recipes, gave them rides, taught them the idioms they didn't know, brought them food when they were sick. It was perhaps the grace of this welcome that inoculated them against the defensiveness and nostalgia that so often infect immigrants. They still loved India, but they never looked back. They spoke often of "Indian values," but these were abstractions meant to suffuse our being rather than commandments to live in this way or that. They accepted and came to savor the American way of life.

And yet we were unmistakably Indian, too. Indianness in those days was like a secret garden to which the society around us lacked access. You needn't have gone there if you didn't want to, but it was there, a hidden world of mysteries. We had a past that others didn't; we had our little secrets of what we ate and wore when we attended a family wedding; we had dinner table stories about places and people from an almost mythical past. We had history, history being the only thing that America's abundant shores could not offer.

We were raised with a different idea of family: family as the fount of everything, family as more important than friends or schools or teachers could ever be. We were raised with an Indian docility: we didn't hit or fight; we didn't play contact sports such as football or hockey but stuck to swimming and tennis. We didn't—not then and still not today—call our parents by their first names or curse in their presence. We got paid for losing teeth but not for doing chores. ("Should I start charging you for cooking?" my mother would ask.) We wore American clothes around the house and to school, but we were asked to wear Indian clothes for weddings and other important occasions. We ate *baingan ka bharta* and *rajma chawal* and *mutter paneer* on some days and penne with tomato sauce on others. We ate meat only occasionally at home, and usually just chicken, but in restaurants we were free to explore the animal kingdom. My mother observed the Indian festival of *karva chauth*, in which women fast for their husbands' prosperity and well-being; in their American rendition of it, however, my father fasted for my mother, too.

And so I grew up with only a faint idea that another country was also somehow mine. My notion of it was never based on India's history or traditions, its long civilizational parade; it was a first-generation idea of a place in our shared past, nostalgically shared but blessedly past. It came not through anthems and ritual feasts and the taut emotions of an Independence Day, but through the stories we were told at meals and on holidays and the characters within our extended clan. As I conjured up the country, I squeezed these things for all the juice that they possessed, searched for meaning where it may not have been, deduced from personal history the history of a people. I forged a memory of events I didn't witness, from times and places I didn't know.

Reflected from afar, India was late-night phone calls that sparked the fear of a far-off death. It was calling back relatives who could not afford to call us. It was Hindu ceremonies with rice, saffron, and Kit Kat bars arrayed on a silver platter. It was the particular strain of British-public-school-meets-Bombay-boulevard English that my parents spoke, prim and propah. It was the sensible frugality of getting books from the library rather than the bookstore and of cautious restaurant ordering—always one main course less than the number of diners, with the dishes shared communally. It was observing that none of the Indian-Americans around us were professors or poets or lawyers, but rather engineers or doctors or, if particularly rambunctious, economists.

Once every two or three years, we would fly east to India. The country offered a foretaste of itself in New York, in the survivalist pushing and pulling to board an airplane with assigned seats. On the other end of the voyage, coming out of the plane door, the machine-cooled air vanished at our backs, and the hot, dank, subtropical atmosphere drank us in. The lighting went from soft yellow to cheap fluorescent white. I remember the workers waiting in the aerobridge, smaller, meeker, scrawnier than the workers on the other end, laborers with the bodies of ballerinas.

Consumed on these visits east, India was being picked up from the airport by my grandparents in the middle of the night. It was cramming more people into their little Maruti than that car could safely hold. It was cousins who knew how to slide their posteriors forward or backward in the car to make such cramming possible. It was the piping-hot *aloo parathas* that my grandmother unfailingly cooked for us upon arrival. It was sideways hugs with my female relatives that strove to avoid breast contact. It was the chauvinism of retired uncles who probed my aspirations and asked nothing of my sister's. It was the ceaseless chatter among the women of making jewelry, making clothes, making dinner. It was the acceptability of reporting toilet success and toilet failure at the breakfast table.

I had the feeling in those days that we, the departed, were doing India a favor by returning. We used to pack our suitcases with gifts of what could not easily be obtained in India, from Johnnie Walker Black Label whiskey to Stilton cheese to Gap khakis. In a young child, this ferrying of goods fed a notion of scarcity in the motherland, casting us as benefactors from a land of abundance. My cousins used to ask me on these December visits if I felt Indian or American, and I remember sensing how much their self-esteem was riding on my answer. With a proudly defiant tone, I always replied "American," an answer that I knew would hurt them; this was because I felt so, and because I felt that to answer otherwise would be somehow to debase myself, to accept a lower berth in the world.

India felt frozen. It was frozen in poverty, and I sensed, even as a child, that everything was shaped by scarcity: the pushing to get on the airplane, the reluctance of the wealthy to spend the most trivial sums of money, the obsession with lucrative careers and snobbery toward other pursuits. India was frozen in socialist bureaucracy, so that it was advisable to have an uncle working in the ministry if you wanted a phone connection before next year. It was frozen in beliefs: I quickly tired of going to yet another dinner party where yet another retiree would drink one whiskey too many and take me aside to condemn an imperialistic and materialistic America whose foreign policy choices, he seemed to imply, were basically my fault—even though I was ten years old, yawning, and up way past my bedtime. To this day, I cringe every time I hear the words, "Why is your America supporting Pakistan?"

"Yes, Uncle," I feel like saying, "the State Department got the idea from me."

India was not supposed to feel foreign to me. I looked Indian, was raised by Indian parents, mingled in America with their Indian friends, and grew up devouring Indian food, having *rakhi* tied on my wrist by my sister, and wearing fresh clothes and lighting candles every Diwali. But in India all this dissipated, as if these ways of being Indian brought me no closer to India itself.

Inevitably, time soothed some of these surface irritations and culture shocks. What endured was a wordless revulsion, deep and inarticulable, at what seemed to be the wastage of human possibility in India. Here was a great civilization of the world, once among the wealthiest and most powerful of nations, and yet, in ways that I was only beginning to grasp, so many were trapped in their boxes: the schoolchildren with brains crammed full of notes, fearful of voicing an opinion in front of their parents; the elders whose doctrines about marriage and childbearing seldom budged, no matter how the world changed; the women to whom few listened, no matter the wisdom of their words. India, in my limited and impressionistic view, seemed a land of replicated lives, where most people grew up to be exactly like their parents—cracking the same jokes, bearing the same prejudices, pursuing vocations not too far afield.

The place seemed to function on low expectations and almost otherworldly powers of acceptance. The dinner party conversations were dull and repetitive and sprinkled with awkward silences; but people accepted. There was only one television channel, beaming tinny and overacted shows that no one with broader choices would ever watch; but people accepted. The poverty—those children with puffed-out bellies and matted hair on the streets, and whose skin color and facial features were jarringly similar to my own—was bloodcurdling; but people, the poor themselves and my well-off relatives, accepted. Women seemed to accept the normalcy of being told that their skin was too dark, that their weight should be increased or decreased, that they should marry this man or that one. People with vegetarian parents seemed to accept that they, too, must be vegetarian. The children of Hindu refugees from what became Pakistan accepted that it was their duty to carry forward their parents' hatred of Muslims. History was heavy. The old went unquestioned. Resignation choked dreams.

The country that gathered in my mind over the years was contradictory and complex and yet also oversimple: it seemed to be a place kind and decent, generous and sacrificial, repressed and narrow, wretched and hopeless; a land short on dynamism and initiative, long on caution, niggling judgment, subservience, and fear; a land where people didn't come into their own as they did in America; a land that had ultimately failed to persuade my father, who loved it dearly, to stay.

A wall of wet, smoky night air hit me as I came out of the terminal in Bombay. The orange of the streetlamps' glow, ripened by smog, told me at once how far I had come. A quarter century had passed since my parents left India, and now I was reentering it to fulfill promptings of my own.

A year earlier, in 2002, I had visited Bombay and Delhi on a vacation from college. I was traveling alone, not with my family, and for some reason I felt a personal connection with the country for the first time. I saw new flecks in the landscape that suggested a turning: a cousin in Bombay took me to a Barista espresso bar with a guitar hanging on the wall and to a nightclub called J49, packed with fashionable young people drinking and smoking and dancing without care; I found an Internet café near my grandparents' home in Delhi, which made me feel less cut off than on past visits. But it was also that I was growing up, learning about the world, and realizing that India was no longer an embarrassing and frustrating place, but rather one that needed to be understood.

I visited a slum in Delhi where my grandmother did charitable work. In a diary, I wrote of a place that was "visually splendid, meaning economically ravaged," its homes ranging "from upscale brick to middle-class mud to impoverished plastic." When I read my words now, I sense a young man awakening to the reality he has neglected. "So much of the world, so much of what happens, seems irrelevant," I wrote, "when you watch a 4-year-old boy, scantily clad, with bruises on his face, bringing a bottle to the tap and waiting thirstily for replenishment."

I wanted to be a writer after college, as the overwrought prose of my diary suggests, but as graduation neared, I saw no easy way into the profession. With the memory of my visit still fresh, an alternative idea came to me: I could move to India. On a whim, I applied to work at the management-consulting firm McKinsey & Company, where my father had gotten his first job in America. I was offered a position and chose the Bombay office because I loved the city and because I had fewer relatives there. I was determined once in India to escape the cocoon of extended family and pave my own road, to discover my roots on my own terms.

When I landed in Bombay on that orange night, a driver dressed in white was waiting at the airport, holding a placard with my name. He was to bring me to the Peregrine, the McKinsey "guest-house" for out-of-town consultants, where, to save money on hotel bills, the company made employees who worked together by day share apartments by night.

It is frightening to land in a city at night and see it lifeless just when you need proof of its life. The cars had mostly deserted the streets; the workaday ruckus of buying and selling stood suspended; not a restaurant or bar was serving. But I woke up the next morning and gazed down on a heaving, boiling, maximal Bombay. The city was like one of those meals so intricately arrayed on the plate, so intimidating that you hesitate to bite into it: millions of human creatures moving by train, bus, car, and foot through their morning routines, opening shops, sweeping sidewalks, giving money, taking money, stopping for a jolt of morning tea. At first, I enjoyed the small mercies of India from the safety of my room at the Peregrine: cooks who made me omelets and processed my laundry, servants who made my bed. Slowly, it became my base for brief incursions into Bombay. I learned the city through small tasks. I had two suits made at Raymond. I met the few people I knew in town for dinner. I went to see my future office, opened a bank account, and bought a cell phone from a traveling salesman with Nokias stashed in a gray briefcase.

Later I began making my forays into the Bombay throng. The instant I left my home, a glaze of sweat coated me. I dissolved into the city's layers of humanity: the frantic bees of the new middle class, tethered by hands-free devices to their just-bought phones, streaking through the crowd faster than the crowd was willing to move; the lowly but securely employed office clerks, known to their bosses as "peons" or "boys," men carrying plastic bags instead of briefcases, bush shirts untucked, feet spilling out of rubber sandals; the impoverished flotsam of the city who moved slower than the common speed, their black hair rendered brown by a lack of nutrients, begging sometimes but mostly just drifting; the hawkers of fruits and vibrators and books; the touts and the vagabonds; the striving and the resigned; the migrants and the deeply entrenched; the weather-beaten and the freshly perfumed.

As I neared the end of my three comfortable weeks at the Peregrine, granted by McKinsey to help me settle in, I was thrust into reality, which always begins with house hunting. A mustachioed, motorcycle-mounted broker named Salim found me a place within my budget. It was a "PG," a paying-guest apartment, which meant that it was a room in someone's house, sealed off and rented on the black market. It was the size of a spacious bathroom, located in the Churchgate area, and made for a humble home, with its fluorescent light, its plastic counters, its too-small bed, its gritty cockroaches.

But I wouldn't be spending much time in the room anyway. McKinsey's business model is to send young people like me, barely aware of what a business model even is, to work with clients in their far-flung headquarters. You can transform a company, they say, only by inhabiting it, dining with its employees, weaving yourself into its fabric. This was a polite way of saying that I now had to live during the week in Ahmedabad, a textile-weaving industrial city in the state of Gujarat, and return to Bombay (where I knew nobody and had nothing to return to) on weekends. This might have seemed a fair deal to anyone unfamiliar with Ahmedabad. It is the leading city in a puritanical, overwhelmingly vegetarian, prohibition-dry state whose most recent bout of fame was for a days-long extravaganza of religious violence that had killed some two thousand Muslims and scores of Hindus the year before my arrival. To make matters worse, my client was a drug maker whose managers spoke in an indecipherable pharmaceuticalese of APIs and NDAs and DTC marketing and whose mission was about as inspiring as Ahmedabad's nightlife.

In my first days at work in Ahmedabad, I used to go to the restroom as often as possible, just to escape. People spoke a variant of English that I didn't understand: they said they were "on tour" when you called to arrange a meeting (they had not joined the Rolling Stones but were traveling); they pressed three fingers together and asked you to wait "two minutes" (they meant an hour); "Please do the needful," they would say when they wanted you to take care of something; there would be "an S & M meeting with PRP in second half" (an afternoon sales-and-marketing meeting with the chairman, identified by his initials). Further, the man in charge of "S & M" was a tall, razor-bald man named Ganesh, after the Hindu elephant god, who was rumored to wear a pistol tucked into his sock. In meetings, you thought twice before questioning his numbers.

The most mystical new concept, though, was "native place," which I eventually discovered was the village where my ancestors had most recently milked cows, even if "recent" meant the year 1500.

"Where are you from?" a typical conversation would begin.

"Washington, D.C." (My family had left Shaker Heights when I was seven years old and eventually settled just outside the capital, in suburban Maryland.)

"Yes, yes, that is OK." *Pause.* "But where are you *from*?"

"America."

"No, no. That is very good. In fact, my brother is in New Jersey, Trenton. I have been to USA, New York, and California also. Twice." *Pause.* "But what I mean to say is, What is your native place?"

"I was born in Cleveland, Ohio, in the Midwest."

"No, no—your *native place*. Basically, you are an Indian only, no?"

"Yes, yes, of course."

"So what is your native place? That only is what I'm asking."

"My parents grew up in Bombay."

"So, basically, you are a Maharashtrian. But your name, Giridharadas . . ."

"Actually, I'm half Tamil and half Punjabi."

"Tamil and Punjabi!" my interlocutor would exclaim, eyes bulging at the thought of such brazen regional miscegenation. (Tamil Nadu is in the southern extreme of the country, jutting into the Indian Ocean; Punjab is high in the north, abutting Pakistan.) "But how could that be?"

"They met in Bombay."

"So basically—basically, you are a Punjabi, correct?"

"Well . . ."

"Basically, your father is a Punjabi."

"No, my mother is Punjabi."

"OK, I see, I see. So your father is a south Indian?"

"Exactly."

"OK, OK, OK." *Pause. Relief. The pigeon had been pigeon-holed.* "So, basically speaking, you are a south Indian."

"Sure. Whatever you want."

Of course, some of the new language was familiar from my parents' usage—"chockablock full," "prepone," "piping hot"—and now had to be relearned as assiduously as it had been unlearned by a first-generation child eager to downplay his differences in America.

On most days in Ahmedabad I ate a plate of *bhel puri*, tamarind-laced street food, for lunch. On special occasions we did the all-you-can-eat at U.S. Pizza, which was located in a nearby mall and which, name aside, packed as many Indian ingredients and spices into its pies as was chemically possible. Slowly I got used to evening *samosa* breaks, to the incessant male touching and hand holding, to the fact that no one listens to you in India until you are old enough to use a cane. After dusk, the McKinsey team would retire to the hotel. Most of my Indian colleagues were graduates of the same engineering school who had then earned MBAs from the same business school, and they shared an intricate, impenetrable culture. This involved several men sitting on a bed, having tossed shoes and socks onto the floor, drinking as their fingers rifled through their toes. They would make raunchy jokes that were not actually that raunchy, because the closest that many of them had been to a woman was the telling of a raunchy joke on a bed with a bunch of other men.

In America, Indians were repressed by the standards of the general population. We were the nerds, the model immigrants who toiled while others indulged. Now in India, though I remained the same person, I was surrounded by people considerably more repressed than I. One colleague told me that he would like to move to America but feared his wife's becoming liberated. Another colleague, nearing thirty, told me that her parents had given her much freedom and that she would never violate it by kissing her fiancé before the wedding. So I took on a new role, which was stunningly unfamiliar to me, of Funmaster. I became the guy who could score alcohol from bootleggers in Gujarat. My colleagues huddled around me on Mondays to ask what scandals I had caused on the weekend, such that I was almost tempted to invent some. I became a jester, a light guy in a serious group, when I had always been on the serious side in America. To be Indian-American in America and Indian-American in India was to be, because of how others saw you, two different people.

On my visits east as a child, we had always been lovingly received by relatives, lavished with food and hugs and time. We were made to feel like heroes. And perhaps I returned to India with a quiet expectation that the country was mine for the taking, that I could reclaim it whenever I wished, that it would welcome me effusively, would need me and make space for me. But the reception was distinctly cooler than I expected. My colleagues felt, and not unfairly, that they had worked harder than I had to reach the same point. I had been admitted to an American university with a double-digit acceptance rate, they to Indian institutions that took in 1 percent of a vast applicant pool. I had traveled the world, eaten in fancy restaurants, studied the mind-widening liberal arts, and done internships, and so I had a facility with aspects of our work that most Indians could not possess: how to conduct myself at a business dinner, or converse confidently with a senior partner, or connect an idea to some recent happening elsewhere in the world. They admired me for this, but they also seemed to resent what felt to them like profiteering from my family's desertion.

But, more than that, India had simply changed. There was a new self-confidence in the country now, and Indians didn't need their émigrés anymore. The country was its own ecology now, was less of a colony, with its own logic and its own pride. Now that it suited me, I was claiming myself as Indian, but Indians were no longer scrambling to claim me. I began to realize that those two-week winter-vacation trips in childhood belonged to a vanishing age when Indians had been cut off from the world and insecure, and they had unfolded in a family context in which love could be taken for granted.

"The skeptics who abandoned ship in the '60s no longer know where either home or heart is," Shobhaa Dé, a popular newspaper columnist, wrote in her recent book *Superstar India*. "'We are Americans,' they once used to boast, proudly telling us deprived folks about the glory that is the USA. Armed with work permits and green cards, they'd arrive for their annual 'staying in touch with the motherland' trips, with countless complaints on their lips." And: "The rest of us would be made to feel diminished on several counts for lacking the 'guts' to pick up lives anew in the land of milk and honey." Now, she noted, the children of the departed were returning because the "party's over" in the West. "But sorry," she says, "nobody wants latecomers to the one happening in India."

One of my clearest impressions about India as a child was that my parents' stories would have been impossible had they stayed. Of course, such a vision was self-serving, for it made a virtue of our displacement. But I looked at my father, a management consultant whose talents would later reveal him to be a masterful writer and wonderfully empathetic teacher, and I knew that in India he could never have dreamed of a career in such things. His father was an engineer whose sons became engineers. They did not question. Likewise, my mother found in America a new liberty to fashion a life undefined by others. She had known little freedom in India to live and spend her time as she pleased. Older relatives would comment on the complexion of her skin. She was scolded about what she ate and what conditions were folklorically believed to flow from her eating habits. In America, where no one judged or supervised her, where my father was too busy eating her cooking to notice whether she was eating it, too, my mother found herself newly enchanted by the taste of food.

They had met in French class, the two of them. My father had never studied the language but needed some bon mots for his job selling Indian trucks and buses in Francophone Africa; my mother, studying French in college, was burnishing her spoken skills. It was he, knowing nothing, who raised his hand constantly, becoming the teacher's pet, and she, knowing it all, who sat in silence, taking note of an eager engineer. The most she allowed herself was to stop her parents' chauffeur-driven car every day at the bus stop where he was waiting and offer him a ride. My father showed none of her restraint. He asked her out again and again, accepting rejection each time. He brought his gold medal from business school to class one day and pulled it slyly out of his pocket to show her. She beamed with admiration, but that was all.

My mother had good reason for her coyness. She was Punjabi, from the very north; he was Tamil, from the very south. She told herself from the beginning that it could never work between them. Even if she let her mind go there, she knew it wouldn't happen in the end. They came from different universes, and she didn't want to lead a good man on.

Her parents were refugees of partition, the traumatic moment in 1947 when the subcontinent was cut in two by the departing British and a chunk of northwestern India became, overnight, the Islamic Republic of Pakistan. Her parents, my Nanu and Nani, grew up in Lahore, in comfortable and educated families that suddenly lost their possessions and their bearings in the world. In a newly independent India, their families, like so many Punjabi families, began anew, educated themselves, slogged their way back into the affluence and respectability that their families had known on the far side of a freshly drawn frontier. Partition's wound had become all but invisible for them by the time my mother was born, in 1955.

My mother's family lived in southern Bombay, the rarefied tip of a rarefied island city, where Nanu worked for Hindustan Lever, the Indian arm of the global Unilever enterprise. They did not feel wealthy, for few did in that age: at times, my grandmother's budgeted grocery money would dry up early, and she had to borrow from the allowance money she had earlier given her daughter. But their world was cosmopolitan and open. Nanu and Nani traveled the world on company-paid business trips, dining in Trafalgar Square in London, seeing the Lido in Paris, even attending a strip show in Amsterdam. Sitting on white cane chairs on his veranda, Nanu would leaf through one newspaper after another and by noon could dissect the politics of any country with more sophistication than many of its own citizens. He wore impeccably cut blazers, and his talk was peppered with "Well, you know, when I was in London in '57 . . ." My grandparents lived in some of Bombay's finest buildings, including a famous seaside property called Bakhtavar. There they entertained my grandfather's equally worldly colleagues with tumblers of whiskey as the velvet whine of Miles Davis's trumpet slid along the walls.

My mother grew up strong. She was a charismatic leader among her peers, staging plays, organizing projects, raising money for charity; she was fiercely protective of her younger brother, with whom she shared a passion for jazz and rock and roll. She read books by Enid Blyton and Jane Austen and W. Somerset Maugham, and listened to the regular Western music hour on All India Radio as well as to Hindi film songs.

But the Westernization and modernity of their setting could be something of an illusion. Miles Davis notwithstanding, my mother was subject to the same culture of *izzat*—honor—that her mother had grown up with in Lahore, eased but never lifted with each successive generation of women. Running through the stories my mother would later tell of India was a theme of stifling, needless repression. As a teenager and even into her twenties, she was seldom allowed to go to parties. On one occasion, the adults let her and her cousins go to a discotheque, but on one condition: they had to take their towering, white-*sari*-clad, widowed grandmother along. (So deprived were they of entertainment that they accepted this deal.) As my mother got older, she was forbidden to go out to meals with male friends. Her mother feared that "society" would talk.

In her twenties, working as a French translator, my mother was the only woman in her office who was not a secretary. Starved gazes would follow her short hair and almond eyes as she navigated the desks. Some men showed interest in her at work, but she gave them no thought, for she quietly assumed that her parents would arrange her marriage and, with it, the rest of her life: in all likelihood to some nice Punjabi boy who would also live in Bombay, whose parents would distantly know her parents, who wouldn't upset the mango cart. The notion of marrying otherwise or, stranger still, migrating to America would have seemed far-fetched to her at the time. It would take a man no less persuasive than my father to bend her mind.

He lived close by and a world apart. He came from a family of Tamil Brahmins, a caste that deserved its reputation for piety verging on sanctimony and purity verging on the total absence of fun. There was little whiskey and even less Miles Davis in their home. His father was a stern, brilliant engineer in the Central Indian Railways who would rise to become one of its highest officials. Thatha was the archetype of the Indian paterfamilias: staunchly protective of his family, emotionally remote, verbally economical, above the fray of daily life, functioning like a chief justice who framed his family's values and monitored their compliance. He married a cheerful wife, tender and docile and eternally absorptive of his temper, who raised their four sons and one daughter with a gentleness and permissiveness that were rare in India.

My father, the middle child, spent much of his childhood in boarding schools, with his parents moving constantly for railway projects, and in those schools he forged a steely self-reliance that was also improbably un-Indian. When at home, he entered and left the apartment as he pleased. He played Ping-Pong and badminton and, in later years, bridge with friends whom his parents did not vet. He was trusted to fend for himself or lean on his siblings for help with homework or getting to after-school activities. I knew, from my mother's stories and those of others, that this style of childhood was not typical, that the norm was guilt-tripping micromanagement. When he would return to India later in life, the deep patience he showed in America would crack when faced with the endless interference in other people's affairs that was so endemically Indian but so foreign to him.

The story of his childhood shaped my earliest narratives about America, where he would one day choose to make his life. He had fallen for America and thrived there, I believed, because he had known freedom and self-determination as a child. I began to see those traits as peculiarly American, and I began to see my father as an American separated at birth from, and later reunited with, a land to which he naturally, psychologically belonged.

His path to America was through education. Education was every generation's duty to its progeny, in the Indian way; the rest was in the progeny's hands. This idea was passed on to my sister and me in America. Sports, television, talking on the phone after school—these were the indulgences of Americans, of a land of plenty. For our family, learning was everything; homework came first; books, being sacred, were never to be left on the floor. But it was a lesson that my father had learned the hard way. In an early grade, he fared poorly in virtually every class. He brought home his report card, which had to be signed. His father flew into a rage, tearing the paper to shreds and spewing words that have remained with my father to this day: "I have no money to leave you. All I can give you is an education." In an instant, my father learned the concept of accountability: no one would tell him how to organize his Thursdays, but if he messed up at year's end, he would suffer for it.

That incident became a point of no return. My father studied like a monk from that day forward, threading the successive needles of India's higher-education system. He trained for a year to get into the Indian Institutes of Technology, the country's ultra-selective engineering school, and he did. He attended a leading business school and topped the class. He struggled, fought, succeeded. But then as he entered his middle twenties, all that drive and energy, the fruits of a bitterly learned lesson, collided with the stagnancy of a country that was not making the fullest use of its people.

It was the 1970s, and he worked in the export division of the Tata conglomerate, based in Bombay. It was a period of social and political turmoil known as the Emergency, in which massive civic unrest had prompted Prime Minister Indira Gandhi to suspend the constitution and take matters into her own hands. The society was tense; mass sterilizations were in progress, opposition leaders languished in jail, and protest was being squelched. But it was not politics that drove my father away. It was that he saw no future in a company where, as in most Indian companies of the era, success favored the tenured. Longevity, not talent, ruled. He saw his superiors, twenty years ahead of him in line, and concluded that he didn't want to spend his life becoming them. The thought was reinforced on those mornings when he trudged through the monsoon to work, as those executives, encased in their company cars, streaked through the water past their drenched trainees.

And yet he began to think about America almost casually, for he was not raised to ponder introspectively. He had heard of people crossing that ocean; some friends were applying to study at Harvard Business School. Why not? A photograph from his farewell party at Tata shows a young man, almost unrecognizable from the seasoned, worldly man who would become my father—beaming, skinny, fresh-faced, innocent, with curly black hair. He is receiving a leather jacket as a parting gift, about to embark on what my young mind would come to see as his actual life: a new beginning in a continent of new beginnings.

My mother had given him no reason to stay. Now he was gone. He wrote her regularly from Boston, and she wrote back. Their friendship deepened. He found a job in Cleveland as graduation approached and returned to India for a summer break before starting his new job in America. Two years had passed, and my parents' correspondence had worked its effects. When at last he asked my mother to marry him on that trip, in the dark of a cinema, it took days of stunned silence before she found her voice, but in the end that voice said "Yes." Her parents, who she feared would oppose her marrying outside the tribe, were broader minded than she realized, and they were impressed by my father's education and temperament. The world was changing, and Harvard graduates, whatever their family histories, were now a marriageable clan of their own. They were wedded ten days later, in my grandparents' home in Bakhtavar, because it was impossible to rent a venue so hurriedly. My father left immediately thereafter for America, alone, while my mother waited months for a visa. Her first steps outside India would come in leaving it for good.

So started their lonely, thrilling adventure. It was not long before my mother was backing a red Oldsmobile, larger than many Indian dwellings, down an icy driveway in Shaker Heights, not long before my father, with his Indian accent, was counseling the executives of America's leading companies. They learned together to drive, to shop in malls, to paint a house. The women in the neighborhood would stop to ask my mother the meaning of the red dot on her forehead; one preempted her by suggesting that it was blood from a hole in her head. She learned from an elderly Jewish neighbor the recipe for cheesecake. They found a regular restaurant they favored, Pearl of the Orient. They shoveled snow for the first time in their lives. They began a family.

What distinguished them in my eyes from the Indians in the

Old Country was their perpetual growth and self-renewal. They discovered new music that was not their own music, new food not their own food. They took up new styles of dressing. They soaked in the world. They allowed their ideas to be upset by better ideas. They clung to pieties that made sense and jettisoned those that didn't. They kept reinventing themselves, discarding the invention, starting anew. My father would become an entrepreneur, then a human-resources executive, then a PhD candidate in his fifties, then a professor. My mother, who began as a homemaker, would learn ceramics, become a ceramics teacher, and then a school administrator. They moved us from Ohio to Paris, then back to Ohio, then to the suburbs of Washington, D.C. They refreshed themselves constantly and, what's more, came to see such refreshment as life's very goal.

It was extraordinary, and ordinary: this is what America did to people, what it always has done. They raised us with this borrowed heritage of self-invention. It was not our Indian heritage, a heritage they sought by and large to preserve. But this was one sphere of American life where the Old Country's values were not permitted to intrude. We were taught to respect our elders as Indians did, to sacrifice for family in the Indian way, to abstain from America's addictive consumption. But we were taught time and again to invent ourselves, to write our own stories. They never pushed us, as other Indian parents did, to become engineers or doctors: to do so would have stripped us of the liberties that they had come to savor for themselves. They selected for us not the math-and-science magnet schools that émigrés adored, but liberally minded private schools that taught painting and history and literature, instilling in us the sense of open-road possibility, of the worthiness of multiple alternative existences, that their own childhoods had lacked. In high school, when I was reading *The Great Gatsby* and becoming enthralled by the novel's seductive, ominous vision of self-invention, my parents were paying steeply for me to become everything India taught the young not to be.

And so it was strange that now I had come to reinvent myself in, of all places, India. It was not a fate that they or I could have imagined. I wondered at times if they felt abandoned, not just by me but also by the invisible forces of history that make countries rise and fall. And I thought to myself: if they left that frozen land for us, if they built from scratch a new life in the West for us, if they slogged, saved, sacrificed to make our lives lighter than theirs, what did it mean when we returned to the place they left?

At first, India had felt alien to me: alien in its crowds and strange phraseology, alien in its probing of my native place, alien in its lack of enthusiasm for my arrival. My old lenses were still in place— India the exhausting, difficult country—and so I saw only what I had always seen. In fact, working at McKinsey shielded me from India's hardships, and I sensed after a time that this was part of the problem. Working in business, I was prancing on the surface of things, not going below and confronting what had fascinated, angered, and humiliated me about India all these years.

Writing would turn out to be a worthier mode of confrontation. I had, of course, put my writing dreams on hold after college. But a year into living in Bombay, I was becoming restless and the dream stirred again. I had written freelance articles for *The New York Times* starting in my last year of high school and continuing through college, and I treasured the paper. I had tried, without success, to write for the *Times* from India fresh from college. One year into living in India, there were new possibilities: the company had acquired full control of the *International Herald Tribune* as its global edition and needed new correspondents in Asia. After some interviews in Paris and New Delhi, and a test article about the names "Mumbai" and "Bombay," I was hired as the company's first Bombay-based correspondent in modern times. I was not sorry to say good-bye to consulting.

I plunged into my new life as a newspaperman and dove deeper than before into India. I filled my shelves with books on India, and on the weekends I would sit with a dozen titles on my bed, as though their presence alone would teach me about caste, Indian democracy, Kashmir, the leading industrialists. I began to study Hindi. I made a list of all the people whom I thought I should know in Bombay and went to see them one by one. I pressed everyone I could for story ideas.

All of this early commotion reflected an insecurity: it was terrific to have gotten the job, but how was I supposed to explain to others a country that I had yet to explain to myself? I eventually realized that ignorance could be my ally: it was my own burning need to understand India that told me where to roam and what to ask. I traveled from one end of the country to another, from Ladakh in the north to Madras in the south, testing the India of my childhood imaginings against the new realities. My work took me to mosques and temples and churches, bleak villages and hungry slums and lavish apartments in Delhi and Bombay, mom-and-pop grocers and glass-and-steel-wrapped software companies. I began my own Indian existence, learning to forge Indian friendships, to love an Indian woman, to haggle in the sweaty bazaar.

India was changing when I arrived, and it continued to change dramatically, viscerally, improbably. The freeze I had sensed as a child seemed to be thawing. It was partly the enormous physical churn: the quantities of earth being moved, the malls and office towers and gated communities being built, the restaurants opening, the factories pumping out cars, the blue jeans being sewn. It was the new verticality of the big cities, the slum dwellers in Bombay moving into towering apartments financed by New York investors, the mushrooming of village backwaters into congested satellite cities such as Gurgaon and Navi Mumbai and Electronics City. It was the villagers who had been moved off their land so that Tata Motors, the once-stagnant company where my father worked, whose lifeless culture had pushed him toward America, could build the world's cheapest car, priced at a little more than $2,000.

To the world, the car became a symbol of India's stirring, and its story hints at what had turned in India. It was not that the old constraints had lifted. The bureaucracy, the corruption, the tax code, the labor laws, the poverty, the potholed roads—these burdens endured. But in my father's day, such hindrances might have been interpreted as an excuse to make shoddy products. Yes, the vehicles are rickety, but India is a very poor country—what to do? A generation later, those same constraints were interpreted in a fresh way. They were unique hardships that gave Tata a special opportunity to build a world-beating car. Because Indian roads were bumpier than the West's, the suspension system had to be even better. Because income levels were low, Tata had to innovate twice as hard to rein in costs—installing one windshield wiper, not two; a hollowed-out steering shaft to save steel; a rear-mounted engine no more powerful than a lawn mower's. It was not so much India's context that had changed. It was a new style of hopeful defiance.

The deepest change that I witnessed in India was not in what its factories were building or what its programmers were coding. It was in the mind, in how people conceived of their possibilities: Indians now seemed to know that they didn't have to leave, as my father had, to have their personal revolutions. Children of the lower castes were hoisting themselves up, one diploma at a time. Women were becoming breadwinners through microcredit and decentralized manufacturing. The young were finding in their cell phones a first zone of privacy and individual identity. Couples were ending marriages no matter what "society" thought, then finding love again. Servants whose mothers and grandmothers had been servants were deciding that their daughters would not be servants, enrolling them in private English-language schools.

Vegetarians were embracing meat, and meat eaters were turning vegetarian, defining themselves by taste and trend, not by caste and faith.

What seemed in decline, in short, was what had most afflicted me about India once: that serene acceptance by people of life as it merely is.

Newspaper and book writers were breathless about the pace and scale of change in "the new India." It was a seductive story of a country unbound, an elephant stirred, a planet-changing model of democracy, pluralism, and growth. The truth was subtler. India's economy was not growing as fast as it could. The country was cutting the poverty rate gently, but nowhere near enough. It was trading anew with the world, but only at a fraction of its potential. It was flexing new muscles overseas militarily and diplomatically, but only sporadically and aimlessly, with little sense of what kind of power it wanted to become. But one thing needed no such qualification: India was erupting in dreams.

It was the dream to own a microwave or refrigerator or motorcycle. The dream of a roof of one's own. The dream to break caste. The dream to bring a cell phone to every Indian with someone to call. The dream to buy out businesses in the kingdom that once colonized you. The dream to marry for love, all the complicated family considerations be damned. The dream to become rich. The dream to overthrow the rich in revolution.

These dreams were brilliant in some instances and in others delusional. They were by turns farsighted and far-fetched, practical and impractical, generous and selfish, principled and cynical, focused and vague, passionate and drifting. They were tempered by countervailing dreams and, as ever in India, by the dogged pull of the past. Some were changing India palpably; others had no chance from the beginning. But that was never the point. It was the very existence of such brazen, unapologetic dreams, and their diffuse flowering from one end of India to the other, that so decisively separated the present from the past—and separated the India my parents had left from the India to which I had now returned.

The Indian revolution was within. It was a revolution in private life, in the tenor of emotions and the nature of human relationships. The very fabric of Indianness—the meaning of being a husband or wife, a factory owner or factory worker, a mother-in-law or daughter-in-law, a student or teacher—was slowly, gently unraveling by the force of these dreams, and allowing itself to be woven in new ways.

Such dreams throbbed aboard the Pushpak Express, which for six dollars in third class ferried migrants from the impoverished northern heartland of India to coastal, moneyed Bombay.

Four years after my initial airplane trip from America, I was setting out on a twenty-four-hour train journey that possessed a certain resonance with that earlier voyage. I had come from privilege in America, whereas the migrants were preparing to join Bombay's vulnerable underclass of taxi drivers and shoe polishers and grocery delivery boys. But in the hope that they placed in the city, in the displacement and bewilderment that they felt, in their exhilaration and fear, they reminded me of the young man who had come to Bombay in 2003 and who was swallowed, as they soon would be, into its terrifying and enthralling maw.

On the platform of the train station in the provincial capital Lucknow, flickering machines offered to weigh passengers for one rupee, about two cents. Burlap sacks sat filled with grain, sent by gaunt farmers on the plains to paunchy shoppers in the cities. Vendors sold toys, eggs, vinyl belts. A woman wearing no shoes fingered her cell phone. Migrants squatted, quietly waiting for the train, as coolies in red jackets flitted across the platform, promising to secure a seat. To ignore them was to risk standing for twenty-four hours. I promptly paid their fifty-rupee charge.

Clickety-clack-clickety-clack, the Pushpak lumbered in. The hordes rose and, with the train still decelerating, mob rule erupted. New acquaintances, in friendly conversation a minute earlier, now pushed one another. An infant, clinging to her father's back, was not spared flying elbows as travelers vied to fling themselves through the door of car Number 05407. When we entered, there was, in fact, a great surplus of space.

The train was a carnival of commerce. Hawkers of *samosas* and *pakodas* and *vadas* came aboard at station stops, screaming their sales pitches. The most impressive vendors were those of tea. As the train hurtled past a green blur of corn and wheat, I saw one standing in the doorway, with neatly parted hair atop his wiry frame. He waited for the perfect moment, then suddenly he jumped.

But he did this to live, not die. Having popped out of the door, he clung to the knobs of the train's exterior with one hand. His other hand clutched a vat of scalding tea. He glided like a climber across the train's skin, one foothold to the next. He crossed the steel beam between the cars like a tightrope walker. Then, arriving at the next car, he repeated his pattern and ducked inside yelling, "*Chai*! *Chai*! Get your hot *chai*!" Such acrobatics were not required on other trains or in that train's first- and second-class cars, which were connected from the inside. But, as if to replicate on board the caste regimes they were fleeing in their villages, the men of third class were cut off from the carriages of the better born.

Deepak Kumar was riding in third class without baggage and without a ticket. He owned nothing more than the pants and plaid shirt he was wearing, his cell phone SIM card (with no phone), his wallet (with no cash), his address book (with no contacts), and a talisman around his neck. He was eighteen, and his light, watery eyes gave him a raw beauty. His fingers were thick and darkened with days' worth of grime. His brown cowlick flailed in the wind as he sat in the train door, watching the landscape fly past.

He had grown up in Delhi. Some years earlier, his mother had died. When his father remarried, the new wife saw him as a hold-over from an ousted regime and began to taunt and beat him. "She swears at me," he said. "She abuses me. She says to me, 'You're not my child.'" His father, working nights as a security guard, was seldom there to intervene. Not long before, Deepak had gone to Lucknow to visit his uncle. While there, he received a phone call from childhood friends who had migrated to Bombay in search of work. When they heard the sadness in his voice, they urged him to join them in the city. At first, he thought the idea fanciful. His father and stepmother relied on his income, and he lived under their roof.

But he called back three days later to say that he would be in Bombay by week's end. His friends promised to meet him at the station. And now, aboard this train, the gravity of his decision was sinking in. He was quieter than the migrants who had gone back and forth many times. He kept to himself. When he began to tell me his story, and got to the part about abuse, his eyes swelled with tears. The migrants around us, hearing this, swung into a routine that almost seemed practiced. Some clowned around to make him laugh. One held his hand. An older migrant named Alok launched into funny stories about his own travails in Bombay. Everyone seemed to say, "We went through this, too. You will survive."

It was Alok's third migration. Deepak's story brought back memories of his own first time. "You see in the movies Bombay, Bombay, Bombay," he said, striking a different cinematic pose at each utterance of the city's name. "So people think, 'I want to go to Bombay.'"

"Bombay is our *sapna nagar*, the place of our dreams," Alok went on. His own dream had once been to become a movie star and work with his greatest idol, the actor Amitabh Bachchan. But now reality had set in. "Everyone goes there and thinks that Amitabh Bachchan will stroke your hair and say, 'Son, how you doing?' But you go there, and you don't even meet him." Alok was wearing a skin-tight zipped-up turquoise sweatshirt. He had worked variously as a parking valet and a waiter. "We are poor, so we don't have any hands to hold, any connections to use, any high-ranking friends," he said. "So we must do it all alone. And nothing in the world can be done all alone."

"Dreams don't go away in Mumbai," he said a few moments later. "They just get smaller."

And yet there were more and more of these dreams. It was said that thirty-one new migrants were arriving in an Indian city every minute. Two out of three Indians still lived in the villages, and this slow emptying was predicted to continue for forty years. It promised to rewire the basic patterns of Indian life: from rural to urban, familial to atomized, from the stoicism of the village to the burning aspiration of the city. The passengers in the railway car were rolling from a warm collectivism into a cool new anonymity. But on the train, in these last few hours, collectivism had its last hurrah. To ride the Pushpak Express was to realize that India remained in so many ways a village-reared nation: the effortless involvement of people in other people's lives, the ceaseless generosity.

The quarters were tight. A baby lay across her mother's lap sipping bottled milk, her legs dangling across a strange man's thigh; he said nothing. Two men facing each other had drifted off to sleep. They appeared not to know each other, but one suddenly woke and nudged the other with his foot to request, wordlessly, some room to rest his legs. The other man reciprocated, and they returned to sleep, their feet now on each other's seats. Throughout the journey passengers switched seats, moved from the benches to the bunks and back. Strangers used one another's backpacks as pillows. As an outsider, I found it hard to tell which clusters of passengers were journeying together and which had met on board.

As the train left the Gangetic Plain, dipping through Kanpur, Bhopal, and Khandwa, then into the wine country of Nashik and toward Bombay, visible misfortune bled into a new rural plenty. The fields turned lusher, plot sizes swelled, and commodities such as wheat gave way to grapes and other cash crops. Bombay released sneak previews of itself with occasional mansions in the middle of the fields, the weekend homes of the wealthy. And before long, we pulled into a station on the margins of the city, and the urban overtook us. Trains whizzed by every minute: the constant click-clack of wheels on tracks; then the slums came, their bright washing on display; and then, at last, the terrifying, exhilarating Bombay throng.

It was into this throng that I had been swept four years earlier. I remembered staring out from the Peregrine's windows and down into the vital, menacing city, too fearful to touch it. I remembered my first bewildered strolls through the crowded streets, the fresh sweat on my arms, and the hope and terror in my heart. As the Pushpak Express pulled in that night, I felt in small measure like a newcomer once again. I wondered what it was like to be a first-time migrant on that train, awakened by roosters all your life, protected by bonds with a dozen relatives, and then flung into this maelstrom of concrete and glass and seawater— this island city of nineteen million people who got here before you.

Upon arriving, Deepak's friends were nowhere to be found. We looked everywhere, on the platform, in the waiting area, in the departure zone. I had heard too many stories of desperate migrants whisked into the grimy underside of the city in circumstances like these. So I took him to the station supervisor and asked about cheap nearby hotels. I gave Deepak my phone number and a few hundred rupees for a room. I kept my phone audible that night. But I imagined him getting absorbed somehow into the rapids of the city. I never expected to hear from him again.

Shortly before nine the next morning, the phone rang. It was Deepak. He said that he had found his friends outside the station the next morning. They had come the night before, failed to see him, and returned again in the morning. Deepak thanked me for the room. Now his Bombay adventure would begin. Once again, I expected him to disappear. But he called again the next day, and then again a few days later, and again and again and again.

He spent the first many days roaming around Bombay with his friends, seeking work as an electrician. Jobs were scarce, and he felt intense pressure to find something quickly. He decided to settle for a steadier, salaried position wrapping takeaway packages in a canteen. He rented a bed in a tiny, dark room, which he shared with other migrants. When I took him to dinner at the Leopold Café six weeks after our train voyage, I learned that he had bought himself English textbooks soon after arriving and was spending an hour or two with them each night after work. He had acquired a taste for tourism, having already visited famous sites, such as Elephanta Island, that I still hadn't seen after four years.

I could track Deepak's progress through the consistency of his cell phone number. When he was doing well, earning regular money, his number stayed the same. When Bombay rattled him, his number changed: it was a pay-as-you-go connection, and if he did not recharge it for several weeks, the number lapsed. He thrived for a time. He quit his first job and found work as an in-house electrician in an affluent apartment block. His number held. But some months later he began to call from a new number each time. I now had half a dozen Deepaks in my phone address book: at first, I labeled them "deepak new" and "deepak new new"; then, becoming wiser, I used "deepak september," "deepak october." At one point he told me that he had been forced out of the electrician job and was at risk of losing his room. He sounded desperate for the first time since that night at the station. I felt an awkwardness as I faced my choices. Should I help him, as I was inclined to do? Or should I guide and advise him but let him figure out Bombay on his own? Would my subsidy help or hurt?

One of India's puzzles is that the country is overrun by workers who cannot find jobs and employers who cannot find workers. I sent an e-mail to friends who ran businesses, asking if they needed someone. Several messages fired back, and Deepak was soon working in a modish home-decor store. I didn't see him for a long spell, and when we finally had dinner again, a year after our initial encounter, he was a new man. He spread his arms across the adjacent chair at the café and slouched in his seat; he seemed cocky, in a nice way; he showed me none of the deference that I had seen on the train. He had saved up thousands of rupees, more than many Indians will ever have in reserve. He was teaching himself conversational English and insisted on answering my questions, posed in Hindi, in the new language he was learning. He said that he had found a girlfriend; he boasted that she was a student at one of Bombay's best colleges, whose father was a businessman with a house on a posh Bombay boulevard. (But I wondered, because he never made her available for a meeting, despite several requests.) Deepak had plans: he was going to bolster his English, then seek a respectable office job. The girl might be flush with love for him now, but Deepak knew that he needed to be bigger to hold her.

I felt great pride in him. He seemed to distill, in a single being, the new sense of hope gusting through India. Some months passed. Then one day I went to buy something at the store where he worked. I hadn't seen him there the last few times, and I asked the manager about him. He took me aside and, measuring his words carefully, told me that Deepak had been fired for stealing. He had taken some bottle openers from the store, which a manager found stashed nearby. They had warned him, but he had stolen again, and so he was dismissed.

And, in hindsight, it was only at this moment that Deepak's story became an all-inclusive story about the new India. Only at this moment did it possess the full range of realities. There was the ambition and confidence and sky-wide sense of possibility.

The tendency toward exaggeration. The faith in self-improvement. The idea of the man without context, the man all his own. The drift toward bewildering big cities. The dashed hopes in those cities. The fraying family and the new rootlessness. Love for its own sake, defiant and boundary breaking. And, amid the dreams of progress, the absence of any restraint on those dreams, of people or rituals or convictions that might have anchored Deepak, might have inspired him to ask whether it was worth it, after all.

The India I grew up with was made in my mind. Now I had to confront the reality of the country it had become. It was a thriving, bustling land, redolent more of the future than the past, hopeful, desperate, wise, naive, raring to go, full of dreams. And it was through my encounters with Indians and their dreams that my old India was slowly revealed to be a country of illusions.

I had forged a whole nation from the fragments of things briefly seen and merely heard. I had absorbed all the simple verities: Indians are simple; Indians know sacrifice; Indians obey elders: the nation as Aesop's fable. But these accustomed ideas were rooted in earth that was moving now, and they were ideas that I believed in part because I needed to believe them, needed some grand narrative to justify, in retrospect, the bend in my family's history.

These ideas had great power to distort, as I had been reminded in the hours before boarding the Pushpak Express. I had gone to see the house in Lucknow where my mother's grandparents once lived. I had tracked down its address and wanted to visit a place whose grandeur lingered in my memories.

My great-grandfather had been a big businessman, and my great-grandmother a woman about town, with a fiery, *sari*-swathed presence that terrified and quickened everyone. My mother used to tell me stories of visiting the Lucknow house as a child, sleeping outdoors with cousins under mosquito nets and the vast sky.

Food flowed like water there, and the corridors bustled with servants; my secondhand memories had them as handsome, hair neatly parted, wearing starched white. Badi Nani, my great-grandmother, with her two patches of undyed hair near her temples to disguise the dyeing of the rest, was known for her gardening skills and her swollen roses. No one entertained as she did, my mother used to say. The Prakashes were somebody in Lucknow, we were told: everyone—carpet sellers, local potentates, other well-born families—would have known us. Men crisscrossed the subcontinent to seek the hands of the Prakash daughters.

A childhood's worth of breakfasts and dinners, of mealtime family reminiscences, had given me a picture of that house. It was a folk memory, inherited rather than directly recalled, but its colors ran vivid in the mind. And now, four decades after we surrendered that house, three decades after my parents surrendered India, I finally saw it. When I arrived, a towering, turbaned Sikh guard stopped me. I told him that the place once belonged to my family, which confused matters further: a phone call and logbook entry were now in order. And then I walked toward a vast structure, labyrinthine like a palace, with roofs of many heights. A sign welcomed me to the road-building division of the government of Uttar Pradesh, a state known more for its divisions than its roads.

The foyer announced itself with a vast swirling staircase, as if to reassure that the memories of grandeur didn't lie. In the hallways through which hot meals once coursed, civil servants now shuffled with files, planning to fill potholes. The courtyard, once home to roses and jasmine, was flowerless; I later discovered, when relaying my impressions to my mother, that its size had been curtailed, apparently to create more office space.

My arrival caused something of a flutter in this sleepy agency, and word soon reached an important man there. He came to see me and told me that he had known my great-grandparents.

He first worked for Badé Nanu in his company, then switched to the agency when my family, struck by financial distress, sold the government their home. He was an accountant, and very old, less of a bridge to the past than a reminder of how far past it was.

When I returned to the car, the driver told me that I had narrowly escaped a confrontation. A few days earlier, in what had become national news, a Hindu mob had terrorized some British tourists, descendants of colonial soldiers who had come to commemorate the 150th anniversary of the 1857 Indian uprising—the Sepoy Mutiny, to the British; to Indians, the First War of Independence. Some Hindu activists were still prowling for foreign tourists, and I had intrigued them. The driver had swatted them away. But the feeling of tension and upheaval, which I sensed now in so much of India, hung especially thick in Lucknow. Clusters of somber, underemployed young men milled about at high noon, aspiring but idle, bored, susceptible to messiahs peddling causes.

Much separated my vision of that house from the house it had become. One day, my mother had eaten for the last time on the lawns, and for a while longer there had been roses, servants, mosquito nets, and cocktail hours. Then history had struck. A collapse in Badé Nanu's tube-well business. The sale of the house to a metastasizing socialist state. The conversion of that state to a brutal new capitalism. The rise of Hindu fanaticism. The new sense, palpable across India, of violence just around the bend. My parents' journey out of India. My own return.

But the change was not only in the events of time. It was also within. My mind was filled with visions of that house, and of India, that were not quite right. This idea came to me when I was looking at an old photograph of the property. It was from the 1960s, and a wedding reception was in progress. A sartorial detail arrested my eye. At any wedding today of my family or of families like it, a number of the men, perhaps most, would wear *kurtas*, *sherwanis*, Nehru jackets—various Indian garments. But in this image from decades ago, the men wore crisply cut Western suits. This puzzled me at first, until I connected it with other developments that I had witnessed upon returning to India. Even as Western ways pour into the country, there has been, simultaneously, a great new confidence in the indigenous: children buzzing with thickly Indian accents and throwing Hindi words into their slang even as their parents spoke in coolly British tones.

But this idea—that in this way, at least, India was becoming less, rather than more, Westernized—upset one of the many casual assumptions that I had held growing up in America as the son of Indian émigrés: our Indian relatives ate their stove-fresh *rotis*, while we made do with toaster-oven-warmed Mexican tortillas; they sacrificed for their elders, while we were selfish enough to ask for money for our chores; they dressed in their traditional garb, while we, pesky immigrant children that we were, wanted only to look Western. But, as the old photograph reminded me, the simple dualisms I had constructed, those ideas about our lives and theirs, were products not of memory but of ideas passively, unquestioningly collected.

What separated me from that house was more than just the barriers of time. There was the further distance of my own false visions and of the need for revisions. Fragments of memory floated in me. Some were once true but had, in the time of my parents' absence from India, become false; some were true from the start and so remained; some were never true. To return to India in this way, as the son of those who had left, was to know dizzying change—and change as much in the seer as in the seen. My vocation was to witness, with supposed detachment, the spectacle of an old country turning new. But I could not pretend to be so detached. India's new realities were undoing not only

India's old realities, but also the old facsimiles of reality in my mind and in the minds of many others in the world. To see India clearly would require an excavation of my own buried imaginings, and a sifting of what had endured from what had withered and mutated and pivoted in new ways.

TWO

Ambition

We rang the doorbell of the old apartment on Carmichael Road. There was the pitter-patter of a servant's footsteps, a glance through the peephole, and then the door flung open as we entered. The servant retreated, back flush against the wall, as if to make himself invisible. My parents and sister were in town, a few years after my arrival in India, and we were having breakfast at a friend's home. The servant escorted us into the living room. Our hosts walked in; we chatted for a time, then moved to the dining room. Breakfast was omelets and toast and coffee, served in the Indian way: we ate as the servant scampered back and forth, serving. We raved about the coffee that the family trumpeted as the servant's specialty, and he nervously, hesitantly accepted our praise.

We returned to my apartment, at which time I realized that I had forgotten to return a mattress we had borrowed from the same friends. I rolled it up and went back. I rang the doorbell. Our friends were no longer home, but the servant was around. The peephole opened, revealing a skeptical, wary eye. "Who is it?" he barked with a new hostility in his voice. I thought that my identity was obvious to him, so I spoke only of my mission: I had a mattress to deliver. The door opened, but this time with no back against the wall. With impatience on his face, he continued his barking, commanding me to place the mattress over there, quickly. He had switched to calling me "*tum*" instead of "*aap*," the more respectful form of "you." I was puzzled and gently amused.

Then it hit me. He didn't recognize me. He assumed that I was a deliveryman, perhaps because I had changed into a T-shirt and shorts, perhaps because most respectable Indians would not carry a mattress themselves. As he grimaced and waved for me to leave, I locked eyes with him and reminded him of our breakfast a brief time earlier. And then I witnessed a metamorphosis that I will never forget: he shriveled before my eyes from master to servant. His erect body deflated; his shoulders slouched; his head bowed down; his eyes reclaimed their unthreatening docility; his flailing arms returned to his sides. "Yes, sir. Sorry, sir. OK, sir. Sorry, sir," he muttered in rhythmic succession. A few seconds earlier, he had been the man and I the boy, in the Indian way; now he was the boy again, begging for my forgiveness, hoping I would tell no one, terrified, reverent.

I had a privilege that morning that I never knew before or afterward. I saw the truth of what it means to be Indian, an ordinary Indian, not a foreigner like me, not an educated elite. I had felt impotence and then omnipotence in the same minute; I had gazed up from, and then down into, the Indian abyss. For the Indians around me, it was the calculus that governed life: Am I his *sahib* or is he mine? Who should shout at whom? Whose body must apologize for its presence and whose must swagger? Whose eyes must stay down? Who can use "*tum*" and who "*aap*"? Who must hide his hands behind his back and who can gesticulate with them?

The only anomaly that morning was that an Indian had made a mistake in this calculation. It was a mistake Indians rarely made. There was no more urgent knowledge in India than the knowledge of one's place, and to commit such an error with any frequency was to risk one's survival.

To my childhood eyes, the starkest difference between America and India was always servants. In America we spent a fair amount of time rinsing our own plates and loading the dishwasher. We mowed the lawn and trimmed our own hedges. We mounted ladders to replace lightbulbs and spent Saturdays assembling IKEA furniture. My mother cooked hot dinners night after night and drove my sister and me everywhere we needed to go. It was the American way of life, and it all seemed normal, even inevitable, until our vacation journeys to India.

There we encountered a new kind of human: the servant. This was not a housekeeper or cleaning lady or chauffeur. Such words belong to someone treated as a professional, hired to turn up, perform a discrete task, and leave. The servant, unlike such professionals, lived in his masters' home, usually had family far enough away as to consume little of his time, ate his masters' food, and responded to their every shout, day or night. He was trained to sublimate his own sense of time to that of his masters, to know the precise moment to bring them tea in the morning or to serve them dinner during their favorite soap opera. And, because he came from the countryside and had few connections, he had little choice once hired but to stay.

These servants, I began to observe, were not people who just happened to have fallen into this work and whose children might just as readily rise out. Servitude was almost genetic. Servants had different physiologies, looking younger than their years from hunger until their late teens, then older than their years under the strain of wrenching work and a lack of medical care. They carried themselves differently, stooping before their masters, hands behind their back, fear and worship in their eyes. They agreed with whatever the masters had to say. Masters ate vegetables and meat at dinner; servants' plates were covered with rice and lentils. At first, I cringed when the lower-caste sweeper woman came to my grandparents' home in Delhi and scuttled on the floor in a permanent, self-deprecating squat when she cleaned; then, like anyone with enough hours in India, I, too, stopped seeing her. When the nanny who raised my mother returned to Delhi many years later to offer a final farewell to the family, she sat beneath us on a stool as we all sat in bed, even though she was in her eighties, even though she had come on the belief that she would soon die, even though we, like so many Indians, told ourselves that she was not a servant but was "family."

The hierarchy that seemed so new to me was, of course, a very old fact of the world, from European feudalism to American slavery to Russian serfdom. But in India it was inextricable from the institution of caste, which for millennia had ordered Indians to lay bricks if born bricklayers, to skin cattle if born cattle skinners, to preach if born priests, and to do these duties without complaint or protest, knowing that the reward in a future life would be proportional to one's degree of acceptance in this one. The caste system stacked the cattle skinners below the bricklayers and the bricklayers below the priests, and ensured that the designations were reflected in family names. In theory, anyone from a low caste could hop on a train, cross over to the other side of the country, and launch a new life where no one knew his caste. It is testimony to the fierce psychological power of caste that this kind of "passing," as anthropologists call it, was taken up by so few Indians.

But in modern India caste was no longer what it once was. Untouchability, the heart of the evil, which dictated certain castes to be so low as to be impure and untouchable, had been outlawed before my parents were born, and over the course of their youths India had taken long strides toward dismantling the regime. The country had set aside millions of government jobs and university seats for the lower castes; its laws were used to punish and deter acts of "casteism"; its democracy had gradually made space for the leaders of the trampled, such that many Indians now asserted their low-caste status as a badge of solidarity and pride. In the villages, less touched by these changes, caste endured: many still knew and cared who was who, and many still performed jobs related to their caste. In the cities, when riding on a bus or working in an office or hiring a servant, in my parents' time and certainly now, people were often unaware of the caste of those they dealt with, and they often didn't care. But even in the cities, below the surface of polite conversation, life was easier or harder for many because of caste. What endured of the caste system, then, was not the rigid classifications themselves but a shadow of the theory behind them: an intuition in the Indian mind that humanity is tiered, that some are born as masters and others are born to serve them.

In the new Indian hierarchy, a waiter in a restaurant might be a Brahmin and his customer an untouchable: that much, at least, had been shaken up. But the customer will still speak to the waiter in the way their roles—if no longer their castes—have traditionally required: snidely, dismissively, without empathy. And the waiter will listen and absorb and smile and bob his head in the way that servants have always done.

It was this diluted, casteless regime of caste that I discovered upon moving to India. In the elevator at McKinsey's office in Bombay, I noticed the men to be of two heights. There were the executives and the deliverymen. The executives were a foot taller, on average. Their faces seemed fuller, their features better formed. They were without limps, body lumps, or skin discolorations, for they had the means to treat such things. The deliverymen were darker, more deformed, worn down by their own histories. They had bowlegs, lazy eyes, misshapen fingers. Because they were mostly just bone, their feet and hands were large for their frames, giving them the proportions of skeletons more than living men. And, of course, it was not just the deliverymen, but their brothers

and sisters everywhere. The lowly police constable directing traffic, his waist the circumference of a rich man's thigh, a man of
the law projecting no authority and inspiring no fear. The waiter
in the elegant restaurant, his tuxedo too loose for his undernour-
ished frame, bowing and groveling and overdosing on the word
"sir" as he serves. The helpers in the restrooms in five-star hotels
in Bombay, saluting as you approach the sink, turning on the tap,
squeezing soap into your hands, dangling a towel and saluting
again and muttering, "Right, sir. OK, sir. Thank you, sir." The servants in the posh apartments on Nepean Sea Road in Bombay who
work inside by day and sleep in the outside hallway by night,
never trusted, men who clean the toilets within but are not permitted to use them.

In encountering these scenes as an outsider, my first reaction
was a mix of revulsion and pride: revulsion at the degradation all
around and pride at my own marvelous sympathy. In watching
the apologetic waiter or scuttling sweeper, I would tell myself that,
where I come from, I would never treat anyone like this. Maybe I
was right. But Indians would always tell me, when I put it to them,
that I didn't understand, that there was no choice here, that I was
being idealistic. And then time wore on, and what once repulsed
me slowly became normal, and then it slowly became my own. I
found myself lapsing into the attitudes of old India. For the first
time in my life, I had my own, part-time servants. Our relations
were warm and professional. I gave them overall instructions but
left them free to make decisions. I learned about their families and
joked around with them. But over time I also felt myself becoming
more dismissive, more ready to snap at their mistakes or to deem
them slothful or forgetful. First I stopped turning my head to give
my maid eye contact when thanking her for doing a task for me;
then I stopped thanking her at all, just nodding or grunting in the
smug way of the privileged. I began to harden, to become ruder
and less patient with those who served me, to omit apologies and
expressions of thanks.

After getting a haircut one evening, I hailed a taxi in downtown Bombay. I got in, but when I stated my address the driver refused. I needed him to turn right under the Kemps Corner bridge, but it was time for his shift change and he had to get the car to his night driver, who was in another direction. He asked me, politely, to find another cab. I knew that there were few out at rush hour. It was hot and muggy. I felt the frustrated anger, deepened by heat, that so often comes in Indian cities. So I refused to move and insisted, and he argued and raised his own voice, and I raised mine further and bullied him; finally he turned right under the bridge and wove himself into the traffic jam that he knew would come if we followed this course.

Now he said nothing further. And in the new silence I heard the small, glowing machine on his dashboard that was playing the Gayatri mantra, a simple Hindu religious chant asking for guidance from divine wisdom, repeated over and over, cyclical and soothing as a lullaby. I had screamed at the man. The horns now screamed at him. The night-shift driver would surely scream at him. His mother might scream at him later that night. For now he had only those gentle, lilting words, and their ability to remove him from the present moment, a transcendence essential for surviving in a world like his.

I felt a sudden pain in my chest, the pain not of this one indignity he had endured but of what must have been many gathered years of them. It came from seeing him as a person, and from realizing that he had been less than that to me a moment earlier. Now that I saw him so, I felt like crying. I saw that my own deed was only one of so many ill deeds he had borne. I had exposed a chasm that was too terrifying to explore. And in that moment I saw more clearly than before the source of the Indian callousness. It was that the chasm is too deep. How many are you going to save? Ten? A thousand? A million? You see that look in the eyes of the powerless, blank and simple; it yearns for your approval; you know how far one kind word from you would go. And yet something compels you not to say it. The dependency scares you, as a needy lover's demands scare you, for it suggests a bottomless pit of giving that will devour you if you give in just slightly and allow yourself to care.

And so he retreats into his world, defeated, and you retreat into yours, ridden with guilt. And then you tell yourself: don't cry for him. Indian shit, more than other shit, flows downward. It was the lesson I had learned after the mattress incident that morning. Just as you have them, they have someone, too. You lose your temper at the taxi driver. He has his wife to beat up. She has her daughter-in-law. That woman has the sweeper. The sweeper has a wife. The wife has a daughter-in-law of her own. And so it goes, humiliation leading to humiliation, master to servant, master to servant, all the miserable way down.

You drive past dark slums or through aching villages, and you ask yourself: If this were your world, how would you break out? Against the idea of your unworthiness, would you have the energy to rebel? How much rage, how much calm, how much grit would it ask of you? How would you do it?

How?

I found an answer in Umred, a speck in the dead center of India, a small town of fifty thousand. To get there, I flew from Bombay to the rapidly growing city of Nagpur, where a glimmering new airport was being built, and then drove on a bone-shaking highway away from that islet of order. The sense of life's preciousness, having already diminished from Bombay to Nagpur, eroded further from Nagpur to Umred as highway machismo became progressively deadlier. Drivers began to linger in the center of the road even when there was nothing to overtake; and, when there was, they hooked violently right and then violently left just before a head-on collision with the oncoming vehicle. A 1 percent chance of death became a tolerable level of risk in these parts. The disposition of living and dying became a matter for God's hands, not the hands on the wheel.

The city fell behind and the plains opened wide. Roofs of corrugated tin held down by rocks appeared. Men ferrying clusters of twigs and burlap-bagged produce on bicycles drifted left and right as they scaled hills for which their spindly legs were no match, their labor at once harder and less efficient than in the city. The ground yellowed and dried by the mile, declaring ever more loudly its craving of the monsoon.

Umred was bigger than a village and smaller than a proper town, still in transit from the rural to the urban world. It began as a market serving the oceans of surrounding farmland. Remnants of the rural life still lingered, transposed strangely to concrete streets. It remained possible to raise cattle in the heart of Umred. Clumps of manure and hay lined the roads, flattening day by day under the weight of buses. Farmers in knotted white turbans, perched high on tractors, sputtered into town to run errands from their villages not far away. In fact, for the visitor, Umred had an unsettling tendency to vanish. Stroll down its main thoroughfare, turn onto a side lane, walk three blocks, and, without warning, the town would disappear and the farms would swallow you. Umred came and went just like that, a flicker of civilization.

In the teeming bazaar, under the blazing sun, the languid salesmen stood at their roller carts, hawking Hindu devotional videos, frilly panties, and cheap, fraudulently branded electronics. There were few sales to be made. Across from a row of fruit sellers, seven cobblers squatted idly, with no shoes to mend. It seemed not to have occurred to any of them to squat somewhere else, away from six rivals. At a taxi stand not far away, potbellied drivers in look-alike Ray-Bans milled around, puffing on cigarettes, waiting for their seven-seating four-by-fours to fill up with a dozen sweaty bodies before departing for the next town. There was no urgency. If it took an hour to achieve the desired economies of scale, then you waited an hour. Umred was used to waiting.

But there were hints, visible not just in Umred but across India, of a new restlessness, of a new yearning to break fate, to pursue a vocation not one's father's, to die other than where one was born. It was visible in the makeshift advertisements pasted all over town for hole-in-the-wall "institutes" and "academies" and "schools" that taught saleable skills, mostly software programming and spoken English, to the young. The ads promised that, for a few thousand rupees, you could pick up a skill and get a job out of town, away from your family. A poster commending cell phones showed a beaming pilot talking on one, playing on that oldest small-town fantasy of the wide world beyond. Another ad used a Caucasian model to promote a skin-whitening lotion from Ponds, as if to whisper to the gullible: "You can be rich and successful and, yes, even white!"

I had come to Umred to write about a riot. A few months earlier, power blackouts that millions of passive rural dwellers across India had suffered silently for years had suddenly triggered a violent backlash here, with police jeeps and a government building burned to their frames by an angry, untamable crowd. I had spoken with many in the town, and a theory emerged: it was a small town in the middle of nowhere, dusty and underwhelming and dead, but it had begun to dream, the townspeople said again and again, because of satellite television, because of migrant cousins with tales of call center jobs and girlfriends and freedom in the city. Once Umred contracted ambition, blackouts tolerated earlier became intolerable.

"Electricity is essential to ambition," an energetic young man named Ravindra had told me that day, "because I need it to do my homework, I need it to listen to music if I am a dancer, I need it to listen to tapes of great speakers, I need it to surf the Internet. But I cannot, so people get angry. They have bigger expectations, but electricity is becoming a hurdle on their path."

Until that day, my principal gauge for change in India had been physical. The metropolises were changing physically, dramatically swiftly; the small towns were inching forward, with perhaps a new mall here or a new call center there; the villages were barely moving at all. It was a way of seeing India that simplified the chaos, and it guided many chroniclers of this new India. What I discovered in Umred that day was that little had to change in the physical world for a revolution to have taken place. The revolution could be a simple idea, like the one expressed when Abhay, one of Ravindra's friends, was told that in Bombay the electricity never stops. "Why?" he snapped, sitting in the hole-in-the-wall sporting goods store that he owned. "They're humans in Bombay but we're only animals here?"

Growth had scarcely come to places like Umred, but the longings created by growth elsewhere were spreading. I remember the precise moment when I received this insight from Ravindra. We were sitting in a tiny restaurant that specialized in the region's fiery *saoji* cuisine. Quarter plates of mutton and chicken were strewn across the table. Ravindra and Abhay were offering examples of the little things that were changing in Umred: young men surfing online for wives, farmers' sons deserting the farms to work at a bank in a nearby town, young women going to fashion school, a deluge of students signing up for English classes. But it was not these facts that arrested me. It was the mention of a local pageant.

"I see Fashion TV on television, Miss India contests in the big cities," Ravindra said. "So I thought, Why can't we have that also?" And so he had organized, some months earlier, the first-ever Mr. and Miss Umred Personality Contest, which seemed to be half about physical appearance and half about the communication skills that were the new rage in small-town India. I didn't know whether to believe him. There was no train station in Umred, no shopping center, but there was a pageant? He saw my puzzled, delighted expression. "We gave them a crown," he reassured me. "It was plastic, but it was good."

The town and the image of that crown stayed with me. Some months later, I happened to call Ravindra to check in with him.

By a strange coincidence, I had reached him on the very day of the second annual Mr. and Miss Personality Contest, for which he was frantically preparing. He invited me, somewhat whimsically, to join them that evening. I decided to pack a bag and drive to the airport that very hour, buying a ticket over the phone in my taxi. I didn't realize at the time that I would learn more about the new ambitions and new impatience, more about the spreading hunger of servants to become masters, from Ravindra than from any of his contestants.

The twenty-two contestants for the Mr. and Miss Umred Personality Contest sat anxiously on white plastic chairs at the front of the gymnasium. The eight women were dressed as if for their own weddings, with gold decorating the center partings of their hair, clunky necklaces on their necks, and sequined *saris* in pink, green, and orange draped around them, pinned with white laminated contestant-number tags. The men had taken their inspiration from Bollywood gangster movies, with leafy collars drooping over the lapels of their ill-fitting suits. Their belts, the belts of the Indian underclass, were too long for their waists, traveling all the way around their backs, such that two belts would have furnished enough leather for three men.

The pageant began with the talent contest. Some of the contenders, most of them engineers from local colleges, sang; some danced; others told jokes. All of them seemed to plagiarize television, which was their main portal to the world. The pouts were lifted from Fashion TV, the breast shimmying from Channel V, the joke timing from *The Great Indian Laughter Challenge* on STAR One. The question-and-answer segment was next. The contestants took turns coming to the front of the stage and facing a panel of conservative local graybeards, who seemed determined to keep the pouting and shimmying in check with their nostalgic questions. One contestant had to reassure the crowd that she would dutifully cook after marriage, even if she won the contest. Another was goaded about her decision to answer the question in English, then grilled as to whether she spoke Marathi, the regional language. These were among the other responses:

Female Contestant Number Two, an electrical engineer, said, "My aim in life is to become a newsreader."

Female Contestant Number Four listed among her hobbies decorating her room and making friends.

Male Contestant Number One said, "I follow the Darwin's principle: the survival of the fittest, that the one who is fittest will survive. That is why I have come to this contest."

Male Contestant Number Three declared, "My aim is to become the ideal son of my parents and to be a good engineer."

Male Contestant Number Fourteen told the judges, somewhat puzzlingly, "I love Hitler's book most. I'm a big Hitler fan." (When I asked Ravindra about this later, he shrugged and blamed the quality of local education: "Actually, we do not have any details about Hitler.")

After a catwalk round, which involved the perplexity of men and women who were probably not allowed to have lunch with a member of the opposite sex strutting down a ramp, it was time to crown the winners. The judges whisperingly reached their verdict and came onstage. (I had been designated the "chief guest" of the ceremony, being an out-of-town guest. This had required me to give a brief speech in English, a language that most of the audience did not understand, and now I was onstage, too.) One by one, the contestants came to thank us, their hands touching our feet. The two winners were announced and handed their prize, which was six hundred rupees each and a gold-colored tiara. Mr. Umred, too, wore a tiara. Two banners on the stage declaring the name of the contest were removed and, reimagined as sashes, were tied around the winners' torsos.

• • •

I realized as I watched Ravindra that night, dressed in a crisp white and purple shirt and a dark tie emblazoned with the crest of a family not his own, that he had made himself Umred's ambassador of escape: part motivational speaker, part revivalist preacher of the gospel of ambition. When he established the Mr. and Miss Umred Personality Contest, he was not bringing a new idea to Umred so much as giving expression to an existing idea. What he had understood was that the young craved an exit, and he had built a personal empire that gave them the means to leave.

Everyone knew Ravindra. Everyone, regardless of age, called him "sir." Later, when he drove me around on his motorcycle, he repeatedly risked our lives by lifting his hands to offer people he knew on the streets a greeting of clasped hands. To reach Nagpur or Pune or Bombay, you had to seek his advice, learn English from his English academy, learn roller skating from his roller-skating academy, reach into his network of contacts, compete in his pageant, learn to dress and think and enunciate like him.

And I began to wonder: who was this man, seemingly descended from a higher place and bigger things, who had made it his business to give a bleak town in the center of India a way out?

On the day after the pageant, Ravindra took me to a restaurant called Uttam, which, in the small-town Indian way, served every kind of Indian cuisine except the local cuisine. Children were waiting tables. I had spent the morning meeting some of the contestants in his pageant, who had oozed praise for their *guru* Ravindra. But now, as he began to tell me his own story, I realized how wrong I had been: the truth about Ravindra was that he had swept into Umred not from above but from below, from hundreds of the Indian gradations below.

He was born in a village called Bhiwapur, a half-hour drive and many social light-years from Umred. It was one of hundreds of thousands of such villages in India, trapped in an earlier age. His family lived in a small house with three rooms, concrete walls, an outdoor latrine, and a thatched roof. They had had no land to cultivate, just a small yard with some anemic trees. His father worked as a coolie, loading foodstuffs on and off trucks. His mother was a farmhand. Neither parent had advanced past the fourth grade, and they spoke Marathi, the local language, but not Hindi. "We are daily wages people," Ravindra said, betraying elements of the old Indian thinking that he hadn't wholly shaken: daily wages as social identity, not economic circumstance.

He grew up eating the kind of meals that I saw my relatives' servants eating: plates heaped with rice, covered with watery lentil *dal*, with a small dollop of chutney on the side to lend piquancy and sometimes a thin piece of *roti*. From time to time, the family splurged on eggplants. In the winters, the air on the central plains would cool, but when Ravindra and his siblings—two younger brothers and one younger sister—were children, there were no blankets, only sheets, and these were too small to reach from neck to feet. They bought their clothes secondhand from the village bazaar, making them poor even by the standards of the poor. They never possessed more than a few hundred rupees in savings, barely enough for a one-way train ride to a neighboring state.

Ravindra's family lived in a particular area of the village, a *mohalla*, a ghetto, whose significance would have been lost on a young boy. But as he grew up, he learned that his *mohalla* was reserved for low-caste laboring families like his. Their caste, traditionally tasked with crushing oil seeds, stood some rungs above the untouchables. And, because they were not untouchable, they were considered too well-born to benefit from the special preferences and spoils that untouchability now brought, but they were still laggard enough to qualify for some, belonging as they did to the bureaucratic category of "Other Backward Classes."

Having grown up in relative privilege, I always wondered how the idea of inferiority first imposed itself on those who had not grown up so. For Ravindra, it was noticing at school that the Jaiswals and Agarwals and Guptas, the children of merchants and shopkeepers in the village, bought two-rupee ice creams at recess, while his *mohalla* friends bought the fifty-paise kind. It was realizing that, when guest speakers came to the school, the children of daily wages people were rarely chosen to introduce them. It was being told at the wedding of a big man in Bhiwapur to wait until the "guests" had eaten. "You come afterwards," he remembered being scolded. It was waiting in queues all the time, for free food from the temple, for his mother's weekly wages, the line coming to signify for Ravindra all the impotence of poverty.

He used to watch his classmates roar into the school yard on the backs of their parents' motorcycles. He did not even have the two modes of transportation below motorcycles on the Indian staircase of affluence: the bicycle and plastic sandals. He wore no footwear until the ninth grade. "Whenever I saw other people wearing expensive shoes and socks and slippers, I used to get very angry, and I felt very bad," he said. "Why am I not getting all these things? Why only I don't have all these things? And at that time I decided that I will earn great money, and I will remove my poverty. I considered poverty as a disease."

This was not the old Indian orthodoxy: for Ravindra, the world was not illusion, *maya*; it was not enough simply to do one's duty and do it well and be satisfied with what God gave. "I just believed that we all are equal human beings, so why do we have differences, as far as social status is concerned, economical status is concerned, social recognition and honor and respect?" he said. "What I used to believe every time is that if one person is getting something big, better, and best, that should be my right."

"Most Indians don't think like that," I interrupted.

"They don't think like that," he said. "They just want to compromise: it's OK, we're having sufficient things; let's be settled. But—I don't know—right from the beginning, I had great anger of my poverty. The generations after me will not live this kind of life—that's what I decided. I will change my destiny. I will be good. I will be rich."

In the eighth grade, the village school held a public-speaking contest. Ravindra had never stood on a stage before. But now here he was, with hundreds of people sitting below him, watching. He spoke for five minutes; the crowd applauded three times. He discovered that night a power in himself that he had not known: to connect, to inspire, to cut into people's hearts with his words. And, having contracted his thirst for money through its absence, he now felt the first flush of respect, of being somebody in a sea of nobodies. "I felt that I am something different, I am something special," he said.

His speech, which won the prize, was about the impact of television on society, and by that time a new television bought by the family was having a great impact on Ravindra himself. He would spend hours each day watching *He-Man*, *Spider-Man*, and *Batman*, piously balanced with the Hindutainment of the *Mahabharata* and *Ramayana* miniseries. I had grown up with Indian parents transplanted to America who regarded television as a threat to our minds and to the onward transmission of Indian values. We were barely allowed to watch it. But in Ravindra's world, deep in small-town India, television was seen differently, even by parents, as a force of liberation.

"TV is the very hi-fi form of everything," Ravindra said. "It's the extreme level of ideas, where they show you everything at top level, so that certainly gives you motivation. On TV you see the things of world-class standard. When you see some person on Discovery catching anaconda, you are looking at the best person in the world for catching anaconda. On TV we never see the strugglers or something like that; we see the people who have achieved what they wanted to be."

But, for all his dreams, Ravindra was just another village kid who didn't have connections and didn't speak English, the language of success in the India that was beginning to flourish in the 1990s. At the end of tenth grade, he decided to enroll himself in an English-language school in Umred, the nearest town, even though he didn't speak English. He and the others from the villages sat in the back of the classroom, gaining fragments of vocabulary and grammar day by day, learning by immersion.

He graduated and moved on to a college in Umred, choosing commerce as his major. But he was working after school to support his family back in the village; the strains eventually became too much, and he failed his second-year exams. He was kicked out. In my parents' India, that might have been his story's end: there were no second chances then; there were no other routes. Diplomas were the only currency. Knowledge was the rampart that protected the well-born from the rest. In an earlier age, that had meant confining Sanskrit learning to the priestly castes; in more recent times, it had translated into massive public investment in elite colleges and universities—such as my father's Indian Institutes of Technology—and the utter neglect of basic schooling for most Indians. Even today, the quality of college instruction at all but the best institutions is miserable, as I learned by sitting in many classrooms myself. And so if you were like Ravindra, you were probably not getting a very good education to begin with, even before an unforgiving examination system cut you loose.

But the ambitions stirring below had created a market for a new breed of middle-class finishing schools. They catered to young people born into the lower orders, filled with dreams but shut out by the old system. The schools were often single-room institutions, taking cash only, with dubious teaching methods. One I came across in Bombay offered diplomas in aviation, hospital management, medical transcription, French, German, Arabic, shipping and logistics, hospitality, and fashion. Another taught everything from early childhood care to interior design. But the most common subject was English. It was not the archaic English curriculum of India's schools and colleges, with Shakespearean sonnets memorized and not understood, the *guru* talking down to his disciples. It was spoken English that could be used in the workplace tomorrow, language the quick and dirty way. It gave students the idioms, vocabulary, and placeless accent that would render your lowly origins untraceable in a land where so much could be deduced when you opened your mouth.

Ravindra coated himself with one finishing school skill after another, learning everything from the work of electricians to desktop publishing. One of the schools sensed his talent with people and hired him as a teacher, paying him 360 rupees a month. Another school soon poached him for more than double that amount. He began to sense, once again, that he was more than just an achiever. People liked him. They listened to him. Students sought him out for advice. With the finishing school cult spreading, the company was opening branches in the villages, including in Bhiwapur. Ravindra was sent to manage a school there. He had left the village as the boy who ate last at weddings; he returned as that loftiest of Indian creatures, a teacher, and, better still, a purveyor of new-economy skills. He was earning 1,800 rupees a month now. He had become a big man.

On his twenty-first birthday, in September 2002, he bought a motorcycle. It was the first motorized vehicle owned in the history of his family. He drove it from the showroom to his home and took his mother for a spin around the village. "She didn't say anything," he recalled. "She just cried. And she said, 'Take care of the bike.'"

But Ravindra was restless. He felt obstructed in Bhiwapur, as if his long adventure had merely deposited him back to where he began. He found work in Nagpur, a further step up the urban ladder from Umred, at a travel agency that sold something called the "Five-Year Family Amusement Package," an all-inclusive combination platter of weekend getaways and religious pilgrimages and amusement park tickets. The package cost 100,000 rupees, about $2,000, for a family of four. Customers would come into the agency's office, curious about the product but needing persuasion. A staff of persuaders, which Ravindra joined, would seek to sell the product, earning a 4 percent commission for every sale.

It was Ravindra's first real contact with successful people—merchants, lawyers, doctors, people who could afford to buy a vacation package. And he quickly realized a value in his customers beyond the commissions they brought.

Ravindra's past, his traditions, the lessons of his parents—these offered no preparation for the man he wished to become. In most countries, at most times, the gulf between the generations is narrower. One might break from one's parents, pursuing a different vocation, living in a different place. But you eat the way they eat—with your hands, or with a fork and knife, or with chopsticks. You drive a different model of the same machine they drive. You wear differently cut versions of the same garments—pants and shirts and skirts, or *kurtas* and *saris*. You construct your own identity, or so the mythology goes, and yet not every component of that identity needs to be created from scratch. But a usable past was not one of Ravindra's luxuries. Everything that he wanted to become had to be carefully, calculatingly borrowed from someone else. And so a client who walked into the travel agency, thinking that he had come for a presentation, was actually offering himself to Ravindra as an exemplar of possible traits. Ravindra was an anthropologist, then an actor, observing and then mimicking.

One day, as he sat with colleagues on a tea break, a fancy car swerved into the parking lot. A middle-aged man got out with his wife and two sons. "They were so smart, handsome," Ravindra recalled. "Their car was so fantastic. They had very expensive opticals—goggles—on their faces, all four. And I saw that family: my God, they looked so rich. They looked so rich. I stopped taking my tea, and I was just staring at them." Seeing them stirred a fantasy in his mind: what would it be like to be them? The images flickered in his mind: "I am going to some big hotel. I am coming out of my car. I have big sunglasses. I'm with my wife and my son, with my family members. A waiter is coming out. He's taking my key. He is parking my car."

By a stroke of luck, the family was assigned to Ravindra. He made his presentation over an hour and a half. They were enchanted, and they bought the package. At the end of the presentation, the man, impressed by Ravindra's demeanor, said to him, "You have that spark. What are you doing here?" He slipped a business card across the table.

But Ravindra said he never called the man, as a consequence of his anthropological researches. He saw an underlying pattern in the successes of those who came in: they had succeeded by working for themselves, not for others. No one could scream at them like the truckers screamed at his father and the landlords screamed at his mother; no one could tell them when it was time for them to eat. They had not just money, but also a degree of control over their lives, of autonomy, that would have appealed to a boy from Bhiwapur. "They were entrepreneurs," Ravindra said. "That was the word which really impressed me—entrepreneurship. If you have something of your own, you can really be a leader of your life, you can really go much more ahead than anybody else, and that really gives you happiness."

This idea of control intrigued me. What did he think of the idea, so prevalent in India, of *kismet*, of fate?

"The new generation does not believe so much in fate," he said. "They have come to know that all rich people have become rich because of their hard work, not by their fate."

"In India," he went on, "many people believe in God and they think that, 'OK, if there is something written in my destiny, then it will happen.' They don't make it happen. But now the new generation is getting changed. Mumbai, Pune, and big-city people, people like me who think more on skills and practical orientation in life—they don't depend on destiny. They plan their lives. They have their goals to achieve. If I plan properly and execute it nicely, then I will get what I want."

He also rejected the idea of *karma*, that one is born into a particular station in life because of one's good or ill deeds in past lives. "Many Indians believe in a rebirth system, but I believe that life is only a one-time chance," he said. "You have to give your best." He said that the "prejudice" and "false beliefs" of the old religion were breaking: "Now we believe in progress and results, and for that you just need hard work—no other thing. All that is superstitious thing."

There was a strange stew of philosophies here: progress, results, opportunity—the language of business—blended with a Marxist critique of the dulling effect of religion, garnished with the vocabulary of American self-help culture. He said that his favorite book was Dale Carnegie's *How to Win Friends and Influence People*, with its tale of the writer's poor childhood in Missouri, his contemplation of suicide, and then his discovery of a talent for public speaking. "I have read that twenty-eight times so far," he said. "Whenever I feel nervous or depressed, I open that book."

The travel agency shut down in 2004. Ravindra decided to return to Umred to become its local Dale Carnegie, to start a finishing school of his own. He set up roller-skating classes and an event-management firm, but the heart of his work was a spoken-English academy that became a port of embarkation for Umred's restive young students. It offered ninety hours of classes over forty-five days for just 1,000 rupees, the cost of a fancy meal in Bombay. The students trickled in at first; then the trickle gathered into a gush, and before long Ravindra was arguably the most important and well-known young man in Umred.

"Seeing my past, when I go in flashback, I really think that, 'My God, this is really unbelievable. This is like a dream,'" he said.

Toward the end of my visit, after hours of conversations, I came back to my original question. Yes, he had come from the villages. But he had grown into one of the brightest, most articulate, energetic people I had met in small-town India. He could go anywhere, make it big. Why was he still here? He brimmed with potential and had risen so far, so quickly, and yet it all seemed to me to have culminated in this rather dreary, mediocre setting. It made little sense: a man with so much verve and drive, a man wholly his own creation, who now wanted nothing more than to be the biggest man in little Umred.

I asked him one day if he was ever tempted to leave, as so many of his disciples were.

"No, no, no. I am not going to leave this place. I am getting everything here, no problem," he said. "One fear is there always in my mind. We can make much more money in Bombay, but it's such a crowded place. No one recognizes you. No one talks with you. No one takes interest in you. It's like a robot life: get up, wake up, get in the trains, get in the vehicles, go to office, come back."

And buried in those words was an idea that I had not seen, that was not easily seen when you come from where I come from. We are all running from something, and Ravindra was running from being a nobody—not just a poor man but less than a full man. And, after his long, wind-tossed odyssey, Bombay or Delhi or Banga-lore would be a cruel port of arrival, restoring him to the very hell of anonymity from which he had come.

A year passed after that visit. One day, as I meandered in a department store in northern India, my phone buzzed with a text message from Ravindra:

> Sir, last couple of months are full of achievements 4 me. My 2 skat-ing kids represented India in international skating comp in Belgium. It ws my greatest dream, turned into reality. I ws busy in passports, visas n other formalities. Nw im going 2 Hongkong 4 international Skating Championship as India team manager on sep 26. My life is transforming rapidly this time. My faith on my abilities raised. Its rising time 4me. My image is getting new shape. Im proving n improv-

ing at personal, social, family n financial areas nicely. At present im contributory english lecturer at 6 dif school n colleges. Im constructing my new home also.

The man never stopped. And in the time since the pageant, he and Umred had lingered in me. They had given me a new way of seeing India, a thread that seemed to connect so much else of what I was seeing. I had begun to see self-invention as a theme of India's unfolding drama. It was an idea that resonated with me, naturally, because of my own family's story: the story of parents who left India to reinvent themselves and then had a son who found his own new beginning in India. Everywhere I went in India, I saw the layers of humiliation and repression, the culture of masters and servants, under siege. It was the unintended consequence of degradation: so much energy, passion, and talent had been locked in the Indian tiers and shaken over and over again by want; the impossibility of rising had only intensified the hunger to rise. And now the society had begun to feel like an aluminum can on the verge of explosion.

I saw it everywhere: in the growing confidence of my maid, her talking back, her taste for fancy watches and shoes that would have seemed unthinkable to her mother, her enrollment of her children in an English-language boarding school; in the airline worker who, when I asked, "How are you?," smiled and patted me on the arm, a democratic touch between blue collar and white collar that would still be rare in the small towns where flight attendants were recruited; in the younger waiters, working alongside their older colleagues, who looked me in the eye and told me plainly that my choice was actually not that tasty; in the women working in factories in southern India who had become the primary breadwinners, leaving the children in the care of their idle, drunken husbands back home. And now Ravindra, the shoeless son of a porter, the one who ate last at weddings and sat in the back rows at school, was the manager of the Indian skating team, was going to Hong Kong, was teaching at six colleges, and was building a house. I had to go see him again.

We met at the same tea stall where we had first been introduced, in Umred's Bypass Square. It had been a year and a half since my last visit, and I was excited to see him. He came on his motorcycle, looking more muscular and adult than I remembered. He seemed, to my delight, to treat me more as a peer and less as a "sir," though he still called me Mr. Anand. As if to defy the heat, he was dressed in a silk shirt with green and blue diagonal stripes and a vast collar, over black polyester pants streaked by a strong pinstripe. He ordered two cups of tea from the owner, whom, of course, he knew well. Well-fed flies buzzed everywhere, jumping from the *pakodas* to the *jalebis* to the vat of brewing tea.

He gushed for a time about how wonderful it was that I had come to visit, and I praised him in return and told him how much his story had moved me. And then he wanted to get down to business. Life was moving in Umred, and there was a long list of developments to report.

The construction of his new home, where his parents and three siblings would eventually live, had begun on the outskirts of Umred. He had moved his parents from Bhiwapur to a rental property in town until the construction was complete. Their days in the village were over. His siblings were doing well, if not as well as he, working variously as a karate coach, a technician for a phone company, and a clerk at a local building firm. He noted some changes in the town since my last visit: he pointed to a black-and-yellow elevated concrete divider that now bisected a large road; he mentioned a new shopping center. He had also become considerably more plugged in: he showed me his new cell phone, a Nokia N91, and he had bought a laptop, his "long-awaited dream." He was already plotting his next moves up the consumption ladder: first a BlackBerry, then a van.

The money for all these things had come, I gathered, from a change in his financial picture. The English academy continued to do well, but it was his roller-skating classes that had taken off. Roller skating was, in fact, gathering speed as a major pastime in small-town India, part of the new frenzy for competitions of any kind. Ravindra had signed a lucrative deal to be the area's exclusive distributor of a brand of high-end skates that he recommended to his students. Meanwhile, he was becoming known in Indian roller-skating circles as a serial groomer of great skaters. One day, he got a call from the Roller Skating Federation of India. The group knew of his skills as a teacher, the man on the line said, and they wanted to appoint him manager of the Indian national roller-skating team. Should he accept, he would be leading the team to Hong Kong for a global competition within weeks. He accepted and went on that trip, marveling at the skyscrapers and the armies of people dressed in coats and ties and dresses.

As he delivered this update, Ravindra received a phone call. It seemed, from the blend of swagger and nervousness in his voice, to be a call of love. The last time we had met, I had asked Ravindra about his romantic affairs and had been surprised. For all his daring, he was a dutiful Indian son on the question of marriage. Forget love: he would marry a woman to his parents' liking, chosen by them with the family's interests in mind. It was so across much of the society: young people bold and mutinous in matters of status and hierarchy, yet wholly willing to submit in this other sphere.

When his call ended, I asked who it was.

Giggle. "That was my best friend, Sunita." *Giggle.*

"Best friend or girlfriend?"

"No, no, best friend, best friend." *Giggle.* "Maybe girlfriend." *Giggle.*

Well, this was new. He said that she was leaving town in a few hours, and I asked if we could meet her. We drove to a school, just outside of town, where she was the supervisor of teachers and he was a lecturer in English. On the way, he told me that they were friends, not boyfriend-girlfriend, but that he was "willing" and that maybe it would happen someday soon. Sunita was also an aspiring trainer and public speaker; she, too, emceed events like the pageant.

"Since we are coming together by means of this profession, she is getting much popular, she is getting improved, her personality is getting much fragranced—she said many times to me," he said. He described her in the language of self-help books that had become a dominant language for him and for so many Indian strivers. "She is getting very much PR," he said. "She gives all credit to me for that. She says, 'You're in my life, and that's why there are so many changes occurring.' And I always say, 'You deserve it. I'm just the medium, maybe.' And she always says, 'You are the best motivator I've ever had.' Since I have been in her life, she has been very positive; she has started thinking differently."

We walked into the school and into the principal's office, where she was sitting along with the principal. She was short, pudgy, pretty, with boxy metal-framed glasses. She was dressed in a white *salwar kameez* with printed flowers. She was the second-ranking official at the school and Ravindra was just a guest lecturer, but I noticed that she called him "sir." As Ravindra, the principal, and I made conversation, she stayed silent. When the principal gushed to me about Ravindra's galvanizing effect on Umred, she grinned quietly.

I accompanied them on an errand of hers, to print out and mail some forms. They both got out of the car at the post office and asked me to wait. A few minutes later Sunita returned on her own. She got back in the car, offering no explanation. I sensed that she wanted to talk. She was leaving town in a few hours, so I thought I would cut to the chase. What was her relationship with Ravindra? Were they just friends or boyfriend-girlfriend? She instantly became shy and retreated into herself. But then something in her stirred, and she said that she liked him very much but that it was complicated.

They had met in the computer institute where he used to teach; she was one of his students. They had fallen out of touch and then come into contact again. She was enchanted by his lectures at the school where she taught. "As a person, I like him very much," she said. "Caring. Hard worker. He has a helping nature. I don't take his name—I call him 'sir'—because I met him first as a teacher."

When I asked if they had a future together, she demurred at first. Then she chose to answer once again, as if realizing the back-channel diplomatic possibilities that I offered. She had thought about marrying him, she said, but he had never spoken of any feelings for her. Her mother, meanwhile, was opposed to the notion. They were from the same caste and even the same subcaste. But there is always a catch in India: they were not from the same sub-subcaste. They were, alas, the descendants of oil-seed crushers of different varieties. This could be overcome, but it would require some labor, so Ravindra had to make up his mind.

Love, like tennis, is not a sport for three. But I promised Sunita that I would see what I could do.

On the outskirts of Umred was a restaurant called Machan, whose village theme, including the terra-cotta oxcart in the muddy court-yard, suggested an anticipatory nostalgia for the world now evaporating. Ravindra and I ordered the peppery plates of chicken and mutton that we had eaten together on my first visit. During lunch, Ravindra took call after call, struggling to peel his eyes from the Nokia screen. And yet in another way he showed a sensitivity that was rare in India. My driver was sitting at another table in the restaurant, and Ravindra repeatedly made sure that a waiter was taking his order, that he was getting what he wanted, that the food was enough and to his liking: an empathy born of having known the other side.

I asked him about Sunita, and suddenly it was as though he were describing another woman.

"She's my first love. I never had such kind of feelings for someone before," he said.

I asked how he knew that it was love. "I used to share everything with her," he said. "If I don't talk with her one day, I just feel very much different, maybe something missing. She takes care of me; I also take care of her. We share good news, bad news, sorrows." Sometimes, he said, she calls him at midnight, from under her bedsheets, just to say good night. "The one day I don't go to school, she always calls me: 'You didn't come today? What's the problem? Everything OK?' If I don't send her some message, she asks, 'What's the problem? You didn't send me message.'"

A moment later, he added, "I'm thankful to God that He has put that love feeling in my heart." But then he suggested that it was her indifference that worried him; he didn't know if she felt the same. But I suggested that it might be the other way around. How was she to know of his interest?

With the prompting of my question, it seemed to dawn on Ravindra that Sunita may have been dropping hints for some time. "Many times she talks about marriage—in general," he said, reflecting as he spoke. "She says, 'I will not get a good husband; I don't know what kind of husband will I get.' Then I ask her, 'What kind of husband do you want?' So maybe she wanted to tell me her expectations through that." He was now listening to himself as carefully as I was listening to him.

"I will get married in two years," he said, rather abruptly. "It's planned already. That's the age of thirty. At that time, I will have many things: my house, my vehicle, a couple of international tours."

But how and when did he intend to reveal this plan to her?

"Obviously, I will tell her," he said. "I will just tell her that I love her and that I would like to marry her—after completion of my home. That is the most important priority and responsibility at present for me."

"But you can tell her before also," I said. "You don't have to marry her now, but you can tell her before. Otherwise, she'll get married to someone else."

"Yeah, that's right." *Giggle.*

"Why are you so fixed about two years from now?" I asked. "If you love someone, wouldn't you put that first?"

"There are so many goals, and I have my sequence set. I believe that you should get right thing at right stage," he said.

This obliviousness to Sunita and her needs was strange. Ravindra was in other ways so acute and insightful and empathetic, so sensitive to the little signals that people gave each other. But I saw, too, that love was just another item in his checklist of success.

"In two years, I would have become national trainer of the Jaycees," he said, referring to a local civic organization for which he led training workshops. "Now I'm zone trainer. This year I'm going to qualify for the national trainer, and I'm going to be first person from whole Umred region to qualify for that exam. So I want to get married with maximum accomplishments under my belt. My wife should feel better about me, that she is getting married to a man of accomplishment."

And the lessons of success in other spheres were applied to romance: "What I believe is, if you want something by heart, really truly, you will get it. That is my experience so far. And I think this will be true for this incident also, as far as the marriage part is concerned. We have many things in common. She is also very public; me, too. I just like to talk; she also. She's also in Jaycees; me, too. She also has good looks; me, too." And he giggled some more.

I wanted to see the house that was sucking Ravindra's attention away from Sunita—his priority, as he had said. He had given the house a name, as if it were a British estate: Rajkamal, a blend of his father's and mother's names. It stood outside town on a vast ground that resembled an empty trailer park. In the scattering of finished homes, the washing hung outdoors and animals wandered outside.

The house was at this moment a structure of drying concrete, with bamboo scaffolding everywhere. There was a living room in the front, a kitchen-cum-dining-room, a master bedroom with an attached bath, and a second bedroom without one. In a suspension of his filial piety, Ravindra mentioned that the master bedroom "hopefully" would be his. He said he had carefully planned the width of the house to leave enough space for a driveway, one that could fit a "four-wheeler." An Omni van from Maruti Suzuki was his next priority down the line—after the house, but before Sunita.

We climbed to the roof. Water was dripping from the still-curing concrete. He walked from one rectangular pool of liquid to the next. In the fields around us were piles of rocks and other unfinished homes with metal rods poking needle-like into the sky. In front of us was a Hindu temple. "So this is my dream home," he announced after a moment's silence.

In that moment, he somehow reminded me of my own immigrant parents and their long journey, with the singularity of his focus and the simplicity of his longing, for dignity and his own small palace and some quantum of control in the world. And yet he was an immigrant not between lands but between the worlds of his own land, between a world of servants and a world of masters that were in many ways further apart than the India my parents left and the America they found.

His success was careful and sequenced and incremental. It was a gradual evolution in his mode of transportation: bare feet, then flip-flops, then shoes, then a motorcycle. It was sleeping outdoors and then indoors, on a *charpoy* and then on a bed, in a shared room and then in a room of his own, under a sheet too small to cover his legs and then under blankets when he needed them. Success was a refrigerator, then a TV, then a stereo, then a video player. It was a cell phone that just made calls, then one that could store hundreds of numbers, too. It was knowing nobody and then accumulating hundreds of numbers to store. Success was a streak of small victories, each nudging Ravindra further away from the world into which he was born.

Ravindra had become famous because of his motivational teaching. But I had never seen him teach. His duties had multiplied since my last visit, and he now lectured at several local schools and colleges. (Ever aware of power gradients and resistant to being a supplicant to another's graces, he made a point of noting that the principals had reached out to him: "I've never given any application. Everywhere they have called me, by knowing my abilities in outer world.") I went to see him teach the next day, first at the high school where Sunita worked, then at a polytechnic college.

He was a commanding figure in the classroom. His personality filled the air and the students' eyes were fastened to him. There seemed to be little daydreaming going on. He paced around the classroom, only a decade older than his students but, unlike them, a man of his own making, at peace in his skin. They sat before him in their half-sleeved shirts and ties and white tube socks and black shoes, listening raptly.

The first class was ostensibly in English communication; the second was in DLS, as Ravindra called it—Development of Life Skills. But all his classes were really just different versions of what was now known as the "personality development" curriculum in India, which taught everything from how to pronounce words to what to wear to an interview, from how to work in teams to how to build self-confidence. It was what the call centers and high-technology firms insisted on: they claimed to receive too many résumés from brilliant engineers who could not string together a coherent sentence, could not work with others, could not make a presentation, could not calm an angry customer. It was what I had seen even at McKinsey in Bombay, where the astounding cerebral powers of my colleagues were rarely matched by their social skills.

Indeed, the very idea of a personality, of unique selfhood, felt like an alien imposition on the traditional Indian world. Hinduism had always cultivated a sublimation of the self, aimed at realizing *moksha*, or liberation, through transcendence and renunciation of the material world, which it saw as illusion. But, more than that, it was the social fixedness of Indian life that had limited the usefulness of a compelling personality. Your station in life was said to be determined by *karma*. Your position in the family was determined by your gender and birth order, not by your artistic skills or manners. Your early peer relationships in traditional households were with cousins more than friends, which meant that you didn't face the pressure that young people faced in the West to become appealing to others: you didn't have to lock down a distinctive niche on the social free market. Your marriage was organized by others, based on family reputation, not your charm. Within a clan, individual members were seen as interchangeable, as when my grandfather's family, foiled in their attempt to marry him to the woman of his choice, turned to the next daughter in the same family, my grandmother. In the corporate universe, your boss would treat your "senior" at work (as he was invariably called) better than you simply because he was your senior, and there were few rewards for a better workplace personality, for speaking or presenting or networking in an exceptional way. Indians were, in a sense, not self-made but other-made, and the system of social incentives traditionally led people to put other pursuits ahead of standing out in the crowd.

Ravindra, like the students he taught, was in revolt against the old fixedness. But, once that revolt was complete, a man could find himself utterly alone. Under the traditional system, such a man may have been low-born, but at least he had a domain of certainties. He knew which foods were his foods. He knew which things his people considered to be polluting and which were thought to be clean. He had a language that may not have let him work in Bangalore but that was at least securely his. He had a way of gesturing and an accent and a wardrobe tested by time. And so when he chose to strike out as self-made, he would need—even before a job and a house and a car—the rudiments of selfhood. He would need a personality.

In his personality classes, Ravindra was a teacher of a kind that I had never seen in India: a democratic one. He was funny. He was plainly in charge but not a monarch. He asked the class to clap when a student took a risk to speak aloud. He encouraged student participation. He was straight out of a self-help book: empowering, giving feedback, motivating, enabling. He was not the sage *guru*, dispensing pearls of wisdom from up high, who had so confined Indian learning.

Ravindra's mission seemed to be to draw the students out of themselves. He called on them to participate, to try creating sentences out loud. One girl summoned him to her desk so that she could whisper her answer first and minimize her social risk. He offered the class an acronym, JAM, which he told them was a common expression in English—though one I had never heard of—to request "just a minute." Then he went over the difference between "affirmative" and "interrogative" and "exclamatory" sentences: the affirmative was a basic sentence, like rice without cumin, he said; the exclamatory was the kind of remark he uttered— "Wow!"—when he first saw the sea, in Bombay. And one could sense he knew that much of his value came simply in dropping the word "Bombay," leaving it to crackle as a dream in his students' minds.

In the DLS class, for college students, he fired up his motivational energies for the students, who were in their late teens, a light black fuzz darkening the boys' faces. "There is always gap at the top," he said, and it took three things to get there: knowledge, attitude, and skill. Here Ravindra taught watered-down versions of MBA precepts, but the ideas were applied, in line with his own self-obsession, to the students' personalities.

Today's lesson was SWOT analysis, by which business executives around the world assess a company's strengths, weaknesses, opportunities, and threats within a competitive industry. But here in Umred, SWOT was part of the relentless cultivation of the self. "SWOT is the method by which we can evaluate ourselves," a lanky teenage boy stood up to say when Ravindra asked for a definition. And I had a sense, from this and earlier visits to Indian finishing schools, of a whole generation's being trained rather than educated, with nothing to which to apply their frameworks. They knew nothing about industry, art, history, literature, science. They would one day be little more than the sum of their self-help ideas.

Ravindra and I drove to Nagpur later that night. I was flying out in the morning. We made conversation in the car, but I could feel myself tiring somewhat of his talk. His total absorption in achievement was grating on me. Then, as these thoughts were simmering, he broke the silence by asking, "Sir, what are your suggestions for me?"

It was a request for feedback: a foreign corporate practice crudely imported into this setting. I thought for a moment. I thought of the narrowness that I had begun to see in the midst of these burgeoning aspirations. The idea of Umred that had come to me at first was of ambition, energy, self-invention: the restlessness that I had known in my own America. It was an idea of hope, at war now with the old degradations. But, precisely because those degradations ran so deep, emancipation would come only to those with a terrifying singularity of purpose. Ravindra could not afford to learn a less practical kind of English, could not afford to spend time understanding the woman he loved, could not afford to take a vacation, could not afford to read books other than motivational tracts with seven tips for solving this or that.

But there were now thousands, tens of thousands, hundreds of thousands, perhaps millions of Indians who were making this bargain and adopting this focus. And they were liberating India, undoing what to me had always seemed its most unpardonable fact. But I wondered what kind of country they would make when there came to be enough of them to change its essential character. They were loyal to their families and yet so cut off from the broader Indian inheritance. The past scarcely inspired them now; it was little more than a set of family rituals, ceremonies to be performed. Their heads were filled with SWOT analysis and ways to win friends and influence people and JAM, not with the tolerance of Ashoka, the poetry of Kabir, the universalism of Tagore. The best sellers in the bookstores they frequented tended to answer questions of "how," not of "why." They were all motion and no reflection, fabricating themselves without reference to history. I wondered if, in rejecting all that was unseemly of the Indian past, they would also eliminate much that was good.

Sitting in the car now, with these ideas washing within me, I chewed on Ravindra's question. I weighed the relative merits of candor and tact. I knew that he relied on my advice and took it seriously, and that I was perhaps the only person who would tell him this. So I chose candor. I told him that my suggestion would be to have a well-rounded idea of life, to pursue interests other than his own success, to be humble, to keep space for friends and family and love.

And I realized, even as the words poured out, and in the moments of silent incomprehension that followed, how empty and out of tune they must have sounded. When you come from where I do, love and leisure and broad reading and a well-rounded mind are vital parts of living, not luxuries. But where he came from, it was remarkable simply to have surfaced fully human, to have shut out all the voices telling you who you could not be, to have listened instead to your inner voice, whispering at first, then rising with every proof of its veracity. Ravindra did not have the luxury of losing focus, of chasing a wider vision: because if he did, the world of degradations that he had escaped would be delighted to have him back.

Some days after leaving Umred, I received a text message from Ravindra:

> Bad news! Sunita denied my love. Her parents r fixing her marriage with some1 else. I think she is unwilling 4 this. Bt cant resist against family.

That trip she had taken out of town had been for an engagement. When she spoke to me in the car, in secret, it was perhaps a last, hopeless attempt. She had given him the opportunity, and now she was gone. She refused even to talk to him now. He begged me all day to call her, which seemed like a terrible idea. But he said that his very life was at stake and that he needed my support. So I called. Her answer, in five words, resolved all ambiguities.

"I love my family more," she said simply.

They had said more to each other through me or with their thumbs tapping tirelessly at their phones than they had ever dared to say in person.

"You're the kind of friend who is difficult to forget," she had once texted him.

"I miss you very much here," he had replied.

And this went for the whole of Umred, not only the two of them and not only for potential lovers. When Ravindra showed me the thousands of text messages he had stashed in his computer, sent and received, they seemed to brim with borrowed emotions: trite proverbs, made-up sayings, quotations from people they scarcely knew, such as Abraham Lincoln. Ravindra and his friends were in their late twenties, but these messages seemed to belong to hyperemotional children.

IF YOU FIND YOUR SELF IN A DARK ROOM+VIBRATING WALLS AND FULL OF BLOOD, THEN DON'T WORRY. YOU ARE AT SAFE PLACE, YOU ARE IN MY HEART!

LOVE is 4 LIFE. LIFE is not 4 LOVE. LOVE may fail in LIFE. LIFE should never fail in LOVE. So dnt spoil LIFE in LOVE. But dnt 4get 2 LOVE in LIFE!

Ice is a cream, luv is a dream, bt frndship is ever green. Dont mak frnds b4 understanding, & dont break ur frndship after misunder-standing.

F'rank
R'ecovers
I'nsults
E'motions
N'ose cuts
D'edications
S'entiments
these all happen wth FRIENDS

Ninety percent of the messages appeared to be forwards. It was as if they had so much to say to each other, and no language of their own in which to say it. The past offered no instruction for the lives these young people were living. A new day had dawned, and with it a new idea of human relationships, relationships not of hierarchical authority but of democratic amity. There had been no time for these new relationships to develop, and they had not yet gained their own vocabulary. There was so much raw energy but no context, nothing to guide it. And it was strange to see Ravindra, with all that he had seen and done, behave on his phone like a little boy.

So it was with him and Sunita. He had nothing more than his self-confidence to offer. He had come so far and planned so thoroughly, but he had never realized that he might inform her of these plans. He did not understand that she felt confused and adrift. He was his own man now, self-made and not other-made, and was, in a sense, oblivious to the ways of his society. He had not realized that one had to lay the Indian groundwork: declare intentions, speak to the parents, and burrow in gently. In his meticulous planning, it had not occurred to him that a woman, unlike an exam, is not conquered simply by willing that you get her. I had urged him to say something to her, give her a sign. And he had sent more and more of those messages. But on the occasions when she called back, he was formal and upright and proper, as if the man sending those texts did not own the voice she now heard.

Now Ravindra would suffer for a time. But then he would resume the great project of his life, which was the project of himself. He would continue down the path of becoming everything that India once told boys like him they could not be. And yet my thoughts on that afternoon kept returning to a message that he had sent me some months earlier, before the latest events could be foreseen:

> "Life sometime becomes so selfish that it wants everything. And while trying 4 everything we miss something that is worth everything."
> Hello Anand Sir, hw r u?

THREE

Pride

My grandfather has always had a thing for tweed blazers, embellished with leather elbow patches and, if the evening is important, a silk pocket square. He sometimes adds a tie clip or cuff links. I have never seen him wear Indian clothes apart from when he sleeps. India is a tropical country, and the common man on the street tends to leave his shirttails hanging loose. Not Nanu: I think he would consider that uncouth. In the tardiest of nations, he is highly punctual; if left to his own, without my grandmother's delays, he would probably turn up early when invited out. He spends his mornings like an English gentleman, sitting on the veranda sipping tea in a floral cup, leafing through the newspapers, pausing now and again to fret about how corrupt and criminal this country—his country—is becoming. He says these things in an elegant Anglo-Indian accent that only widens the seeming distance between him and the land whose citizenship he proudly holds.

Nanu is, in other words, what the British statesman and historian Thomas Babington Macaulay had in mind when in 1835, at the height of the Raj, he proposed an educational regime that would groom a local elite of brown-skinned Englishmen. "We must at present do our best," he said, "to form a class who may be interpreters between us and the millions whom we govern; a class of persons, Indian in blood and colour, but English in taste, in opinions, in morals, and in intellect. To that class we may leave it to refine the vernacular dialects of the country, to enrich those dialects with terms of science borrowed from the Western nomenclature, and to render them by degrees fit vehicles for conveying knowledge to the great mass of the population."

It was testimony to the dramatic success of this idea that, in the first hours of August 15, 1947, as a new Indian republic won freedom from the British, the speech by its leader heralding that freedom was uttered in English—a language that most Indians, huddled around their transistor radios, did not understand. But Jawaharlal Nehru, who approached India with a foreigner's sense of romance, was Harrow- and Cambridge-schooled and, like Nanu, an Englishman at heart. Mohandas Gandhi, who seemed less English in his homespun cloth, was a London-trained barrister who wrote in the colonizer's language more eloquently than most of the colonizers. And, if Nehru and Gandhi could be respectable Englishmen and still held up as passionate, patriotic Indians, then surely their countrymen could follow their lead.

What I saw of India as a child was homogeneous and whole. I had no idea as yet of the country's different worlds, no sense that my reality was only a partial reality. Looking back, though, I realize how British my relatives' India was. Alongside the spiced food and family devotion and chilling poverty that were specially Indian was so much that was borrowed. At parties, my relatives favored triangular sandwiches (with crusts removed); they spoke without embarrassment of convening "high tea." Their English was perfect, though peppered occasionally with choice Hindi and Punjabi and Tamil words. They had their own eating restrictions, with some of them vegetarian, but they were never of the typical Indian level of complexity or obsessiveness, and they never prevented my sister and me from eating what we wanted.

There was never talk of our caste, a notion that seemed beneath their cosmopolitan air. There was no feet touching that I saw, although feet touching was almost as universal in India as gravity. They didn't do the typical Indian things: didn't seek to involve us in religious rituals, didn't constantly ask how much things cost, didn't cut in line.

Back in America, our membership in this Anglicized class was impressed upon us in only the subtlest ways. My mother would use such phrases as "our kind of people," "educated people," and "good upbringing" from time to time. These seemed like perfectly nice, perfectly banal things to say, and it took a while for me to discover their deeper connotations. All they meant at the time was that, unlike so many other Indian-Americans, we bought into the American ethos, believed in the American dream, did not make snide comments about "the whites," as many other Indians did, and harbored none of the overwrought nostalgia for the motherland that prevailed in many immigrant communities. My parents had no problems with American girlfriends and boy-friends. We rarely ate Indian food outside of the home, so as to taste others' cooking. My parents rejected the survivalist ethics that could sometimes prevail in India, making a point of teaching us to pay our taxes happily and in full and to inform the waiter when we were undercharged in a restaurant, not just when we were overcharged. When summer came, and my mother recom-mended books for me to read, they were almost always English or American titles, not Indian ones.

It was only many years later, with my arrival in India, that I began to understand that our ways were not the ways of the Indian mainstream, but of a particular class of Indians. This class called itself "middle class" but formed something of a benign cul-tural aristocracy. It was made up of Anglophiles whose children had attended school at J. B. Petit and Campion and Cathedral and St. Xavier's and St. Stephen's and Elphinstone. Our grandfathers had worked as civil servants, or *boxwallahs*, British-behaving salarymen in big, respectable companies; they had resisted the grime of actual commerce. Our parents spoke Hindi but had grown up reading and writing and reasoning in English. Our relatives in India loved their country, but their affection was an idea more than a visceral emotion. And, because it is impossible to define who is in without defining who is out, there lurked in our self-appraisal an unconscious dismissal of those whose families were different: those who spoke in emphatic and syllable-hugging Indian accents, who prayed and fasted all the time, who talked constantly of money, who displayed their wealth but lacked what we thought to be taste.

I came of age in the interstices of two civilizations, with the inevitable confusions of identity. On the more difficult days, it was possible to feel that I didn't quite belong anywhere and that the burden of winning a place was heavier for me than for the other American kids. And, even though I did not love India, I suppose that I extracted a certain comfort from the knowledge that I belonged to this rooted, rarefied Indian breed. My parents had education, bearing, and class. They spoke in sparklingly enunciated English that made the neighbors marvel. My family had a longer history of education than many of the established American families around us. I knew in the back of my mind that we were somebody somewhere—insiders, not outsiders; proud, respected. And so when I returned to India, I took for granted that it still existed, that country—a place that belonged to our kind of families, to Indians who dressed and thought, dreamed and talked, as we did.

Except that it didn't anymore.

Arriving in the city my parents had left, I insisted on calling it "Bombay." Its official name had been changed to "Mumbai" some years earlier by a political party intent on purging the colonial legacy. But I had grown up hearing tales of Bombay, and I refused to switch. My insistence on this matter was aided by another of my insistences. I brooked no option but living in the southern sliver of Bombay whose geography my parents had passed down to me—the world of Churchgate, Colaba, Marine Drive, Oval Maidan, the Taj Mahal hotel. And because South Bombay was home to the descendants of Macaulay's Anglicized elite, I heard no complaint from my neighbors about my choice of nomenclature. They, too, called it "Bombay."

It was silly to insist on living in South Bombay: I was making a modest salary, and so it was the equivalent of a newcomer to New York demanding to live on Park Avenue for $200 a month. That was how I ended up sleeping on a bed shorter than my body, above teams of hardworking cockroaches: the neighborhood was prestigious, but all I could afford within it was a glorified closet in someone else's home. And it was silly, too, because I had come to India to venture beyond my comfort zone, to encounter the world, not to replicate my family's worldview and geography.

As I settled into my new surroundings, it was possible to believe that the world of Anglicized South Bombay remained intact. I spent many weekend evenings at Indigo, an elegant restaurant that attracted the city's prosperous young. The atmosphere was new, but the people I met there were, I realized, the children of my parents' former peers: the people I might have grown up with had my parents stayed in India. They spoke in the South Bombay accent that I knew so well. They remarked every few minutes at the smallness of the world. When they gave directions, they relied not on landmarks but on the whereabouts of other families like them: "You know Anju's house, *na*? Take a left there. Pratap's mother's house is on the right. Go past that and take a left at Bunty's sister-in-law's place . . ." And they walked and talked with that careless swagger of people who know that a society is theirs: that there are people they can call, connections they can use; that the world operates and will always operate according to laws conceived by and for them.

There was something immediately familiar to me about the members of this class, but there was also something unsettling about their remoteness from India. The poet Langston Hughes once wrote of black Americans who wished that they were white. It required the death of that wish, he wrote, for blacks to be "free within ourselves." I wondered whether Indian Anglophiles were free in that way. In the sepia-tinted photographs of grandparents and great-grandparents that hung on their walls, the men were almost always wearing Western clothes. Anglophile parents, seeking an edge on the matrimonial markets, described their daughters as "convented," meaning that they had received a British-style convent education. These Indians rarely read Hindi novels, not even in English translation. The categories of their imagination, the habits of their logic, and their literary reference points were all Western. They judged arguments by the crispness of their articulation, rather than in the way familiar to more Indians—by their narrative and emotional force. The octogenarian grandmother of friends of mine put it this way once: she had realized only as an adult that everything she had learned in childhood had taught her to hate the Indianness within. What is it like to grow up in a society and be told from the beginning, in a thousand unconscious moments, that the ways of its streets, the cut of its gestures, the rhythms of its speech are beneath you?

But I realized, as I sunk into the society, that things were changing, both within the Anglicized community and beyond it. I tried in my early days in Bombay to mix my social circles, to bring together my McKinsey friends and my Anglophile Indigo friends. But I grasped very quickly that I was causing a collision between old and new elites who had little interest in or regard for each other. My Indigo friends seemed to find my McKinsey friends, who were products of the new meritocracy in India, uncool, unsophisticated, raw, ignorant of the world outside McKinsey, moralistic, and boringly averse to merrymaking. The animosity was mutual. When I mentioned my movements on the weekends, I would see judgment creeping across my colleagues' faces: a blend of jealousy and scorn. They seemed to think of my Indigo friends as shallow, pretentious, loose, unprincipled, spoiled brats, members of a lazy and effete ancien régime whose hearts were not truly in India.

My colleagues were not the tweed-draped Indians remembered from childhood. They tended not to come from privilege; their parents were almost uniformly less well-off and less educated than they now were, although hardly poor. In everything from their food habits to their way of speaking to their cultural preferences, they were the Indians that the Anglicized dismissed for being too Indian. And now they were the Indians rising into influence, getting the best banking and consulting jobs, anchoring television shows, winning elections, and defining the new code of manners.

They had none of the old guard's escapism. They might try this or that cuisine in a restaurant, but they spoke openly and unapologetically about preferring their *ghar ka khana*, their "home food," in the authentic regional style, to everything else. They preferred Bollywood music to Western sounds. And they spoke very differently from my Indian relatives. My colleagues' accents had the exaggerated, staccato tone of the India that Macaulay never reached, lurching from one intensely stated phrase to the next, punching every syllable, from the rigorously rolled "R" to the heavily thwacked "T," singing all the while. They clicked their tongues when arguing to express frustration or incomprehension. They gestured in ways that were familiar from travels in small-town India, rotating a hand back and forth to say, "I don't know," or performing a gradual outward drift of the arm punctuated by a sudden wrist flick to dismiss an idea.

It might not seem remarkable today to find Indian behavior among Indians in Bombay, but a generation ago it would have been. Elite Indians had not been just a more moneyed version of regular Indians; they had been a different kind of Indian, produced in an encounter between East and West, not fully of their own country. A generation ago, the ways of the common Indian would not have been visible at a place as rarefied as McKinsey; and so to find everyday, everyman manners expressed so confidently in the cafeteria of this elite company, by the hands and mouths of a new elite, was to witness a great subversion.

It was not only how they spoke but also the words they used. They had a new language, popularly called "Hinglish," a fusion that involved stirring spicy Hindi words into English sentences, conjugating Hindi verbs with English suffixes, and appropriating the pidgin English of the less-educated classes.

"*Arre*, don't give her any *bhav*. Boys always *lagao chakkars* around her."

"*Chhod*, *yaar*. He is like that only."

"He was just line-*maro*-ing."

"*Chal*, timepass *karte hain*. Shall we *pucca* meet at seven?"

"Come *jaldi se*. *Nahin to* the booze will finish."

"My boss is really acting pricey. All I did was prepone the meeting, *ya*."

Such mixing was not entirely alien to the Anglicized old guard of an earlier generation. But it had been something to put on with friends occasionally, if at all, and not to use in official situations. Status depended on polish, which required a smoothing out of what the colonizers might have seen as rough Indian edges. My colleagues belonged to a generation that was turning the rules around, embracing Hindi and Indianness more generally. And their own speech was echoed in the language of newspapers and entertainment and advertising: Bollywood films were emerging with titles such as *Jab We Met*, *Right Ya Wrong*, and *U Me Aur Hum*; Domino's Pizza was selling pies with the delightful tagline "Hungry, *kya*?"—you hungry or what?

Consider that tagline for a moment more. Domino's was coming to India; it was nudging traditional fare from contention; globalization was on the march. But these advertisements, and the advertisements for indigenous products as well, were more likely to include Hindi or Telugu or Bengali than they were a generation ago. So was India becoming more Westernized or less?

One way to regard the country's evolution, especially by detractors, was as a process of pseudo-Americanization. After all, to tell Ravindra's story is to channel the familiar American vocabulary of self-making, transposed to unfamiliar terrain. But, in fact, a more complex process was unfolding in India: there was the liberation of the self, the fragmenting of the society, the coming of modernity, but there was also, with that freeing, a revival of pride within and a new comfort in brown skin. Ravindra was defying one kind of repression: the traditional repression of a thousand layers, of the landlords who had taunted his parents. But for many Indians, it was not the village betters who had reined them in, who had deprived them and the world of the fullness of themselves. It was, rather, the colonial stain, that residual longing to be someone apart from yourself. But India was now living through an upheaval in the laws of manners. Millions of Indians strove to learn English, but fewer and fewer strove to be English. And so India's revolutions were not merely about success and growth. They were also about a new self-confidence and new liberty to be Indian without apology.

In the eyes of many of the old Anglophiles, the rise of the indigenous was a return to older, coarser days. In some ways, Bombay was becoming less permissive than it had been, even as it became, in another sense, more globalized and connected to the world. When the old guard remained in charge, you could eat and drink everything everywhere; you could stay out all night listening to Ravi Shankar in concert. But with the equations of power now changing, the provincialism of the new middle class was asserting itself in Bombay. New ideas of right and wrong held sway in a city where money and clout had come into the hands of a new breed of Indian. Whole zones of the city had been declared off-limits to

meat, in order to satisfy pious upper-caste Hindu residents, even as
other parts of the city were sprinkled with sushi restaurants and
gelato parlors—and this restriction had a further, and quietly
desired, effect of excluding Muslims from the neighborhood. The
late concerts were gone, too, a casualty of new "moral policing,"
as it was called in the press: the values of the small town applied to
the city, by people for whom such towns offered a framework for
making sense of new times.

I began to see the people who had always shaped my idea of
India, in whose universe my parents had been brought up, to
whose company I had returned, as relics of a passing age. It was an
unpleasant truth to accept. I began to see their lethargy. In many
families, someone, generations earlier, had earned their berth. For
long years after that, life had often been lived on cruise control.
But now the children of the Anglophiles were struggling to win
admission to the same colleges that their parents had attended.
Many of them had wealth but no cash flow in an increasingly
meritocratic society that had fewer and fewer slots for the untal-
ented. They ate at the country club instead of at restaurants, because
the club provided food at cost; memberships could be inherited,
and so to live as if wealthy required only that an ancestor of yours
was actually so. They clung to whatever connections they still had.
Connections mattered less and less; you no longer needed one to
get a telephone or plane ticket. But at their parties they would
brandish their connections anyway, pretending that they still lived
in a closed system of five thousand acquaintances.

They still sat in their old bastions—the Bombay Gymkhana,
the Willingdon Sports Club, and the like. They still sipped their
whiskeys and their fresh-lime sodas and traded gossip about this
one's marriage to that one and how the venue was way too small
and for 10,000 rupees a head, you know, the food should have
been a little better than that. They still used language like "chap"
and "attaboy." They still boasted of their lack of fluency in Hindi.
The rich among them would tell anyone who would listen that

they buy Louis Vuitton only "abroad." They still clung to the sense of their own superiority, calling ordinary Indians by condescending names such as "vernie," for "vernacular." And yet they could no longer deny the gathering evidence that their country was passing into new hands.

In the last years of the 1940s, two men from the merchant castes, my Punjabi grandfather and a young Gujarati named Dhirubhai Ambani, were embarking on their careers. They were both born as *banias*, traders, a caste-bounded community that instructed its sons right from childhood to understand risk and working capital and net profit—and a community that, under the cultural regime of that time, in a new era of public-spiritedness, was regarded as crass and uncouth, trafficking in the vulgarity of actual commerce, with no tie clips or cuff links or tweed to distinguish them from the masses.

Nanu and Dhirubhai had another thing in common: their fathers (and, in Nanu's case, his grandfather, too) had broken with the caste heritage, working with papers and books, not money and goods. Nanu's father, who died when Nanu was twelve, was a lawyer; Dhirubhai's father was the headmaster of a school. Neither man left his son with a business and so, as they prepared to make their lives in the young new republic, each man faced a choice: follow his father's path toward the respectability of the coat and tie or revert to the ways of the trader caste.

For Nanu, it did not even register as a choice. Born in 1924, he was a bright, handsome student in Lahore. Everywhere around him he saw professionals. His father's father had been a well-regarded estate officer for an important landlord. His father was an authority on municipal law who fought cases and wrote books on the field. Everyone he knew had climbed through education. The family name was Agarwal, a *bania* subcaste whose name decorates many grocers' awnings in the country's north. But "business," as it was defined in India—the buying and selling of things, as opposed to "service," the work of a professional who cerebrally manages—was not for Nanu.

His education through eighth grade was in Urdu, with English only a second language. He switched to an English-language program in high school. As graduation neared, he fell in with a group of friends planning to study commerce, with a view to becoming an accountant. He was the highest-ranking student in the college when he graduated in 1944. Now he dreamed of England. He wanted to do the three-year apprenticeship required of accountants in London, so as to return to India a more prestigious manager, a gentleman. But, with war raging in those years, London was in turmoil and tickets for sea passage were scarce. Nanu enrolled in a program for a master's degree in economics instead. By the time the possibility of a boat ticket resurfaced, he was a year into the program and had missed his chance.

One year after his economics course, Nanu was doing his apprenticeship at a firm in Lahore when the partition of the subcontinent came. His native city would now be part of Pakistan. As a Hindu, he needed to make his way south to India, and, luckily, his firm had an office in Delhi, to which he transferred once the dust of those days settled. In 1949, at twenty-five, with his accounting apprenticeship—known as "articles"—complete, he needed a job. On a whim, he traveled with a friend to Calcutta, then the commercial capital of the country and the former headquarters of the colonial administration, where a new Indian aristocracy was in the making.

The colonizers had gone but the companies they had managed remained. A handful of Britons were still at the top, but Indian managers now filled the intermediate rungs. In choosing these managers, the British had been drawn to those Indians who most reminded them of themselves—the *boxwallahs*. At their best, they were Macaulay's stepchildren, the sons of civil servants and lawyers and clerks who had educated their boys in English, taught them how to dress like Englishmen, perhaps even taken them to the club for golf and sent them to boarding school in England. They were little Nehrus, and they were the new business elite. Despite the visible business talent of the Indian street, of the *banias* and the millions more who were *banias* at heart, the British firms preferred managers of a certain gentility, who saw business as a gentleman's game and shared their contempt for tawdry moneymaking.

Nanu began his career at McLeod & Company, a trading firm (engaged in a form much elevated in its practitioners' eyes from *bania* trading) whose interests spanned jute, tea gardens, insurance, shipping, and engineering. Until a few years earlier, the most important social division in Calcutta would have been brown versus white. But it was now covenanted versus noncovenanted. A covenanted officer, brown or white, was like a commissioned officer in the army: he was on a fast track to upper management, receiving perquisites such as six-month vacations in England every third year, even if he was not English. In some cases, the covenanted had use of a separate elevator.

Nanu was covenanted and so whisked into a world that was bewildering to a child of the middle class from Lahore. The work was stimulating. The office was air-conditioned. He and his covenanted colleagues ate side by side in a private dining room. "It was not a buffet," he stressed sixty years later, the distinction still mattering to him: they were served Western food in plated courses. A coat and tie were required in the office. In the summer, however, it was permissible to carry the coat over your shoulder.

The *boxwallahs* finished their work around five each evening and met managers from other companies for tea. On weeknights, Nanu and his friends met at Flury's, which served pastries and cakes. On weekend mornings, they convened at a local eatery on the Chowrangi Road, where they would sip beer and "gossip and chitchat," as he later put it. Business was gentle and gentlemanly. Some managers used to tuck in a round of golf in the morning, reaching the office only at eleven. Subtracting, then, the two-hour gin-and-tonic-soaked lunch that was also customary, the actual working time could be a very manageable four hours. There were evenings at the club; there were cocktail parties at which Indian managers sought to compete at scotch drinking with their burlier British colleagues.

Nanu was further immersed in Englishness when he was assigned to audit the company's tea gardens in Assam and West Bengal. He would travel for six-week stretches, spending a week at each garden. Most of the garden managers were Englishmen, with whom he would interact for twelve hours a day and learn how to talk, carry himself, and even think. They ate breakfast together with the manager's wife. They worked together during the day, punctuated by lunch, again with the manager's wife. There was afternoon tea immediately after work. Then they would retire to their rooms, bathe, and return to the drawing room for a chat before dinner and, in wintertime, a fire. After dinner, there might be a bit of brandy.

"From the unruly chap in Delhi doing my articles, I became a little more polished chap," Nanu said. "I learned a lot of things: behavior, etiquette, attitude, meeting people and talking to them. I picked up how one should behave—how to eat, how to use forks, fish knives. I picked up all those things by observation."

He was now on his way to the upper reaches of Indian society. He was the picture of respectability in those days, with his neatly parted hair, a trim mustache, and shirts and pants to which he paid great attention. He worked for a brief time with Dunlop, then switched to Hindustan Lever. In 1954, he married my grandmother; my mother was born a year later. They remained in Calcutta until 1959, when he moved to the company headquarters in Bombay. He would eventually become the company's chief internal auditor.

He remained sensitive to the contempt for *banias* in that age. It was the time of Gandhi, himself a tradition-breaking *bania*, and a time of causes nobler than the pursuit of profit. "High thinking, simple living" was the phrase of the hour. Ideas mattered, values mattered, causes mattered. Money carried the taint of an imperialism just vanquished; it was greed, after all, in whose service the colonizers had come. In these times, Nanu never dreamed of starting his own business, nor even of knocking people over to rise within Hindustan Lever. The quiet bureaucrat, whether in government or in business, was the picture of respectability. "I felt that I had reached a very honorable, comfortable position," he said. "I never was interested in or involved in running a business. I always wanted to be a professional." He compared himself to some of his *bania* relatives who had actually lived the *bania* life, and he was satisfied by the comparison: "They had a lot of money; I didn't have a lot. But I still felt I was one leg up on them. My education, my background, my knowledge—I was probably more sophisticated in my attitude, behavior, manners."

And it was this worldview that was responsible for a small quirk in our family history. My mother, before she was married, had a different last name from her father. "Agarwal referred to the *bania* community, and I somehow didn't like this *bania*-hood," Nanu explained one day. "So I thought, I can't drop Agarwal from my name, which says that I'm from a *bania* family. But at least for my children I can drop the name and give them my middle name, so they're not associated with *banias*."

Dhirubhai Ambani was born eight years after Nanu, in 1932. His portal into the world was a village in Gujarat called Chorwad, which happens to translate as "settlement of thieves." It was, in fact, a settlement of merchants. The Ambanis were *modh banias*, from the same trading subcaste as Gandhi, and, unlike Nanu, Dhirubhai had a number of role models in the mercantile life. But, as in Nanu's case, Dhirubhai's father was a professional man. Working as a teacher and headmaster, he had never found his footing in business, owing (it was whispered) to an excess of honesty. It was a mistake that his son and later his grandson would never be accused of making.

Dhirubhai had the same choice as Nanu, to follow in his father's footsteps or to try his hand at the *bania* life. His decision was made for him when he bungled his high school examinations. He would later joke of having an MABF degree—"matriculation appeared but failed." With no credentials to ride and no family trade to enter, Dhirubhai decided to do what many young Gujaratis were doing in the late 1940s: he set out for the Arab port of Aden to make some money and build some connections, with the hope of eventually starting his own business. In an age of massive government enterprises, secure salaried jobs, and asphyxiating controls on private enterprise, Dhirubhai swam against the current.

Aden was in those days a city of the world, a popular way station between East and West that teemed with British soldiers, Arab traders, and enterprising Indian migrants. There Dhirubhai found work selling products for Shell Oil, crossing to the Horn of Africa in wooden dhows. Family photographs from that time show a pudgy but handsome man, dapper in his boxy suit, with something of the used-car salesman in his eye. He was fearless and confident. It was said that he paraded stark naked in the shared bathrooms of the employee quarters, while the other Indians walked around coyly in their towels.

He was working for the white man, just as Nanu was doing in those days. But he seemed much less concerned with learning their ways than with giving expression to his own. Colleagues in Aden remembered his *bania* penchant for risk taking and self-confidence. Frustrated with his staid salary job, he prowled the Aden souk after work, taking out positions in future deliveries of commodities, creating his own personal derivatives market. One day, officials in the government treasury noticed that the main unit of exchange, a pure silver coin called the rial, was vanishing from the money supply. Investigators traced the disappearance to Aden and eventually to Dhirubhai. He had discovered that the coin's metal content was worth more than its exchange value and had been melting coins to sell the silver.

In 1954, the year Nanu and Nani were married, Dhirubhai married a young woman, Kokila Patel, selected by his family from within the caste, and returned with her to Aden. They had a son, Mukesh, three years later. As time wore on, Dhirubhai tired of Aden. He was not built to take orders and work for others, as his constant freelancing suggested, and so he decided to return to India and start a business of his own. In the coming years, he and his wife had a second son, Anil, and two daughters, Dipti and Nina.

Dhirubhai returned to his village and recruited as his partner a cousin whose father was willing to supply seed money for a business. Together they set out for Bombay, the bustling commercial capital. Reliance Industries, as it would eventually be called, started in a small office in a packed market, with one table, one telephone, and three chairs. Dhirubhai and his cousin began as simple traders. They bought spices in India and sold them to contacts in Aden. Then they got into trading yarn.

In an age of public purpose, private capital was still held in contempt in India. Taxes were high, regulations were tight, licenses were required to produce anything or even to change the amount of something that you produced. India's leaders remained enamored of homespun cotton, the fabric favored by Gandhi, and used the power of the law to restrict large-scale production of textiles, which had been a principal trade interest of the British. There were also severe limitations on the imports of raw materials, unless you had special ways of dodging them. And it must be noted that the class of men who implemented these regulations, who needed to be pleaded with by business owners, who lorded imperiously over industries they scarcely understood, was largely the same class of men with whom my grandfather dined at Flury's in Calcutta: the Anglicized professionals who, when they didn't enter the *boxwallah* companies, entered the civil service, in those days among the most prestigious lines of work.

Dhirubhai would have been a canny, corrupt, vernie trader in their eyes, beneath their refinement. But he began to display a talent for getting what he wanted. It would become a truism of Indian life within the company's first years that Reliance could bribe, cheat, and steal its way out of anything—although it showed a remarkable ability to prevent these allegations from reaching the pages of newspapers and the verdicts of courts: what was widely suspected was rarely proven. What was apparent was that Dhirubhai managed to secure licenses and special exemptions and forgiveness that few other companies could. He managed to have politicians do his bidding as if they were on his payroll. He made problems go away, over and over again. And he built a reputation for never forgetting the people who helped him. He had a talent for relationships—on Bombay's streets, where he sipped thousands of cups of tea to ingratiate himself with the merchants who mattered, and in Delhi, where coveted licenses were on sale to the highest suitcase-carrying bidder. He quickly emerged as a don of the Indian yarn trade.

It was not business as my grandfather thought of business. It was a no-holds-barred, bottom-up approach that refused to accept "no," that defied the stuffy Anglicized stickler for rules, that put human relationships above everything: commerce as it was played on the streets, not as a parlor game.

The Ambanis lived back then in a modest two-bedroom apartment in the Bhuleshwar neighborhood of Bombay, in a building called Jai Hind Estate. It is part of what is known, somewhat disparagingly, as the *chawls*, the tenements.

I visited Jai Hind Estate one day. It stood in a cluster of buildings with grated windows and balconies among which pigeons ricocheted all day. Dhirubhai's children would have stared out of the windows at other people's laundry flailing in the breeze. In a country where having a housemaid was a hallmark of being stably middle class, Jai Hind Estate was decidedly below that line, then as now. Everywhere homemakers flogged their mattresses clean and plunged soiled clothes into soapy buckets as children scampered around. Bollywood songs wafted through the halls. These were the people to whom Bollywood catered: Indians whose dreams outstripped their grinding realities, who took shelter in the big-screen projection of their fantasies.

I was, of course, encountering the *chawls* through my own eyes. Shortly after visiting the house, I asked Dhirubhai's son Mukesh about those years. He saw them differently, as a time in a special urban space where the warmth of the Indian village endured. Lives were lived in the open. Doors stayed ajar. A single balcony was shared by multiple families. People cooked for others' children, who moved in snack-seeking cohorts from one household to the next. (When Mukesh was a boy, he lost half of his pinky finger on one of these snack missions, when a door slammed in a friend's house.) The noise and chaos of Indian family life—everyone yelling at everyone, a never-ending stream of tasks to perform—had its drawbacks if you liked privacy, quiet, and space. But its blessing was the power of perpetual miniature drama to drown out the deeper, paralytic drama so endemic to modern societies: angst, depression, soul-searching. The *chawls* bred sturdy people, immune somehow to the larger dilemmas of tradition and modernity, Indianness and Westernness, that were confounding another class of Indians coming of age just a few miles away.

Several times a day, Mukesh ran down dark stairwells and out into the streets. Immediately outside were street-food vendors, selling the tamarind-laced *chaat* that he loved. All around was vital, throbbing business: not the genteel business of the *boxwallahs*, but kill-or-be-killed commerce: shops selling *saris* and jewelry and grain. Every inch of space, every moment of time, counted. Pushcarts ferrying cloth and food rolled past every minute. Indian politeness vanished here. Laborers who would bow meekly elsewhere in the city would ram their carts into a person's leg if he did not move. In the *chawls* a child would have drunk in the mythology of the merchant and his sense of battle. Business was a street fight.

By the late 1960s, Reliance was thriving. It had begun to manufacture its own polyester and sell its own Vimal brand of clothes in a chain of retail outlets. Before Mukesh's tenth birthday, Dhirubhai changed the family's surroundings overnight, moving into a lavish apartment in one of Bombay's finest addresses, the Usha Kiran building on Altamount Road. The city's boldface names lived in Usha Kiran; despite the import controls, the parking lot overflowed with Mercedes sedans. It was not far from where my mother was growing up, in Nanu's company-owned apartment. But even as Nanu sought to hide his children's *bania* origins, Dhirubhai had an opposite fear: that money would somehow sap his children's sense of *bania*-hood and deprive them of the street smarts that had propelled him to success. To address this worry, he turned to a man named Mahendra Vyas.

Vyas was a science teacher at the New Era School in Bombay. Dhirubhai hired him for an unusual assignment: to keep his children close to the streets for two hours a day. Other families on Altamount Road sought to insulate their children from the Indian reality and to groom them academically above all. But Dhirubhai told Vyas that academics was off-limits. Formal education is fruitless, he would say; just look at me. He wanted Vyas to take the children on the municipal bus and to public cricket games, to show them how to ride the train in third class and how to buy tickets in the station, one of the rare spaces where the rich were pushed and pulled and made to feel as impotent as everybody else. Once a year, Vyas took the children to live in a village for ten to fifteen days. Mukesh later described these tutorials to me as "one of the best things that happened to me in my life."

This training in the rustic left an impression. In 1979, when Mukesh went to Stanford University for an MBA, he remained steeped in his working-class ways. Upon arriving, he latched on to an Indian classmate, Akhil Gupta, and asked Gupta to accompany him on an urgent mission: to find the perfect plastic mug. Traditionally, most Indians outside the Westernized elite have viewed toilet paper as insufficiently thorough, cleaning themselves instead by hand and water poured from a mug. Mukesh had grown up with this custom and now, arriving at Stanford, insisted on driving around Palo Alto for hours to find a suitable mug, with the handle and spout just so.

Mukesh was remembered on campus as generous, retiring, and chronically homesick. There was a sweetness in his nature that his friends admired. Knowing that Gupta was short of money, Mukesh would suggest that they go food shopping together, pay for the groceries, and casually leave them in Gupta's apartment. He never really settled into Stanford or showed much interest in his surroundings. His heart and his thoughts were always in India. "He was there at Stanford, but he was also not there," Gupta said. "After class, he used to be on the phone with his sister for an hour. He missed home. He missed the food and his family a lot."

On Friday evenings at Stanford, a group of students would go out for ice cream. Gupta, feeling adventurous, picked a new flavor every time. Mukesh never wavered from chocolate. Gupta would turn philosophical, arguing that evolution required the trying of many things and then the selection of the best. His friend's smiling reply still resonates in his ears: "He used to say, 'You keep evolving, I'll keep getting what I want, and we'll see what happens to each other,'" Gupta said.

Mukesh's fidelity to his indigenous manners never left him. Many other Indian business leaders donned finely cut suits and flaunted fussy tastes. Ratan Tata cruised down Marine Drive on Sundays in fast cars and favored Hermès ties with matching pocket squares. Vijay Mallya was said to be trailed in his home by a butler holding a silver tray with a cigar and a scotch. Adi and Parmeshwar Godrej were famous for soirees that attracted Hollywood stars. Mukesh Ambani behaved differently. Among family and close friends, he preferred speaking Gujarati to English. He was openly pious, asking colleagues to stop with him at a temple during business trips to partake in a ritual Hindu prayer. He loathed business suits, preferring a white short-sleeved shirt and black trousers in the style of Indian bureaucrats. His idea of entertainment was not the Jazz Yatra concert series that my mother had relished but Bollywood; he was said regularly to watch films late at night in his private theater. He had a legendary appetite, but mostly for the food of the bustling Bombay streets. He was known to walk out of fancy restaurants in search of *dosas*, south Indian crepes, sold by the roadside. One evening, many years after Stanford, he and Gupta had dined together in New York at Nobu, the well-known Japanese restaurant. Mukesh picked at the fare, finding it bland. At the end of the meal, Gupta recalled him saying, "That was nice. Now should we go have dinner?"

Nandan Nilekani, a friend of Mukesh's and a pioneer of the Indian software industry, put it to me this way: "If you look at his interests, they're very rooted in India. He likes movies; he likes street food. He's very comfortable with himself; he's not trying to impress anyone else. It's part of a broader shift in self-confidence that is happening, where people are no longer looking at Westernized symbols of having arrived."

I asked Mukesh, when we met one afternoon in his office, if he saw himself as part of this larger turning: the ascent of a class of Indians unburdened by the colonial past, more rooted in their own land, less battered by the sense of inferiority that came with trying to emulate another culture: another facet of the Indian opening, another form of release. The thought seemed alien to him. "Now as you're saying it, I relate to what you're saying," he said, thinking aloud as he spoke.

"One thing which I learned from my father," he said, "which is very important to pass on to multiple generations, is to say"—and here he repeatedly thumped the sofa for emphasis—"never have an inferiority complex, never think that this guy is great and I can't do it and all the other stuff." In his college days, he went on, "there was a lot of emulation, and my own view was that that itself compounded the inferiority complex. My view was, 'What the hell, *ya*. We can do what we feel like.' I think what has changed now, and it's changing in multiple generations, is this self-confidence and self-belief. And sometimes we've got too much of it, without proving ourselves. But the right amount of self-belief, the right amount of self-confidence, the right amount of faith in oneself is important. And that's changed."

The success of the Ambani family reflected the rise of the indigenous not just in cultural terms but economically as well. The *boxwallah* firms had operated in a comfortable, closed game of capitalism. It was an era of production ceilings, when more was demanded than could legally be produced. Funds came from banks staffed by fellow *boxwallahs*. Permits were granted by civil servants who dressed and spoke like they did. The companies could survive without doing battle; with no incentive (or permission) to expand, they focused on products that all but ignored the hundreds of millions of Indians who lived in villages such as Ravindra's Bhiwapur and Dhirubhai's Chorwad, Indians who could not dream of buying the creams and toothpastes that Nanu's company produced.

From the beginning, Reliance marketed itself differently, as a company of, by, and for the Indian masses. It bypassed the clubby world of Indian banks and became the first major Indian firm to raise capital from millions of public shareholders. It then used the popular clout of its shareholders, who were, of course, also voters, to bully politicians into cooperation. At company meetings, Dhirubhai Ambani spoke of being a simple man, a middle-class man, just like his investors. The company devoted itself to producing things that would touch every Indian, starting with yarn and polyester and, over the years, moving into oil and gas, petro-chemicals and plastics, cell phones and groceries. The Ambanis were ruthless in their tactics but sweetly patriotic at the same time, with no interest in industries in which success would not seep into the Indian layers.

Mukesh's first project of his own was to set up a plant to pro-duce polyester filament yarn in a rural area called Patalganga. He had been summoned home one year into his two-year Stanford program by a father with little patience for book learning. This MBA stuff was fine, but it was now time for business, Mukesh was told. The plant was completed on schedule and to widespread acclaim, and Mukesh began to emerge as a respected business leader in his own right, with his own style of management: part visionary and part taskmaster, big thinking but achingly detailed. The business burgeoned, entering one new line after another, its reputation for daring and government manipulation growing in tandem.

In the intervening years, India changed. The sun set on the world in which my parents had been born, in which money was tawdry and sacrifice was noble and the professional was exalted. In the early 1990s, India was on the verge of bankruptcy. Com-mand economics and import restrictions and autarky had not worked, and so the doors of the economy were flung open. Con-trols were stripped away, caps abolished, quotas dispensed with, permissions and licenses banished into history. The market was allowed to remake India. There was an explosion of credit cards and refrigerators and soft drinks; the number of television chan-nels multiplied several hundredfold; choices flowered; new wants emerged out of thin air. Wealth as an end in itself became sanc-tioned in law and socially acceptable.

In 2002, Dhirubhai Ambani died. Arun Shourie, a politician and former cabinet minister who in earlier decades as a journal-ist had crusaded against Reliance's behavior, declared that he had made a "180-degree turn" in his assessment of the company. His turnabout spoke in many ways for the country itself. In a speech a year after Dhirubhai's death, he said, referring not just to the Ambanis but to the larger class of *bania* industrialists that they represented, "Dhirubhais are to be thanked not once but twice over. First, they set up world-class companies and facilities in spite of those regulations; and, second, by exceeding the limits and restrictions, they created the case for scrapping those regulations. They made a case for reforms."

Two years after Dhirubhai Ambani's death, the aftershocks began. The company was doing well, with Mukesh as chairman and his brother, Anil, as vice chairman. But now a power struggle broke out, with an only-in-India plot: two brothers, living in the same house, lobbing accusatory firebombs against each other through the press, while a pious Hindu mother labors behind the scenes to divide the multibillion-dollar spoils.

After months of battle, the mother cleaved the empire. Mukesh, cast in this drama as the sober older brother, got the old-economy industries: chemicals, textiles, energy. Anil, cast as the flamboyant smooth talker married to a Bollywood star, got the new-economy firms: electrical power, financial services, and mobile phones. It was agreed that both brothers could use the Reliance name but under separate brands. Meanwhile, they would continue to live in the same house, on different floors of the building, until Mukesh's new house was completed some years later.

Both Reliances outstripped expectations after the split. Anil's slice of the empire grew massively. He now ran one of the largest phone networks in India, and his entertainment firm made inroads into Hollywood, signing several deals with American stars. Anil was said to be the more personable of the two; many who knew both brothers said that it was easier to work for him. And yet it was Mukesh who emerged as his father's true successor—by the scale and daring of his projects, by his conflation of the nation's imperatives with his own, by his childlike and deadly effective gall. Mukesh not only proposed to build a bigger enterprise with greater profits; he also began to speak of his projects as if he were a national leader, describing a raft of challenges that were India's deep, existential concerns—from its energy crisis to its village poverty to its crumbling infrastructure—and proposing for each of them a Reliance solution.

"If we say, 'Can we really banish abject poverty in this country?'—Yes, in ten, fifteen years we can say we would have done that substantially," he told me when I came to see him. "Can we make sure that we create a social structure where we remove untouchability? We're fast moving to a new India where you don't think about this caste and that caste, and you can differentiate yourself between young and old, what you stand for and what you don't stand for. These changes are happening."

The curtain of dusk fell on Bombay, and the stadium lights glared in the darkness. As Mukesh Ambani's cricket team warmed up for its match, the roads leading into the stadium clogged with municipal buses, Mercedes sedans, and Indian-made motorcycles with names such as Hero, Glamour, and X-treme. The air thickened with their fumes. Heat curled up from the ditch-dimpled streets. Those tuned in to their radios were encountering the cognitive dissonance of Bombay's traffic: light, flighty, hopeful Bollywood show tunes pitted valiantly against the hopeless, immovable gridlock of the streets.

One by one, the cricket fans abandoned their rides. The prosperous could pop out without a care because they employed drivers. The slim-waisted, sandal-wearing poor could leap just as easily from their buses into the traffic, wriggling like dancers to dodge car mirrors. The burden was heaviest on the swelling Indian middle class, affluent enough to shun the grimy, fluorescent-lit buses, but not rich enough to hire their own drivers. They stayed in their cars, in groups of four and five, inching forward, honking, waiting.

A few hundred yards away, the stadium compound was jump-ing with the sweat-slicked bodies of those prudent enough to have come early. It was an orgy of the newly moneyed classes: loud, brash, confident, overweight, aggressive. Each cluster was its own private world, bumping obliviously into the other clusters with little apparent concern. There were paunchy young software types, with their trademark blue shirts and dark pants and plastic-wrapped identity cards at their waists; sprawling three-generation clans, whose fathers and children rushed ahead while arthritic grandmothers waddled behind, attended by their daughters-in-law; raucous bachelors draping arms around one another. In a society not long removed from famine, the size and ubiquity of bellies were striking: the marks of a new urban plenty. The crowd spoke in lush, emphatic Hinglish.

Cricket was once a game for the Anglophile gentry, its matches played over several days and watched by the kind of people who had days to spare, people genteel enough to appreciate the sport's genteelness. It then became the defining sport of independent India. And now, on this steamy evening in the Bombay suburbs, cricket was being reinvented again with a new intercity Indian league. Having passed from the colonizers to the colonized and from the gentry to the people, it was now being repackaged as a commodity to be sold to the hopeful masses with cheerleaders (on loan from the Washington Redskins football team), shrill announcers, and over-the-top glimmer more redolent of Bolly-wood than of Lords. To attract "the man on the street," a phrase with sad literality in India, the league had trimmed the matches to three hours, no longer than a Bollywood film.

The Chairman was late. That was what everyone in the box called Mukesh Ambani, all the handlers and press agents and anxiously waiting guests. His box was the size of a tennis court, divided between an air-conditioned interior and terraced seats outdoors. It was encased in glass, to separate his guests from the crowd beyond. The unboxed were loud and fierce and sweating in the heat, squeezed shoulder-to-shoulder outdoors on white plastic chairs. Mukesh's guests in the box sat on chairs upholstered with magenta faux-ostrich pleather. They sipped beer and wine, which those beyond were denied.

Presently Mukesh and his family entered, ringed by boxy security men in gray safari suits. A sense of their arrival spread virally through the crowd. People began to turn around, to stand up, to shake their heads from side to side and smile, to clasp their hands together in greeting and—if they were lucky enough to stand along the Chairman's path—to shake the hand of one of the family members as they descended to their front-row seats.

Mukesh was dressed in his usual villager-made-good style: a long-sleeved Hugo Boss windbreaker and fading navy chino pants. His hair was neatly parted and moist. His largeness was accentuated by pants too short for him, not quite reaching his feet, and a little too tight, riding up between the bulges of his thighs. The Chairman's wife was the more decorous and sociable of the two. She wore a beige *salwar kameez* emblazoned with pink roses and was spotted with a mine's worth of diamonds—on her eyeglasses, on her ring, on her earrings, on the rim of her watch. These shimmered visibly every time she turned around to wave and smile and blink her eyes at her invited guests. To the couple's left, one of their sons was slicing the air with a team flag and leading the crowd in a call-and-response Hindu chant: "*Ganpati Bappa Morya!*"

Mukesh stared ahead at the game, unmoved by the mingling around him. But his obliviousness was not reciprocated. When people are around Mukesh, they change. They flit around at a respectful distance, their eyes never leaving him, their minds never ceasing to dream up ways to engage him in conversation. A minor bureaucrat stood on the steps several rows behind him, strategizing with his aides about the best way to buttonhole the Chairman. Tuxedo-clad waiters took turns venturing to the front of the box to offer Mukesh a snack, but they would become too nervous to seek his attention when they approached.

His awestruck devotees had no mysterious purposes. They wanted only to speak a few flattering words to the Chairman, to call him "sir" and nod reverently, to tell him what an honor it was to meet him. People craved such moments not necessarily because they needed anything from him right now, but because they knew that they would need the Chairman someday.

Mukesh Ambani was now the most powerful private citizen of India since Gandhi. He had become more than a man, more than a businessman, more than the billionaire he was. He was a system to which others felt obliged to belong. Everyone agreed that he had few real friends; they would tell you this, then claim that they were one of them. They derided and praised him in the same sentence. An old friend of his told me that Mukesh reminded him equally of Mother Teresa and a nonviolent Don Corleone. The Chairman would squelch any rival who hindered his business interests, and do it while smiling into the rival's eyes, another friend told me.

Such fear and trembling were by themselves a kind of influence. But Mukesh's more vital power lay in how his story could be interpreted, not by his rich friends in the cricket box but by the Indians beyond the glass, peering in. He was, in many ways, one of them. He would not have had such a box in the India that my parents left. But the world had turned, and with it the hierarchy of manners; now a new kind of Indian, rooted in the local soil, mentally uncolonized, fanatical about his own country, unconstrained by an abstract British-taught morality, was in charge.

The cricket match reached halftime, and the Ambanis rose to eat. As Mukesh approached the buffet, two suited businessmen were brought to him, one a foreigner, one an Indian. He welcomed them warmly and asked them to eat. They demurred. He insisted and pointed them toward a stack of plates, several feet away. They resisted again. So he walked over himself and picked up two plates and handed them to the men, who still seemed shy, until Mukesh pressed the plates into their chests.

Throughout the game, a few privileged souls had been ushered into a conversation with the Chairman. Each one strained to find something to say that would stick. The secret to succeeding in those encounters, his friends had told me, to make him listen and perhaps invite you at a later date to his office, was to give him a "tip-off," in Ambani-speak. Mukesh's currency was information: hot, exclusive, actionable information. He tended to greet visitors with *"To kya ho raha hai?"*—So what is going on?—rather than "How are you?" The question was an invitation to offer Mukesh a valuable tidbit: which stock offering would soon be canceled, which bureaucrat would soon be transferred, which oil company would announce a find.

Information protected an empire that had risen against the system and had then become the system in its own right. Reliance operated like a small country, with an in-house "intelligence agency," as some called it, that was the envy of its rivals. It was said by its admirers and rivals alike to maintain exacting biographical files on everyone who mattered or could one day matter to its business, along with a vast database of the schedules of officials in the Indian government. Reliance executives denied all of this.

A man who worked for Reliance for many years, and left amicably, gave me an illustration of the uses of such information. In the 1990s, when the brothers were still together and Enron still existed, an Enron executive had come to India seeking to set up a power plant. She met one of the brothers in a hotel lounge. She boasted that Enron was now as powerful in India as Reliance. His reply, as it was recounted to the former Reliance manager, went something like this: "Yesterday, at two nineteen p.m., you arrived at the Finance Ministry to meet so-and-so official. You talked about this issue and that issue. You left the office at two thirty-five." The Enron executive was stunned. "OK, maybe almost as powerful," she said meekly.

Reliance maintained a network of hundreds of "moles" and

"stringers," as people who had worked for the company described them: people who had full-time jobs in government ministries or some excuse for hanging around them and leaked important information to Reliance. There was another set of spies within the company, reporting directly to the Chairman, giving him unfiltered facts about the deeds of his own people.

In its various spying activities, and in its suspicion and anxiety, Reliance seemed a throwback to an earlier time, still assuming scarcity in an age of abundance. "Remember, these guys all grew up in the License Raj," a close friend of both brothers told me, referring to the 1970s and '80s, when licenses from the government were required for all economic activity, stunting the growth of enterprises like Reliance. "They grew up as lotuses from the filth. It makes them tough, it makes them suspicious, it makes them vindictive at times, and it makes them come out in a hurry. They always see life as 'Oh God, better not miss an opportunity.' When they were growing up, you didn't get a second chance."

The heart of their manipulation was, of course, money. Reliance paid, and paid well. Nothing was unique about spending money in India to this end. But a longtime veteran of the company told me that two things distinguished Reliance from its rivals. The first was that many Indian companies were often compelled to pay for what they were already entitled to under law. Reliance did that, of course, but, more than others, it also paid for bureaucratic decisions to which it was not entitled, the executive said. Second, although the company used money to secure influence, it had invented many other creative ways to garner leverage.

Among them was its power over the press. Journalists covering the company were made part of the family, as some editors and reporters told me. It was not uncommon for reporters to receive DVD players, mangos, digital cameras, and sometimes even cash as gifts. If a journalist or bureaucrat rode the Ambani gravy train for a while, and did his part in return, he might enter what one of Mukesh's friends called the "nursing home." Those who had been helpful, who had understood the Ambani way, were rewarded not with fruit and gadgets but with foundation grants and consultancy retainers in retirement, in a country where pensions were meager and the support of children was no longer ensured.

"Reliance is like the government of India," a friend of Mukesh's told me one day over Chinese food in Bombay. "Once you join, you're there for life."

Foreign correspondents were normally spared such tactics. But I sensed in dealing with Mukesh's people that they were accustomed to getting their way with reporters. I could feel it in the gentle, coaxing tone they used when asking me not to write something or to let something go. It had no hint of authority in it. It was the tone of a stern but loving father who is telling you what is best for you. When I came to meet Mukesh, for what we had agreed was an on-the-record interview, he began with the tone: "Why don't we leave this—you can leave it as a freewheeling conversation, and you can figure it out between you and—" he said, pointing to his press aide, seated nearby. This was code language. It meant that I should not write anything from the interview that could injure him, that I should check afterward with his people for what I could and could not use. I ignored this.

My favorite Reliance influence-peddling tactic, revealed by the former executive and confirmed by other Ambani associates, was its financing of the American college tuitions of Indian bureaucrats' children. The tactic was invented because some honest bureaucrats simply refused to take bribes. Reliance was not sure how to deal with the truly honest, but it soon found a vulnerability: Indian parents will do anything for their children, and even some honest bureaucrats would allow themselves to be bought just once, for the sake of their children's security. The former executive once conducted the transaction himself. He donated a large sum to an American university. He specified to university officials that the money was not a general gift but was to be channeled into a scholarship for a particular student. The university raised no objections.

When I met Mukesh in his office, I asked him about the tuition payments. And what began as a simple denial opened into a revealing glimpse of his moral reasoning.

"Nah, these are all fables. Not true," he said.

I pressed him: did the company do anything of the sort or didn't it?

"Well, I don't think it's doing or not doing. It's the question of saying, 'Have I used Reliance's money to pay for some of this?'—which I don't think we've ever done. I don't know. If you work for Reliance and you help somebody get admission, that's a different thing. That's what I call a 'relationship.'"

I persisted.

"Would we have paid fees for somebody? The question doesn't arise—never," he said. He paused and recalibrated. "Some foundation would have given some scholarship maybe, but that's all out in the public domain. So we would have never said that 'Here's a check' and all the other stuff." And then he seemed to come around: "A foundation—like, some scholarships that we run openly—those would have happened."

The tuition example, brazen though it was, illustrated something for which Reliance was admired. Unlike many other large Indian companies, Reliance was never called transactional. Its fixers, lobbyists, and executives did not call only when they needed something. They cultivated and nurtured relationships just as Dhirubhai Ambani used to do, just as he had seen his relatives do in the village. They cared genuinely about a person's family and remembered the names of spouses and children. If a bureaucrat known to the company needed a complex surgery that he could not afford, he might be sent to a place like the Mayo Clinic in America at Reliance's expense, even if the company had not had business before him in years.

"Mukesh is not opportunistic," said a friend of the two

brothers. "I know of several industrialists—I deal with them every day—if you're a joint secretary in the government of India, they will treat you differently. The day you retire, you're forgotten. With Mukesh, you're friends for life."

As I continued my conversation with Mukesh, asking him about corruption more generally, he began, once again, with a denial. And then his answer evolved. He drew a distinction between corrupt and upright behavior, with Reliance on the upright side. But even he seemed to realize that there was something ridiculous about his denial, and he now attempted another, finer distinction: between the transactional and relational ways of securing influence.

"Our philosophy was very simple, not complicated at all, in terms of saying we believe in relationships and relationships are critical." *Pause.* "Believing in what I call a cause is important." *Pause.* "So at all times, if you have relationships and somebody says, 'OK, why don't you do this political deal for me,' I say, 'No, our cause is to build industry, and we will build industry.'"

I said that I had heard of Reliance's reputation for not being transactional, but for maintaining long-term financial relationships with those in power.

"The easier way to think about that is, we never got involved in anything that is transactional," he began. "Also, this whole business of trying to—I don't think that payments per se work. I personally think that money can do very little. And this has been my experience all across. We would never—we would run away from any kind of transactional stuff. What we mean by relationships is to effectively stand by. That happens pretty much everywhere else in the world. It's not transactional. If you and I have a relationship, and you need to go to Tirupati and need to have *darshan*"—Tirupati being an important place of Hindu pilgrimage, and *darshan* referring to a coveted spot in line to visit the temple there—"then surely if we have that, you can have that, or if you need an introduction to somebody. That's a faith framework that you have. And then you develop that individual rapport where you can say you can trust the guy."

This word "relationship" was important. It had come up again and again in conversations with Mukesh's friends. Mukesh was a man of relationships. His father understood relationships. A relationship with the Ambanis was a relationship for life. A favorite story that the family's admirers told was that Dhirubhai Ambani had gone to see Indira Gandhi on the day she lost the election of 1977; in some versions of the story, he came with a suitcase of cash. But the cash was beside the point. He had gone to see the loser on the day when no one else would, when every other industrialist was scrambling to schedule tea with the incoming prime minister. And it turned out to be prescient: she would eventually return to power, and Reliance was none the poorer for it.

But Dhirubhai had not gone to meet her simply because he expected her to retake power one day—and understanding this was essential to understanding the story's meaning. It took a special instinct on that election day to gravitate to the loser, and it was an instinct passed down from the villages. Relationships for the Ambanis were not unlike the relationships of their caste ancestors in Gujarat. A shopkeeper or cloth trader in Chorwad did not borrow from the bank that offered the best interest rate at this very hour, or sell to the customers paying today's highest price. In that universe, a living was made through a webbed community of suppliers and partners and patrons whose children married your children, whose taboos were your taboos, who prayed in the same temple, attended the same weddings, and looked after you when you fell ill.

Now the village was far behind them and the world had changed. But the idea of building up a tribe around you and nurturing it, giving limitlessly to it, trusting it with your fortune, had been transplanted to the new landscape. The bureaucrats and politicians were Mukesh's friends. He had an "individual rapport" with them. They had a "faith framework" together. What was wrong if he let them use his private plane to go pray at the temple in Tirupati? What was wrong if he helped their children go to college in America?

Consider the following morality test. Ask yourself which two of the following four statements best reflect your own ideas of right and wrong.

1. It is wrong to cut ahead of someone in line when you're in a hurry.
2. It is wrong to let your parents spend their last years in a nursing home.
3. It is wrong to use your influence to help your nephew get a job in your company.
4. It is wrong to let relatives visit your home without serving them a meal.

Let us imagine for a moment how my grandfather would answer and how Mukesh Ambani would answer. I have not had the chance to administer this test on either, but I am reasonably certain that Nanu would pick one and three, that it is wrong to cut in line and wrong to use influence for a nephew; and that Mukesh would pick two and four, that it is wrong not to tend to one's parents and wrong not to serve visiting relatives a meal. And, before you puzzle over this strange test, let me contend that it distills two visions of morality that are at war in India—a war that Mukesh's vision is now winning.

The first vision, Nanu's vision, is more concerned with a universal fairness, no matter who the person, no matter what the context. It is always wrong to cut in line, and it doesn't matter whether you're in a hurry or not. It is always wrong to give an unfair advantage to your own family member in your company's hiring process, even if you care a great deal about him. The second vision, which I ascribe to Mukesh, is not entirely blind to such norms, but its emphasis is on applying such norms in family situations more than in the public square; it is the ethics of *dharma*, duty, not of abstract rules. It is wrong to slight your parents, relatives, or guests—those in your fold—but it is pragmatically understandable when lateness requires that you break the usual rule of not cutting in front of a bunch of people you do not know. It is understandable to help a nephew rather than upholding some abstract principle that everyone else is probably breaking anyway.

These two visions mingle and compete and combine in Indian life, but the first emphasis has echoes of the Western Judeo-Christian tradition of thought, and the second emphasis is more rooted in the Hindu worldview. A. K. Ramanujan, a distinguished Indian linguist and folklorist, argued in his brilliant essay "Is There an Indian Way of Thinking?" that these different emphases define the fault line between the Indian and Western minds. In the Hindu moral system, there may be different punishments for the same crime of defaming a Brahmin, depending on who defamed him: 100 *panas* for a member of the warrior caste, 150 or 200 for a merchant, and corporal punishment for a laborer. Murder punishments vary in similar fashion. Other sources of Indian philosophy provide instances under which lying is forgivable and even advantageous (such as when an upper-caste Hindu might face death as a result of telling the truth).

Ramanujan wrote of the ancient Indian sage and lawgiver Manu, whose teachings form the basis of much of this context-sensitive morality: "One has only to read Manu after a bit of Kant to be struck by the former's extraordinary lack of universality. He seems to have no clear notion of a universal *human* nature from which one can deduce ethical decrees like 'Man shall not kill', or 'Man shall not tell an untruth'. One is aware of no notion of a 'state', no unitary law of all men." Ramanujan contrasts this with Immanuel Kant's categorical imperative: "Act as if the maxim of your action were to become through your will a Universal Law of Nature." What he concludes is that traditional Indian thinking, moral and otherwise, is "context-sensitive," as opposed to the "context-free" orientation of mainstream Western thought, which aspires to universal principles and norms: "Universalisation means putting oneself in another's place—it is the golden rule of the New Testament, Hobbes' 'law of all men': do not do unto others what you do not want done unto you. The main tradition of Judeo/Christian ethics is based on such a premise of universalisation—Manu will not understand such a premise. To be moral, for Manu, is to particularise—to ask who did what, to whom and when."

Once you begin to see through this prism, it has the power to explain much observed Indian behavior. It is the small Anglicized elite, my grandfather's India, that clings to its firm ideas of right and wrong, sits at cocktail parties and frets about the maddening corruption. They have possessed a disproportionate influence in the years since independence, and so it has seemed at times that their way is the respected Indian way. But the truth is that a more flexible morality is common on the Indian streets, in the villages, among the rising middle class.

In India, the context for moral reasoning has traditionally been one's caste or class or family circle, not the society at large, not the civic commons. Caste laws dictated how one human being was to treat another or be punished for mistreatment, not universal declarations of rights. The important question in deciding whether to extend ethical consideration to someone is "Do they belong to our fold?"

The boundedness of this ethical system explains certain paradoxes of Indian daily life. You could be in a train station and pushed and shoved by the traveler behind you; then, aboard the train, if you strike up a conversation with the same person, there is a good chance that he will offer you food, make space for you where there is none, help you in any way he can. Before you have met, you are anonymous, and the rule of the jungle applies. As soon as you have created a connection, you are part of his extended universe and circle of consideration, and his moral calculations now factor you in. I saw it, too, when I spent ten days in a silent meditation retreat outside Bombay. I noticed that the more Westernized students would practice civic behavior, such as holding doors open for others, waiting patiently in line, and refraining from pushing. The more indigenous Indians tended instead to jump the queue or slip through a just-closing door without propping it open for the next person. And yet I knew from experience that, if I met the same people in the towns or villages where they came from and went to them in need of food or shelter or a phone call, it would be they, more than the Westernized lot, who would rise to the occasion, feed me, clothe me, give of themselves without limit.

For Indians, these Western and Indian moral tendencies have competed for generations. The Western tendency had seemed to dominate in the years before and after independence, in the hands of men such as Nehru and Gandhi, whose writings reveal their own grounding in the Western universalist way. But now things were changing, and one way to construe the rise of Mukesh Ambani and so many others like him, and to make sense of their morality or amorality, was to see their deeds as another aspect of the indigenous reassertion, of the revolution from below. Their influence-peddling, mango-giving, mole-retaining behavior was not simply amorality. It was an alternative morality of the family, a context-sensitive morality that also served to work around the inflexibility of the British-given, Anglophile-staffed bureaucracy. It was a pattern of moral reasoning in which the calculus of right and wrong was made based on the effect of one's choices on those one cared about. And it seemed to be the pattern of the looming future.

Mukesh Ambani was a topic of conversation wherever I went in India, but the conversation took two very different forms. In the cities, the educated old guard would bemoan his ethics over and over again: that he had the government virtually working for him, that he manipulated the law with impunity, that public servants used his private plane as if it were their own. "What is becoming of our country?" the critics would fret, assigning Mukesh a considerable portion of the blame for coarsening the system. Then I would find myself in Umred and other small towns, where young strivers worshipped the Ambani family like gods: their ability to defy smug civil servants, their use of connections, their single-minded focus, their belief that anything could be done in India, their rapid social ascent, the garish twenty-seven-story apartment tower that Mukesh was building for his family in Bombay. For the old rich, Mukesh's skyscraper was a symbol of his lack of taste. For the rising, it was a hint of a changing of the guard.

On one of my visits to Umred, I had mentioned to Ravindra my encounters with Mukesh, and he insisted that I sit beside him and show him every photograph of the Ambani family that I could find on my laptop. For Ravindra's generation of strivers, Mukesh's success telegraphed the coming of a new India that rewarded the gritty and the impatient; an India where the pursuit of wealth overwhelmed all other pursuits; an India whose elite was more frequently refreshed, fortified by the rigors of having to earn the lives they enjoyed; an India anchored, much to the chagrin of the old guard, in India.

I had grown up with the image of Nanu sitting on his bed, knees up, writing up a letter to this or that bureaucrat or politician, mourning, one sliver at a time, the decline of his country. He was a committed citizen, and I never gave his letters much more thought than that. But I realized now that something larger was at work.

Nanu had been born into what felt to him like a society of propriety and principles and ideals. But the abstraction of these ideals, their universal and civic nature, had given them an alien and borrowed quality, and in time the soil below had begun to assert its claims. And, though he faulted those he read of and wrote to, the real trouble was within. It was his idea of India that was, when you came down to it, out of the mainstream. He didn't just loathe corruption. Something in him simply could not understand it, could not understand the burning hunger for advancement, could not grasp why someone would not be content to do his assigned duty and do it well. The letters he wrote to those officials were articulate and elegant, but they had in them an almost willful denial of the country that India actually was. The ideas of right and wrong to which his letters appealed, the summons to uphold principle at any cost, belonged to a worldview that many of his countrymen did not share. His morality was not the only, or even the dominant, Indian morality. He didn't understand hiring some-one because he was your cousin's son—but many Indians would. He didn't understand taking a little kickback on a contract because you wanted to give your daughter a truly splendid wedding—but many Indians would.

And all those letters seem now like the last gasps of a dying regime. A new regime had come, eager after waiting so long to sweep in and sweep the earlier truths away.

FOUR

Anger

On a steaming summer morning in Bombay, I awoke before dawn to accompany Behram Harda on his rounds. Behram had been a dancer in the Bollywood films of the 1970s, shuffling across the set with his twist and his cha-cha. Now in his fifties, with salt-and-pepper stubble and hair slicked back in homage to the Bollywood leading men of old, he worked as a municipal rat catcher. He and three henchmen strode through Bombay's B Ward, cages in hand, waving and smiling at residents to whom their arrival brought daily reassurance. They walked into apartment complexes, zeroed in on the burrows they knew by heart, and dropped in fumigation tablets to gas the rats. They planted sachets of poison garnished with garlic and chutney. They picked up rats sprawled dead on the pavement—proof of the previous day's success.

By five past ten a.m. they had two swarming cages in their possession. It was time for the rats to die. The catchers filled a tin bucket with water and submerged the first cage. But the cage was taller than the bucket, and the more clever rats clawed their way to the top and kept their noses above water. When the catchers restored the cage to dry ground, granting the rats a fleeting reprieve, the surviving animals patiently rearranged their fur, as if nothing had happened, as if the preceding minute had foreshadowed nothing at all. The catchers had a backup plan. They turned the cage on its side, the open door pressed against the pavement, and lifted it slightly from time to time. A tail would pop out before long, and a rat would be pulled from the cage. The assistant would fling each rat down against the ground like a Whac-A-Mole player. Each rat convulsed with shock, then suddenly went still. Many began bleeding at the nose and mouth. In some cases, the limbs gyrated, Elvis-like, for a final few seconds. A few especially resilient souls briefly resurrected themselves to make a last, death-defying jump. And then they, too, died.

The squad killed twenty-six rats in five minutes.

Behram Harda was that rarest of creatures: the impassioned civil servant, content with his narrow function, devoted without limit to the cause. But his occupation was like so many occupations in India: tedious, soul draining, and, in the final analysis, futile. It was the government job incarnate: secure and thankless. As he and I leaned against sacks of grain in a rat-infested warehouse, Behram confessed that he was fighting an unwinnable war. Rats multiplied faster than they could be caught, he said. He knew that in ten years Bombay would have more rats than it did now. "It is impossible to get them," he said.

It was impossible because the equation between the rats and the catchers had changed. When Behram got the job three decades ago, government service still attracted India's brightest minds, and Bombay was a smaller, more genteel town, still clean enough to deprive rats of the garbage on which they snack. But in the following years India turned inside out, with serious implications for the wars of catchers and rats. Bombay became a filthy megalopolis of nineteen million people, more than half of whom lived in a parallel city of shanties. Not far from the malls and luxury apartments sprouting in the city were forgotten byways where old ladies swept human waste into drains, men soaped and bathed themselves in the gutters, and women plucked lice from the heads of their husbands and brothers. They lived in the midst of garbage and, by consequence, of rats. As we walked through a government housing project for the poor, Behram pointed out, with visible irritation, a heap of eggshells and mango peels and butter wrappers and coconut halves thrown from the upper floors, arraying something of a rodent buffet.

While the rats had prospered, the caliber of the catchers had suffered. Men with Behram's dedication no longer turned up in the civil service. In a socialist country turned capitalist, the young and zealous now flocked to call centers and software houses, not municipal pest control. In the rat-catching squad, many posts were vacant, unable to find takers even amid Bombay's throngs. It was distinctly unglamorous work, and it might have been especially so for a man who had once danced in hit Bollywood movies such as *Brahmachari*, and who still looked, in a certain light, like a man of film. But when he was a young dancer, Bollywood was not much of an industry and a municipal job in a socialist country seemed more secure. His father made him trade in dancing for civil service. How were they to know that India, two decades later, would swivel to capitalism, that Bollywood would turn into a cash machine, that government jobs would surrender their appeal?

"I killed all my ambitions," Behram said.

He uttered this last phrase with that calm Indian look in his eyes, a look that suggests obliviousness to the absurdity of one's condition. This is the kind of man whom bitterness could easily seduce. Behram was hardly the poorest Indian I have met, nor by any means the wealthiest. Like Deepak Kumar, who dreamed of middleness, like Ravindra, who had pushed his way into it, like Mukesh Ambani, who had risen from it, Behram Harda was a creature of the great Indian middle. And how ordinary it would be for a man in his place to resent his father, to curse the missed opportunity of a life in the movies, to scowl at an economic revolution that left him stranded. How unremarkable it would be to struggle every morning to pull yourself out of bed and make a cup of tea. But these had been afflictions seldom suffered in India, where a man's place had for so long been something to endure and not overcome.

Behram was not bitter. He possessed, in concentrate, the stoicism that had kept India whole and humming. He was happy with his respectable monthly salary of a little more than $200. His joys were simple. The high point of his civil service career came in 1986, when Bombay's municipal commissioner, having heard of Behram's prowess, came to see his work. He brought to that work an exactitude normally reserved for the execution of humans. Back in his office, he showed me logbooks that he had kept, almost like family photo albums, since 1989. They listed every rat catcher employed by B Ward and the tally of rats slaughtered each month. He had even enlisted an artist friend to design elaborate annual summary pages of the data, decorated with colored markers.

We are all endowed with a power to make our lives seem worthwhile to ourselves. But these faculties of transcendence and self-deception had been specially developed in India. It had been the particular gift of Indians to deny that aspect of the self that simmers resentfully, that wails in the silence of the night, "Why me?"

At first, I had seen India in other ways, through other lenses. I had seen a country frozen in my youth, and then returned to see it bursting with energy. I had seen the new cult of the self and new faith in self-making. I had seen, alongside this flowering of self-confidence, a new cultural confidence in the ascent of the uncolonized Indian. And all of this, in different ways, suggested an Indian awakening, after the darkness in which India had lurked in my imagination. Behram Harda's story stayed with me because it contained another thesis, another truth.

In the ordinary course of human affairs, countries churn slowly.

Landscapes and fashions and balances of power change, but the fundamental laws of nature do not. The world continues to be more or less what it was before. People make choices in their younger days and then, if fortunate, grow up to see their dreams at least partially fulfilled. And then there are moments of special upheaval, when empires depart, when ideologies rotate, when the streets swell in irrepressible anger, when the laws of nature are rather abruptly written afresh. India was in the midst of such a moment. The meanings of destiny, family, love, class—of what it means to be Indian—were being defined anew by millions of people, all at once. That was a hopeful thing for so many. But I began to see in time that there were many Behram Hardas, too: Indians who had lived with the certainties of another world, made their plans in that world, fixed their dreams in that world, and then had woken up one day to discover that that world had been pulled from beneath their feet. It left them behind; it made their own country feel suddenly inaccessible to them. Stoicism—or sometimes, oppositely, anger—would be the only consolation.

My sister and I were never allowed to buy our Halloween costumes. We had to make them. The nonimmigrant children in our neighborhoods in Cleveland and later in Washington were allowed to wear elaborate plastic masks that turned them into Frankensteins and wart-flecked witches and famous athletes and popular (or unpopular) presidents. They went into the costume store and came out as He-Man, Batman, a Power Ranger, Bill Clinton, Mickey Mouse, Alice in Wonderland—you name it. But no: we were Indian, and we didn't believe in spending money frivolously, and we had to make our costumes. Garbage bags, old bedsheets, outmoded clothes, superglue, cardboard—anything we could find was drafted into the costuming process.

I never quite understood it. We lived in nice neighborhoods, drove elegant cars, went to the best schools. But when it came to

Halloween costumes, being Indian required what felt to a young child like insufferable austerity. It required, too, that we watched little or no television, even if that was what all the other kids did. When we craved the latest toys, we would sometimes get them and sometimes not. Either way, my mother would make a point of noting that back in India, back in her day, she and her cousins hadn't played with toys but with one another. Instead of store-bought board games, they piled matches on top of Coca-Cola bottles to pass an afternoon. Instead of store-bought birthday cards, they glued phonebook-flattened flowers onto folded paper.

My parents chose to raise my sister and me in the most acquisitive country on earth. But lurking in my consciousness as a child were certain ideas about money and material things that they had brought over from India, from the precapitalist India in which Behram Harda had made his plans. The ideas blended several traditions: Nehru's Fabian socialism, Gandhi's homespun self-sufficiency, the Hindu rejection of the material world as illusory, the Buddhist commandment to transcend desire, postcolonial anti-imperialism, the we're-all-in-it-together collectivism of a new era of nation building. Of course, when I visited India in childhood, I was entirely unaware of the genesis of these ideas, conscious only of their little manifestations in the lives of my relatives.

My father's parents lived on the sixth floor of an apartment tower in suburban Bombay. They had been very successful by midcentury standards, with Thatha, my grandfather, retiring with a respectable (and very Indian) title: senior deputy general manager of the Central Indian Railways. And yet the rusticity of their lives was a shock every time I returned to India. It was partly that their pension was modest in a time of rising prices. But they had five prosperous children who wished to take care of them, and Thatha and Ammamma proudly rebuffed this generosity most of the time. As much as they loved fruit, they would buy mostly just bananas, the cheapest of the lot. They seemed never to acquire new clothes, with Thatha mending whatever they had on his sewing machine. His own preferred apparel was a white *dhoti* and, when the air cooled, a sleeveless undershirt on top. They rarely dined in restaurants or, in later years, ordered food to the apartment. They rejected their children's offers of washing machines, videocassette players, and other modern conveniences. Thatha would loudly declare such things to be "useless" in his resounding Tamil accent. He was a skillful modern engineer, a man of technology, but in his personal life his renouncing, Brahminical side overwhelmed his other allegiances.

My father ached every time he returned to the apartment and saw how they lived. "We live so well in America," he would say. "It makes me so sad to see them live like this." And yet I realized over time that my grandparents themselves were not sad; they were just wired in a different way, and in India their way had been the way of millions. It was a certain obliviousness to material things. Happiness for them came from elsewhere: from the knowledge that they had given five children a world-class education; from the occasional visits of those devoted children and their loving families; from their deep spiritual practice; from the respect that Thatha commanded in Bombay for his expertise in the Hindu religious texts. I used to look at the cracking paint and white fluorescent tube lights and dank bathrooms and wonder how anyone could be happy in a home like theirs. And I suppose that they might have looked back at me, with my burning and unfulfillable American cravings, and wondered how anyone could be happy with a mind like mine.

The gulf between the rich and poor was eternal in India, and yet in the years of my grandparents' middle age everyone suffered certain things equally, because the wealthy could not as yet buy their way out. When the electricity went, it went for all. There was just one, government-run television broadcaster, no matter how many channels you could afford. When the water ran dry, it ran dry for all. It was hard to get a train ticket at the last minute no matter how rich you were, and harder still to get a telephone line from the bureaucracy-ridden government monopoly, whose waiting lists were famously long. The roads were equally potholed for everyone, and, with only two kinds of cars produced locally, you could not insulate yourself from the bumps much more than the next driver.

It was common in those days, during our visits east, to hear an Indian relative dismiss Americans as "materialistic." But I realize now that they were actually speaking, in the inverse, of themselves. They were really saying, "We aren't materialistic; and aren't we delightful?" It was not easy to live so simply and then see wealthier émigré relatives jet in, shop like maniacs, complain about the poor conditions of things, and jet out. The human need to keep up with one's peers translated, in their case, into outstripping us morally. In their mind, we belonged to a ruthlessly capitalist, money-grabbing, time-starved, family-destroying society; they were part of a society in which everyone sank or swam together, in which spiritual rather than material joys ruled, in which life was confronted with stoic endurance, not acquisitive fever.

My mother would become irritated every time someone attacked us with this speech, and I remember her tart retort: "You think Indians are any less materialistic?" The difference, she said, was that Indians had nothing to be materialistic about right then. Stoicism and self-denial were necessary adaptations in a time of scarcity. How long would they last when scarcity ran dry?

Mothers can be prescient.

By the time I moved to India, the country had become a circus of money, concentrated at the upper levels but not exclusively. The dream of money bound the Indian billionaire to the low-caste boy who realized one day that he could be like the men on his television screen and enrolled at once in $100 classes. Although the changes I was witnessing would take decades to seep into the lowest levels, the culture and manners of India were shaped more and more by its middle and by middleness: by the values of those in the middle, by the ambitions of those seeking middleness, by the resentments of those left out, by the nostalgia of people who sensed their middleness slipping away. A culture of middleness was becoming a dominant national culture, even for those with few means of acting on the culture themselves. After all, to buy a washing machine costs money, but to desire one is free.

The dogma of money and markets was now tearing down other doctrines in its path. And the change, once it happened, seemed to be no change at all. This was who so many Indians had always been, deep in the veins: born moneymakers. Socialism had been an audacious experiment, imposed at independence by a remote, elite governing class taken with borrowed European ideas. And now, at last, Indian policy had come into line with the way that Indians actually were. The society had stopped lying to itself and to the world about its ascetic otherworldliness. Rupees had become God in India, an instant substitute for so many other forms of meaning.

Consumption—condemned as futile by the religious texts, strenuously resisted by my grandparents, who denied its pleasures to my parents, who taught my sister and me to resist it in turn—had become a new religion for millions. The swelling moneyed class loved to shop. They shopped at malls and street stalls and bazaars; they shopped for lipstick and handbags and CDs and jeans; they walked into restaurants without fretting, lingered in coffee shops, gazed into each other's eyes at the popular date spot known as McDonald's. As if to remind me of how old these impulses were, the Indian retail magnate Kishore Biyani once told me that he had designed the aisles of his Big Bazaar supermarkets to be a little narrow, so as to re-create the crowding and chaos that Indians associated with their street bazaars and the bargains they offered: the old brought back as a corporate ruse, to make the disorienting new seem more familiar.

When they walked into the new malls and supermarkets, members of the consuming class were likely to pull out a credit card; this, too, spoke of a new ethos. Gold, not plastic, had been the substance with which money was associated in the Indian imagination. Indians longed for and hoarded and decorated themselves with gold in a world in which the future was something to fear. If you converted the fruits of your past into gold and hid it somewhere or strung it around your wife's neck, then you were at least partially insured against the future: against the tax man who might come after you, against the illness that might cripple you, against inflation and stagnation. In this fearful mode of thinking, you conceived of your worth as the present value of past earnings. Plastic was different. It allowed you to buy today and earn the money to pay tomorrow. It bet on the future, not against it. It suggested a confidence in what was to come, valuing your net worth as the present value of future earnings.

In their homes, upwardly mobile Indians were now obsessed with reality television, and especially with the subset of it that involved competition—singing competitions, comedy competitions, dancing competitions, competitions of any kind. *Indian Idol* was every bit the sensation in India as its British and American counterparts. In small towns such as Umred and Lucknow, the young inevitably cited competition shows as the inspiration for their ambitions. And in this, too, was a hint of the Indian capitalist mind coming again into its own. What so appealed to the millions of viewers was not the singing and dancing itself, but the ruthless fairness that the shows suggested. For many, life in India had not been very fair. So many spheres had required a connection or a bribe or a favor: getting into a school, getting a job, getting the apartment you loved. The competition shows resonated because they suggested the coming of a new world in which everyone would have their chance to sing, and the market would judge, and the best would truly win.

There was a sense now, absent from an earlier generation, that money could solve all problems. If you were wealthy in today's India, there were no power outages, because you could get a generator or an inverter, or you could live in a gated community with its own private power plant. If you had money and were willing to be extragenerous with the priests, certain temples would grant you "VIP *darshan*," which was a shorter, faster queue for idol viewing. If you were too busy even to go to the temple, cell phone providers now offered ways to wire money to a temple by text message, with the donation, plus a small surcharge, added to your next bill. If you owned a luxurious car, the air didn't feel as hot, the traffic as unbearable, or the roads as bumpy as they did for others.

Capitalism had transfixed the Indian imagination. And changes in the norms of money were a revolution in their own right, but they were also powerful as metaphor. There was not simply a rise in consumption, but also a new conception of life itself as something to be consumed rather than endured. There was not simply growth in buy-now-pay-later credit cards, but also a spreading tendency to bet on tomorrow, to believe that it will only improve on today. There was not simply a new audience for reality television, but also a growing belief in the power of unbridled competition to solve all problems. There was not simply the gated community as real-estate offering, but also a new aspiration to opt out of the system, to depart India without leaving.

When I spoke to successful people, their talk was as fiercely materialistic and capitalistic as their parents' had not been. They spoke as if they had just surfaced from an American chamber of commerce seminar. A rising tide lifts all boats. The government that governs least, governs best. Give a man a fishing rod, not a fish. The poor are lazy and idle; that's why they're poor. For a certain population of Indians, the journey from socialism to markets, so wrenching in other parts of the world, was very smooth indeed.

And in all of India, few cities had embraced this conversion more aggressively and wholeheartedly than Hyderabad, in the south. It had given itself over to the new world that was coming, inviting the World Bank and McKinsey to help it reinvent itself. It had privatized its airport, built new roads, and made room for the software and technology companies that it was seeking to attract. People had taken to calling the place "Cyberabad," because of the dozens of global technology companies that had set up operations in glass-encased palaces throughout the city—Microsoft, Google, Oracle, Dell, Deloitte, Motorola, and others.

In the ultimate reward for this skin shedding, Hyderabad was granted a special privilege in 2006. When George W. Bush, a great enthusiast of markets, visited India that year, the city was selected for the American president's only contact with the India beyond official Delhi. He flew into Hyderabad and held a televised roundtable discussion about markets and entrepreneurship with a group of students at the new Indian School of Business, an American-style MBA program that McKinsey had helped to erect in its own image.

But before it became Bush's kind of town, Hyderabad was the seat of a fabled Islamic empire ruled by the Nizams from the early eighteenth century until the mid-twentieth century. By the time of the last Nizam, that empire sprawled over a land mass the size of Italy. The Nizam had a personal fortune in the hundreds of millions of dollars and led one of the richest families on earth. The grotesque fabulousness of his palace, described by William Dalrymple and other writers, was legendary: the dancing girls who performed nightly on ropes tied between their own living quarters and the emperor's; his eleven thousand servants, including thirty-eight for chandelier polishing alone; the hidden lorries stashed with heirloom jewelry, in case the family had to flee; the forty-two concubines and more than two hundred children; the regiment of women soldiers brought from Somalia to guard the segregated female quarters.

It was a closed, feudal world, decadent and remote, callous to the suffering of the peasants, and it was ultimately doomed. The Nizam had been granted special autonomy under the British Raj,

and he continued to assert his empire's autonomy at independence time, after the British had left. But the new Indian republic
could not tolerate a vast alien territory in its gut and, by a mix
of suasion and force (known euphemistically in Hyderabad as the
"Police Action"), brought the empire into its fold in 1948. The city
of Hyderabad, a capital of one of the great kingdoms of the world,
shrunk over the years into its new status as just another Indian
provincial city.

Hyderabad folded into a new India with its own tastes and
ways, a city of Soviet-style apartment towers, vast armies of civil
servants, and a thriving Telugu-language film industry. And now,
all these years later, that city had grown encrusted and was folding
into yet another assertive future. Beginning in the 1990s, Hyderabad had fixed itself the task of becoming a "world city." It wanted
to be the kind of city to which foreign airlines flew directly, a city
that enticed businesses to host conferences, a city with Zara and
Mango and H&M outlets, a city whose fusion menus used the
words "reduction" and "coulis."

At the heart of this strategy was a shiny new airport, built far
outside the city, on lands from which villagers had been removed
and resettled. Everyone was talking about the airport. It was said
to be the best in India, a whiff of the nation's future, and I was
keen to see it for myself.

The airplane landed and taxied to the gate, where the first
hint of newness struck. The long white arm of an aerobridge
reached out and attached itself to the plane. Unlike elsewhere in
India, we would not have to descend onto the tarmac, wait in the
heat for a bus, and cling to the ceiling bars as the bus swerved
this way and that around the taxiway. Every flight was assigned
an aerobridge in the new airport, I was later told, with grave consequences for the corrupt: officials at India's airports had long
used the paucity of aerobridges for domestic flights to exact obeisance and gifts, particularly on Hindu holidays, from airline

staff: no obeisance, no aerobridge. But now that old economy was under threat.

Inside the terminal was a dimly lit lounge in self-consciously world-city style: sofas of differing heights, extra-fat blinds, lamps dimmer than was practical. There were, I was told, sixty-three kinds of whiskey for sale at this world-class airport. The toilets were cleaned no longer with Indian twig brooms but with vacuum cleaners. Security cameras monitored whether the cleaners performed their tasks at the appointed times, and so the familiar noxiousness of the Indian airport restroom was gone. What remained of old India was visible in the colorful folk art that had been etched into the glass walls of the terminal. But it was an India of dancing ladies in *saris*, simplified and packaged for the white man.

"Welcome to the Happening City," one of the many giddy advertisements said. The others were mostly for software companies seeking outsourcing contracts from visiting Westerners, and for gated communities that wanted the software engineers who won those contracts to buy "premium quality luxury villas" with their American dollars.

In the corridor leading out of the airport were drivers, dressed in white, holding signs for their customers, including a "Microsoft Mr. Sridhar" and an "M. Rita Singh Motorola." There were none of the old rickety taxis around, and none of their aggressive, unshaven drivers standing outside arrivals blocking my path and prodding me to hire them. The police had been told to repel drivers who didn't belong to one of two officially sanctioned air-conditioned taxi companies. Some months earlier, when the airport had first opened and some displaced villagers had come to see the site of their former homes, police officers had chased them away. (Airport officials said that a school had been established nearby to teach the villagers' children "airport-related skills," so that they could eventually return to their land in a more remunerative capacity: "upgradation," as they called it in India.)

When I entered the taxi, the driver was eager to know how this new airport compared to airports in Bombay and elsewhere in the world. I knew that he knew that he might never fly out of the airport himself. But he had figured out that his city would be praised every time the question was asked, and he seemed to squeeze from the compliments a dribble of pride for himself.

As we drove into Hyderabad, billboards began to appear, speaking in the new language of Indian aspirations. "Shape your world with LIC's profit plus and Fortune plus," an insurance firm declared. Don't just insure yourself, the ad insisted; shape your world! Another featured a young couple holding a house in their palms and handing it to their parents. Houses were once bought primarily by retirees who could afford them; now even the young, with their fat paychecks and net-present-value mentalities, and with a home-loan industry flourishing, could buy houses, one for themselves and one for the parents, with all the implications for personal liberty.

As the rugged, boulder-strewn villages vanished behind us and downtown presented itself, there was evidence of a new and sudden middle-class plenty. Cell phones were hawked every few yards. English classes were on offer. Recruiting agencies promised to carry the young out of India, to work as flight attendants and software coders and engineers. A place called iStore sold iPods. "Taste the world," a Spencer's supermarket declared. There was a store called Bread Talk, selling Western-style pastries to those who might once have sufficed with stove-made *rotis*. There were ads for Budweiser, Reebok, Citibank. Taken together, the signage hinted at the escalator of middle-class respectability that millions were riding: first a cell phone, then a motorbike, then a car, then a laptop, then a house, then a wife.

It was as if the city had awoken one day and concluded that its past offered it nothing, and had decided to become another city altogether, a city mimicking other cities.

• • •

I had come to Hyderabad to meet a Maoist insurgent named Vara-vara Rao. I had never met a Maoist before and at first struggled to contact him to request a meeting. Then I discovered that a well-to-do woman whom I knew in Bombay knew a writer who was an authority on Indian Maoists; she introduced me to the writer, who introduced me to the Maoist. I reached Rao on his mobile. (Going cellular is one of the practical capitalist exceptions that the Mao-ists make.) He invited me to visit him at his home in Hyderabad, which was a hub not only of India's technology industry but also of its deadliest insurgency.

Varavara Rao would have been considered a terrorist by many Indians. The Indian Maoist movement of which he was an intel-lectual godfather—in the formal role of a "revolutionary poet," as he called it—had been described by India's prime minister as the chief threat to India's security, greater even than the threat of Islamist militants.

The revolutionaries, known sometimes as Maoists and some-times as Naxalites, after the village where their revolt had begun, led an armed peasants' insurgency. The movement had its origins in the peaceful Marxist parties that had flourished in the early days of independence; after a time, the more radical Marxists, concluding that change might not come from within the system, had broken off to pursue their dream of violent revolution. It was a small faction in a vast democracy, but its violent agitations had been growing in recent years. Party cadres moved from village to village in central India, coaxing the poor and forgotten, sometimes peaceably, sometimes coercively, to join the Naxalite cause: to pay unofficial taxes to it, to cease to recognize the state and federal governments, even to take up arms in its service. They asserted control over one village at a time, slowly aggregating them into clusters; the talk now was of an emerging "red corridor" that cut through the belly of the subcontinent. In parts of this corridor, the Indian police no longer dared to go, and the Maoists were effectively in charge. The goal, inspired by the Chinese experience, was to expand the corridor, spread into towns and cities, and eventually conquer the country. They telegraphed these dreams with brazen attacks on police posts and railway stations and other public installations. The government was fighting back by forming civilian militias, arming them, and freeing them to take back Maoist-controlled villages by any means required.

But the Maoists were more than just a security threat. In an age when even those Indian states governed by the Communist Party were dabbling in capitalist ideas, inviting multinational companies in to build factories, the Maoist movement was among the last loud screams of dissent. Indians were converting by the day to the religion of personal success, and there was diminishing patience for those who would divert their attention. The Maoists were hated for their violence but, more than that, for spoiling the Indian parade: for clinging, in the eyes of the upwardly mobile, to an outmoded leftist fantasy that had tried to remake the nation and had failed. It was money, in the emerging view, that would unshackle Indians, erode untouchability, bring fairness; the hammer and sickle would do none of this. And so I had come to Hyderabad to hear a dissenting voice, to understand how Varavara Rao saw the changing scenery around us.

The drive to his apartment took me away from the city of malls and jeans shops and fast-food outlets, into grittier, working-class parts where men shaved bamboo stalks on the street and milled about in *dhotis*. The advertisements fell away; the relentless pressure to buy relaxed for a time; ducking under a railway bridge and crossing an overpass, I came to Varavara's building.

The electricity had gone out, and with it the elevator. I climbed the stairs and knocked on the door. Rao's daughter opened it, wearing a billowing nightgown. She asked me to sit on a bench near the front door. Water came shortly. After a few minutes, Varavara appeared, dressed in a blue and green plaid loincloth, typical of the region, with a white short-sleeved shirt that was slowly migrating toward a soft yellow. He was nearly seventy years old. He wore thin-rimmed glasses that stood askew on his nose. We graduated from the courtesy glass of water to the tongue-loosening cup of tea.

The Maoists, as I understood them, were rebels with two different causes. They were against the present process of globalization, against precisely what had happened to Hyderabad in the last many years—its Citibankification. But their movement had started many years before India's opening to the world, and their earlier focus had been not on white-collar oppressors from the West but on the problems of the countryside, on the village landlords who had trampled on the rural peasantry for long centuries. I wondered which of these causes most gripped Varavara, and I began by asking how his revolutionary ideas had formed.

At first, he said simply that his village, deep in the Telangana region, a few hours by car from where we now sat, was a fertile place for leftist ideas. He was born in 1940, the youngest of ten children. He had older brothers active in the local Congress Party, agitating for independence from the British, and they served as his role models. It was a thrilling time. The winds of change were blowing, the world was at war, and everything was being carved up and remade. New divisions sliced up the globe. Old empires were retreating from their colonies. For India, too, independence was imminent. And so politics was on many Indian minds in those days.

The politically conscious in Varavara's village tended to find their voice through literature and through poetry in particular. Varavara's brothers were highly literate, perpetually "reading books, discussing about the books, reciting the poems," as he recalled. He became infatuated with a poet from the region named Srirangam Srinivasarao, whom they all called Sri Sri, whose words championed the common man and, inspired by events from the Great Depression to the Spanish Civil War to India's own independence struggle, described a world ripe for a remaking. "Poetry gave me an idea of what is the new world," Varavara said. "The idea was to have equality, that there is no discrimination between the people."

I asked how that idea contrasted with the realities he had seen in his village, and it was only now that he revealed his origins: he came from a feudal family. They were Brahmins and landlords, two of the Maoists' most important enemies. His father controlled more than fifty acres of land, and an uncle had nearly twice as much, although the holdings had been larger in his grandfather's time and were gradually dwindling.

To be born a Brahmin and a landlord in that age and place was to inherit a debt of cruelty. Varavara remembered boys of the upper castes who had made elderly untouchables stand before them as they sat and who had barked derogatory names at them for amusement. The untouchables could not wear slippers in front of their betters. When they left an audience with an upper-caste man, they were to walk backward, so as to spare him the sight of their posterior. He remembered some young mothers toiling in the fields of the local landlord, their breasts swelling with milk. When they sought a break to nourish their young, the landlord called for clay pots and asked the women to fill them with their milk. Then he took the pots and sprinkled their contents onto his field.

"Oppression" would become an important word in Varavara's vocabulary, as for any revolutionary. But he said that his first understanding of the idea came from observing his own family. His uncle was a landlord in the traditional mold. In addition to his landholdings, he was the revenue collector for the area. He kept a non-Brahmin concubine, in keeping with the local overlord custom of marrying rigidly and fornicating freely. Varavara claimed that the uncle had feasted on wine and caviar, those Brahmin poisons, in the evenings, which was either a startling degree of opulence for the village or a Maoist-tinted memory. The uncle regularly abused his servants. One day, around the time Varavara was five years old, one of the uncle's sons, taken with the new dreams of equality gusting through the country in the age of Gandhi, decided to challenge his father. The son, who was in his twenties, marched into the house, leading a procession of untouchables from the village. Their mere contact with the home would have sullied it in the father's eyes. Varavara's uncle chased them around in a rage, flogging as many as he could with a stick.

That episode distilled two observations that Varavara made as a child: that he had come into a cruel world of layered humiliations, and that this world was on the cusp of changing. His uncle was carrying on with the old ways, but Varavara's brothers and cousins were engaged in the daring new. They helped young widows in the family remarry, in defiance of the Hindu custom. They took Varavara as a child to eat and sleep in the untouchable quarter of the village, so as to dissolve any early prejudice before it could congeal. They preached against child marriage, against smoking and drinking, and in favor of the education of women. "I could see the change before my eyes," Varavara told me in his slow, carefully parceled English. "It was in my own house. We felt that we were instrumental in these changes."

Inspired by his brothers and drunk on Sri Sri's revolution-themed poetry, Varavara came of age considering himself a socialist. This was not uncommon in an age when Nehru, the socialist father of the nation, was leading India in hatching five-year development plans and erecting dams, which he described as the temples of the new republic. Varavara believed in Nehru, believed in the system: in the first general elections, in 1952, as a twelve-year-old, he campaigned for the Congress Party, marching through his village in a procession led by bullocks, intended to persuade rural constituents of the party's salt-of-the-earth credentials.

As a teenager, Varavara tried his hand at writing poetry, publishing his first work in 1957. It was called "Socialist Moon," a tribute to the Soviet Union's launch of Sputnik, which came just as the Indians and Soviets were warming to each other diplomatically. Over the next several years, Varavara studied literature at university, earning a master's degree. He continued to steep himself in the politics of the age and continued to believe in creating the new world that he dreamed of within the established system of government. When Nehru died in 1964, the young poet eulogized the fallen prime minister in verse. He said that India had become "Dwaraka without Krishna," an ancient kingdom without its god-king.

"This was a very romantic poem," Varavara told me with a trace of nostalgia in his voice, "a very sentimental poem."

In 1965, Varavara dropped out of a PhD course in literature and decided to take a job with the government. He continued to believe that change was possible by peaceful, evolutionary means. In his poetry, he used snow as a metaphor for the establishment. It was cold, frozen, stagnant, but, with the coming of sunrise, it would melt away on its own.

He joined the Department of Audio-Visual Publicity in Delhi, which was effectively the government's propaganda arm. He translated public-service announcements—encouraging people to save money, support new laws, spawn fewer children—into Telugu, the local language of Andhra Pradesh, his native state. The work was an education in the practical power of language. A word choice here or there in an advertisement could send protesters into the streets or keep them at home. When controversial announcements had to be translated, the director of his unit would come to Varavara's desk with food and tea, suddenly showing interest in the young trainee, making sure he did his work as thoroughly and sensitively as possible.

The work awakened Varavara to how the state actually worked. The socialist government had become increasingly paranoid about Communist parties attacking it from the left and had begun to spread defamatory lies about collusion between India's Communist parties and the Chinese army. In this way Varavara learned of the fear and insecurity that plagued officialdom, beneath its air of omniscience and authority. After he befriended a Communist state legislator, his mail began to be read by censors. The government could be mighty and wise, but it could also be grasping and petty.

A year after joining the government, Varavara left. He returned to Andhra Pradesh and found work as a lecturer in literature. With three friends he started a literary magazine called *Srijana*, meaning "creation." They and others in their social world had begun to wrestle with the fact that after twenty years of the new republic, things were not turning out as they had hoped. Life in the villages was largely unchanged, with the old ills of landlordism and caste discrimination enduring. India was in those days drifting into entanglements with the United States and the International Monetary Fund, which the young leftists deplored. Meanwhile, they looked to the Soviet Union and China for inspiration. If there, why not here? they asked one another.

Above all, they felt guilty about the abstractness of their convictions. Varavara remembered his friends saying to one another: "We are sitting, reading, discussing poems, but nothing much is changing. We must bring some change." They had tired of engaging in what he called an "academic exercise."

And then, in May 1967, a small bulletin appeared in the local newspaper that would alter Varavara's life path irrevocably. It said only that there had been a burst of violence in a village called Naxalbari in the state of West Bengal, hundreds of miles to the north. Peasants and landlords had been locked in a dispute, and now the peasants had retaliated against the murder of one of their own by attacking the landlords.

The violence in Naxalbari was the first flash of a movement with high ambitions. The Naxalites began to sow violent uprisings across Bengal, against the landlords and the government that supported them. They formed their own branch of the Communist

Party, to distinguish themselves from those Indian Communists who believed that things could be changed peacefully. And they formed something of an armed insurgency—fragmented at times and uncertain of the ultimate path, but committed to the violent overthrow of the Indian state and the remaking of the country.

Varavara and his friends were delicate creatures with no violent aspirations of their own. But they decided to serve as part of the movement's intellectual wing. In the year after the Naxalbari violence, *Srijana* published a poem in Telugu whose title translates roughly as "Come with Your Finger on the Trigger." It summoned Varavara's generation of cerebral socialists to arms. Two years later, they formed the Revolutionary Writers Association as the permanent literary-intellectual arm of what was now called the Naxalite movement. Varavara wrote poems, marched in processions, debated doctrine at meetings, blocked roads in protest, and rushed into villages where disputes were brewing to bear witness. On many occasions, the police would fire on the crowds or assassinate Naxalite activists. Varavara had lost hundreds of his friends to the government he once served.

He began to be arrested and sent to prison every few years, sometimes only briefly, sometimes for months, sometimes for some years at a time. He would spend eight years of his life in prison, reading and writing and quietly waiting for the chance to be out in the daylight again, facing the problems of the world. In a poem, translated below from the Telugu, he wrote of being jailed.

This is prison
The voice muffled
Movements confined
But the hand scribbles
Torment of the heart doesn't cease
Dreams in lonely darkness float toward
Lighted shores

. . . .

If men turn from crime for self
To that for society
If these guns are loaded with the cause of working class
Before my eyes
The road to armed revolution
Will lead us to our destiny
In the shadow of my eyes
A dream
Soaked in the blood of my heart

Maoism for Varavara was ultimately a revolt against what he had known in childhood: a society of barriers, my people here and your people there, Brahmins and untouchables, nonpolluting and polluting, beating and beaten. He had believed for a time that independence and a new republic would bring new ideas of justice, solidarity, and common humanity. But those ideas had faded into history, and things had remained more or less the same, as he saw it. From his disappointment and the disappointment of a generation of like-minded souls, the Maoist cause was born.

And yet Naxalism in the twenty-first century was much more than an anti-landlord movement. It had become a revolt against the globalized future, not just against the village past. And in hearing Varavara speak of the infants starved of breast milk and the untouchables segregated and scorned, I wondered if the emotions from one battle were being projected onto another. Wasn't the new urban future a form of deliverance from the village past? What did the misdeeds of a cruel old landlord and of Varavara's Brahmin uncle have to do with the coming to India of Citibank and General Electric and Microsoft?

To answer that question, I turned to Varavara Rao's nephew Venugopal, a fellow Maoist poet, born in 1961. I wondered if his story might illuminate what the movement had come to mean for a younger generation.

Venugopal sat in his office under a swirling fan. He wore a purple shirt, untucked and with its sleeves rolled up, and brown pants over brown open-toed sandals. He kept a pen in his shirt pocket. On shelves behind him were hundreds of books, including *The Development Dictionary* and the made-for-airport-bookstores title *World Class in India*, about managers who had turned around sluggish Indian corporations.

He began by telling me, as his uncle had, of his family background. Venugopal's own father was a strict Brahmin who had sensed the country's changing course and allowed his children to break with tradition in their own lives. As Venugopal came of age, the political influences were more radical than they had been in Varavara Rao's youth. At age twelve Venugopal began to work as his uncle's de facto secretary, as Varavara's name grew in prominence and the demands on his time multiplied. Venugopal sorted through the mail each day and read proofs of poetry and essays sent to *Srijana* for consideration. He read Engels, Marx, and the Telugu poets, and he began to develop his own revolutionary notions, influenced by his uncle but reflective of his own anxieties as a son of the 1960s, not the 1940s.

"The root of whatever Marx thought was about human relationships," he said, when I asked what ideas had most arrested him in his early reading. "Human relationships are not in a proper way now. Maybe private property destroyed them; maybe selfishness destroyed them; maybe capital destroyed them. So, though he started with capital, though he started with commodities, the basis of all that was to retrieve the human being for humans."

In his student days, Venugopal felt an alien coldness creeping into Indian life, undermining the traditional spontaneity, warmth, and mutual involvement: people taking the time to visit one another in person, to show up unannounced at one another's homes, to sacrifice for their families. "From the beginning I was thinking that relationships are not as humane as they could be; relationships are not as emotional as they could be," he said. "People are so distant, and they come into contact with each other only with a purpose, only when they have some work to do." He had tried to live differently: "In my office every day, I meet at least twenty, thirty people. I talk to them, they talk to me—with no agenda. There need not be any agenda. I basically believe that man is a social animal. That social content is being eroded. Why is it eroded? I think private property is everything."

It was a fissure between his ideology and his uncle's. For his uncle, hell had been the Indian village, with its primordial humiliations; the idea of a casteless, egalitarian future that had begun to emerge in the 1940s suggested a passage from that world into an urban, anonymous India, an India of crowded city buses where it would be impossible to know who was who. Venugopal's hell, on the other hand, seemed to be the big city, with its coldness and anonymity and fragmentation; the warmth that was vanishing was a village warmth: the round-the-clock card games, the absence of doors, the loving mutual interference.

I asked Venugopal if he and his uncle were fighting the same battle or two different ones.

"Actually, there are two different constraints to the human relationships," he said. "One was the traditional hierarchical structures of caste; that allows one caste to be in solidarity, but not with others. And the other is this globalization and the commoditization of society that is coming more and more."

"The caste hierarchy did not see a human being as a human being," he went on. "It said that each person is assigned a job, and his duty is to do that job, and he should not complain about that job; he should not resist from that job. Only by doing that job will he get *moksha*"—the release of the soul from the cycle of death and rebirth in higher and lower stations of life. "So the traditional Hindu philosophy, the Indian way of life, wanted to divide people and give them some duties. Human potential was curtailed. Human being was jutted into a pigeonhole. It killed a human being, and in the place of human being it wanted to put a machine. It may not be a modern machine, but an old-fashioned machine. Basically, they wanted to see the system reproduce itself smoothly, without overthrowing the privileged."

"Globalization," he continued, "wanted to do that same thing. That's why *dharma* and globalization have common things, though they talk in different languages. Consider the idea of comparative advantage. Comparative advantage is another term for caste division."

The part about caste I understood. But comparative advantage was simply the idea of specialization—that it is more efficient for you to be a tailor and me to be a baker, for you to make my clothes and trade them for bread from me, rather than everybody doing everything for himself. It said nothing about what your children and grandchildren should do, said nothing about your intrinsic human worth. How, then, was it a replication of caste?

"With the division of labor," Venugopal said, "you can do wonders, and, as Adam Smith said, with the same amount of labor you can make forty-eight thousand of the same thing. All that is fine. But with that you are subjecting a creative human being to one kind of work, and you are not allowing him to learn other things. So you are dividing laborers from each other; and, when man is separated from another man, that really means man is separated from himself."

This was the idea of alienation, from Marx: the notion that this narrowing of tasks, while making things more efficient, also made it harder to find meaning in work. What Venugopal was arguing was that what caste did flagrantly, putting humans into their different boxes, globalization was doing more artfully: giving every worker a sliver of a specialized role, making him work harder and harder, depriving him over time of a sense of the whole, and eroding his connections with other humans. Venugopal saw as cousins in deprivation the laborer driven from his land for the software company and the software coder who writes his narrow code, slogs for people he has never met, and suffers the fate of the new-economy worker bee: fifteen-hour days, bumper-to-bumper traffic, sexual and marital frustration, children who ask, "How come Papa never comes home?"

"When caste wanted to separate man from man, it used the concept of *dharma*," Venugopal said. "When capitalism wanted to separate man from man, it used the concept of production, of higher consumption, of better livelihood—whatever. The end result was separating human being from human being and erasing the socialness, the human essence, from the human being."

What Varavara fought was, at bottom, a village society that dehumanized, that saw so many people not as people but as means to an end. What Venugopal now fought was the very different forces that, to me and so many others, appeared as liberators: the new-economy jobs, the malls, the single-family homes that offered space and freedom. Because in India those things seemed so new, so alien to the India with which I had grown up, my attention had dwelled on them. But what Venugopal saw in these forces—in Deepak Kumar's urban reinvention, in Ravindra's seething ambitions, in Mukesh Ambani's gargantuan plans—was a new kind of dehumanization: an obsession with advancement, the erosion of time, the turning of men into robots, and, above all, a fragmenting of the society—no longer into Brahmins here and untouchables there, but into software engineers who lived in gated enclosures and villagers who were told to pack up and make way for a new airport for the software engineers.

For many millions of Indians, globalization could be seen as deliverance from the past. But in Venugopal's telling, it could also be seen as a return to the past, as a concession of the failure of the ideas of independence. There had once been an older India in which the Brahmin's water was exclusively his water and the untouchable's water exclusively his. Then, for a time, there had been the dream of a republic that would erase those differences. Brahmins and untouchables would all pay taxes to the same vast state and all drink water from the same taps and all send their children to public colleges. But that vision of India had not quite been fulfilled, and even if the lines between the castes had blurred, the India of privatization and globalization was a return to an India in which the privileged drank their water (bottled or privately treated by the gated communities) and the rest drank theirs (from the tap or well, laced with chemicals and bacteria).

What had changed, in Venugopal's view, was that the middle class, once the "conscience keepers of society," had become the new Brahmins—aloof from those less fortunate, living in their own world, callous to the plight of others. "Since 1857," he said, giving the date of the Indian colonial uprising, "it was always the middle class which led struggles, which tried to enlighten people, which wrote, which addressed public meetings. Post-'92, this middle class has slowly been bought. And now the middle class has only one goal in mind: to earn money, to earn dollars, and use that money to buy real estate around the city and enjoy life. So the human essence has gone from sociality to pleasure seeking."

If the old Brahmins had cut themselves off from others with their special forehead markings and separate living quarters, the new Brahmins segregated themselves in fresh ways. In the place of bodily markings, they defined themselves by what they consumed, and they flaunted that consumption in others' faces, eating in restaurants, shopping in malls, driving around in fancy cars in ways that an earlier generation of elites did not do and arguably could not have done. The new middle class lived as much of their lives as was possible indoors, in air-conditioned spaces, safely removed from the sun-baked poor: the customer of the roadside *chai wallah* started frequenting the indoor Barista chain of coffee shops; the user of the public bus and train upgraded to the cool bubble of her own car; the bazaar shopper discovered the mall. The new Brahmins ceased to rely on the state and its public provision, which had formerly bound the rich and poor in common cause. It was now possible to buy your way out of the shortages of power and water, to establish a factory in a Special Economic Zone with its own tax laws and without the red tape that still bound ordinary Indians, to pay to send your middlingly bright children to Australia for college while everyone else suffered under an educational regime that would not reform its ways. The new Brahmins lived in their own mental world, as the old Brahmins had done, but in lieu of reading arcane Sanskrit texts, they now read English-language newspapers that airbrushed bad news—of inequity, strife, the displacements of the new world—and spoke mostly of globalization's delights.

Affluence was bringing to India a slow-burning privatization of attitudes. And yet it was not difficult to empathize with the impulse behind this turning inward, this shrinking of concern. In a society like India's, the ideas of consumption and personal success had natural appeal. The old culture had been a thicket of external restraints: families had dictated whom to marry, what to study, where to work; bureaucrats had told you whether you could get a phone line or start a business; a caste had determined the amount of respect that you could command. People were now revolting against those definitions and destinies. They shared a new belief in the power of self-contained individuals: a belief that individuals must not slight elders but must no longer depend on them; must not forget their roots but must now look beyond them; must not crave a government job like their fathers but must now survive as though the state did not exist.

Just as the new self-confidence in India was nourishing a rediscovery of traditional ways, so, too, the individuation ushered in by modernity was, in fact, in Venugopal's eyes, a return to the past, to an older pattern of division known from the villages: a world in which I am ensconced indoors behind glass and you are sweltering outside, in which I am an Inside Kind of Person and you are an Outside Kind of Person. That was how it had been in the villages, and that, he feared, was how it would be in the India that was coming.

There were, of course, other ways of judging these new times, and few institutions could claim more credit for spreading the cheerful interpretation than the *Economic Times*. It was the early morning read for India's stock traders, bankers, and billionaires. It had no intellectual or moral pretensions; it did not cover poverty or the arts or science with depth; it did not exist to hold the powerful to account. Its purpose was to help people make money, which meant giving them the data to make decisions and, equally, putting them in the onward-and-upward mood to perpetuate a boom. In 1998, for example, as Venugopal saw Hyderabad and India stumbling toward a future that he feared, the *ET* (as it is known) ran this feel-good story about the place.

HYDERABAD ON ITS WAY TO BECOMING CYBERABAD

A proactive government, efficient bureaucracy, enthusiastic entrepreneurs, bourgeoning training facilities, a huge talent pool, and an information technology culture are providing a potent mix for IT majors to eye Hyderabad with new interest. It is the packaging that matters. No doubt, global information technology giants have started accepting the signals.

Microsoft Corporation's plan to set up a software development centre in Hyderabad, its first such outfit outside the US, speaks of the attractions the city holds out to prospective investors. . . .

But then, experts say this is only the whimper. The bang is yet to come.

There was nothing unusual in this article. Its breathless vocabulary—proactive, efficient, packaging, whimper, bang: the vocabulary of business journalists who learn to mimic their business sources—was now standard in India's English-language press. There was only one strange feature of the article, although its significance would have been lost on most readers. It was written by Venugopal himself.

I knew from several fleeting mentions that Venugopal had worked as a journalist. I knew that he had his own opinion column in a Telugu newspaper, because he had taken a short pause from our conversation to file it by e-mail. What I didn't realize after our first meeting was that most of the articles under his name were not print versions of his radical propositions, but rather gushing tributes to the new economy, under headlines such as these: "'Small' Is What Makes Microsoft Go"; "IBM's Latest Offers Road to Infinity"; "Car PC Is Technology of the Future"; "Get Ready to Surf the Net Through Your Television."

The nature of this work came up early in our second meeting, when I asked Venugopal about his journalistic endeavors. He told me that he had written for the *ET* in the past, and he explained it this way: "To earn a livelihood, I have to do something, because I'm not a whole-timer for revolution."

It was my first brush with the idea of part-time revolution.

"In a twenty-four-hour day, I have to sell myself for at least four hours or six hours or eight hours, so that the rest of the sixteen hours can be spent on Naxalism," he explained. He conceded that this arrangement was at war with itself. "On one side, you are fighting a state, you are fighting a system, you are going and preaching against the system, you are writing against the system," he said. "But you are working inside the system. This is a contradiction. But I think the basic necessity of a person to be able to do whatever he wants to do, to see whatever he wants to see, even for his freedom of expression—first, he has to live. For living, nobody is going to give free lunches, as they say; so for that I have to earn my lunch."

He had begun with a Telugu newspaper, after editing a Maoist underground journal for a short time. He used to write articles from morning to night and plot the revolution by moonlight. When that newspaper shut down, he struggled to get a job in journalism, since his revolutionary affiliations were becoming known in Hyderabad. So he took a job in Bangalore with a research group, the Institute for Social and Economic Change. His charge was to visit rural areas beset by poverty and drought and to write reports on them. The only catch was that the World Bank, the institution for which he most blamed Hyderabad's metamorphosis, was funding the institute's work. The contradiction was plain once again, but he tried to look on the bright side: "I gained a firsthand experience of how to write reports, how you bring out reality in a nonrevolutionary way, how you bring out reality in numbers and how you crunch numbers."

It gave him another "skill set," he added, sounding very much like the people he disliked.

It was from the institute that he jumped to the *Economic Times*, in 1995. He was sent to Hyderabad as a correspondent. Within weeks of his arrival, a new leader of the state, Chandrababu Naidu, swept into office with a new program of economic reforms and collaboration with the World Bank and global corporations to turn the city into a software hub. Venugopal was assigned to cover the information-technology and outsourcing beat—the subject that was putting India on the world economic map at that time. Venugopal was writing the articles that paved the way for Thomas Friedman to come to India and discover a flattened world.

I began to laugh at that beat assignment, and Venugopal joined in. "God has a sense of humor," I said.

"That gave me a very good chance to go into the belly of the beast," Venugopal said. "I met almost all the leaders of the IT industry at the time, the nascent IT industry. Everybody used to come here, from Infosys to Wipro to Satyam to everybody. And, because I was representing *Economic Times,* I used to be given the first priority."

Venugopal's first months at the *ET* passed uneventfully. He learned how to write to boost a nation's collective ego. He attended some lectures given to the staff by Swaminathan Aiyar, an economist and columnist for the *Times of India,* a sister paper of the *ET.* Aiyar divided his time between Washington, D.C., and India, and his column, titled "Swaminomics," reflected the free-market libertarian sensibilities that had earned him roles with the Cato Institute, the World Bank, and the *Economist.* It was a way of thinking now coming into vogue in India, and he was there to give young reporters a crash course in it.

"He used to tell us that a newspaper is no longer a social service," Venugopal recalled. "It might have been a social service during the independence days, but now it's a business operation. If it is a business operation, then the only thing that matters is how better you package, how better you sell. It's not the content that matters; it's the form that matters. And actually it was from his mouth that I heard the words 'feel-good factor' for the first time. At that time, our office was in Indira Park, near a slum. He said, 'This slum is there. It is a reality. But if you publish this on page one, this doesn't make any difference. This is a disgusting sight.' The newspaper's audience wasn't interested in reading such stories."

In the manner of Reliance Industries, companies began to offer Venugopal gifts, sometimes subtly, sometimes brazenly: pens, boxes of sweets, gadgets, even computers. He said that he declined them all.

For years, his day-night dualism went on undisturbed. But he stirred the pot too heavily when he began to write two different versions of the same stories, one in the *ET,* the other in a Telugu daily that gave him his own regular column—one in the dialect of English Aspiration, the other in the dialect of Telugu Anger.

On one occasion, the state government was moving to privatize some public services and outsource them to a company in Singapore. "I wrote that just as a news story—government services are going to be connected to the Net and then privatized; such and such Singapore company is going to take over—as bland, vanilla news in *Economic Times*," Venugopal said. "But I used the same thing and wrote in my Telugu column that public services have to be in the public domain, and private companies should not come, and why a Singapore company of all the people should not come." He had obtained the scoop as a leak from the government. A senior official, livid to discover Venugopal's dual-use reporting, tried to get him fired.

It seemed to me in listening to this story that the self-interested pragmatism that Venugopal saw in the new middle class, the departure from ideals for money's sake, was evident in his own story as well. And there was more of it. Venugopal remained in journalism until 2005, when he left to cofound the research institute in whose offices we now sat. It published a journal and offered research and report-writing services for hire. And here, again, a compromise: the institute conducted rigorous studies of rural areas, of their economic conditions and political climate, and sold these services to, among others, the Bharatiya Janata Party and the Congress Party. It was surreal to think of the Maoist who, in all sincerity, without any desire to manipulate the work to his Maoist ends, did polling and political research for the two major political parties of the government that he was seeking to overthrow.

Then he offered another way of explaining his years as a parttimer.

"The people in my circuit, maybe 99.9 percent of people, might not have gone to a five-star hotel even once in their lifetimes. They don't know how to conduct themselves in a five-star hotel," he said. "But I used to dine every day in a five-star," thanks to his work for the *Economic Times*. "In the beginning, even I didn't know how to conduct myself, but I learned through ten years of that. The experiences I had, I always think that everyone should have all these experiences. You experience that, and you identify that that is not good—or that, if it is good, it has to be there for everybody else. Only a handful of people have had that kind of luxurious experience, and by virtue of my position I had an opportunity to taste that life."

I asked him if the consumer culture around him had ever tempted him. It was plain enough that he had not chosen the renouncing Gandhian way, had not been inspired to follow his uncle's model as a whole-timer and political prisoner.

"It has a lot of seductive potential," he said of the money world. "But because my convictions were solid and crystallized by then, I was not enamored by that life." And yet when he spoke a few moments later of those who were enamored, it seemed that he knew their sentiments perhaps a little too well.

"If you go to a multiplex," he said, "if you hang around for one hour or two hours, you see the kind of clothing, you see the kind of people there, the kind of accents there. Either you think that you are inferior—you think, 'This is the standard, and I'm deviant; I cannot take this.' Or you think, 'I have to imitate and this is the standard I have to get.' This is human nature.

"If such things are not abundant," he went on, "or if the person who has them now doesn't want to leave them, wants to protect his rights over them, then my jealousy and my aspiration for that will turn into an enmity against that person and a disinterest in that good." And the anger would only intensify, he said, if the machinery of the state, far from righting injustices and narrowing imbalances, threw its weight behind the already privileged: "If that person has the state behind him, if that person has power with him, my enmity grows. This is the natural—the logical—sequence of what is happening."

· · ·

Venugopal was not what he seemed at first. India's complicated relationship with modernity and money cut through his own soul. He blamed the World Bank for tearing the nation apart, but he once lived off its grants. He loathed the drunk and happy middle class that derived much of its euphoria from the newspapers, but he wrote for the most vacuously euphoric paper of them all. His companion, a woman who worked as a documentary filmmaker, had accepted an award from Prime Minister Manmohan Singh, who was the highest target of the insurgency for which Venugopal worked.

What Venugopal despised in the middle class was its self-regard. The new economy and its possibilities were draining principles out of Indian life. All that was left was what car you drove, where you worked, whether you had bought a private "villa" of your own. A market economy was bringing with it a market mentality. There was no place, he felt, for higher purpose, for family, for culture. There were few longings among the rising middle class that did not involve their next promotion, as I had felt so palpably with Ravindra. A singular focus on professional success had saturated the upwardly mobile, and along with the blindness it could cause came an unapologetic pragmatism. Like Mukesh Ambani, these ascendant Indians paid little heed to abstract conceptions of good and bad. They lived by the principle of whatever works. But this seemed to me to be Venugopal's principle, too.

I was coming to understand more fully something Venugopal had told me as I was leaving his office the day before. The middle class, he said, had shifted its loyalties from an ideology that attended to the poor to one that served only themselves: they conceived of themselves now as poorer versions of the fortunate, no longer as fortunate versions of the poor. But this desertion wouldn't deplete the Maoist cause, he said. It would make it more dangerous.

"The potential intellectual leaders, the potential inspirers, the potential writers—we might have lost them," he said. "More and more farmers are thrown out of their land and becoming land-less. I think they'll join the movement with a vengeance. That's why I'm afraid the future conflicts will be more violent. If middle-class leadership was there, at least some liberal rules would have been there."

In his choice of words—his being afraid of violence; his want-ing "liberal rules" to temper conflicts—and in his regret at the loss of the intelligentsia, Venugopal continued to betray his own biases. He was hardly the ruthless, machete-wielding warrior that was the dominant image of the Naxalite. He was at heart a utopian, like his uncle. Together they had dreamed of a differently wired world. But now the utopianism of the educated middle class was bleeding away. Indians had found new strivings; their utopias had shrunk to the size of personal paradises. And, without them, Venugopal seemed to say, the Maoist movement would become volatile and uncontrollable, all muscle and no brain.

I asked him to lay out for me, as vividly as possible, how he imagined that the conquest of India would occur.

He said that there were five thousand, perhaps ten thousand, full-time guerrillas, along with a larger number who belonged to part-time militias. They would convert one village at a time, then seek to connect the dots of their conquests, and slowly develop "liberated zones." When I pressed him for more specific plans, he seemed irritated. "I don't think one could draw a blueprint of that," he said. So I changed tack, asking him what India would look like should they succeed.

There was a long pause. "First, land reforms, in a genuine sense, will happen," he said. "Along with land reforms, I think at least in some parts of the country there has to be cooperative agri-culture, a communal system—not to imitate China, but because the Indian village was always a self-reliant village, and I think even now one can get back a self-reliant, self-sufficient rural vil-lage, but without caste. Older self-reliant, self-sufficient villages had a landlord and an oppressive caste hierarchy, but now that can be removed. Second, the full industrial potential of the country will be released because of its rich natural-resource base." Third, he stated, all multinational corporations and all foreign property would be seized and nationalized, without compensation.

"I may not live under this," he went on, "but one day the society will have this, because I think this is natural and this is social and this is in consonance with the human essence. Leave aside the land reforms and capital and all that. Human beings have to live as human beings, with their human essence, their sociality, their social being. Their relationships should not be on the basis of inequality or power or property. It should be on the basis of their human worth. That will happen."

What made Venugopal's vision most improbable to me was not the daunting territorial task or the differing scale of the insurgent and official armies. It was, rather, this idea of the human essence that he proposed. At bottom, he sought to turn Indians into a people other than themselves. He sought to make them egalitarian in spirit, sought to make them forget who was a master and who was a servant, sought to beat back the karmic, pain-absorbing mentality that had carried the many quiet millions through the night. Capitalism of the kind venerated by Ravindra and Mukesh Ambani seemed in some ways to be agitating against these old traits, and it seemed equally to be reinforcing the vision of a society of compartments. I wondered how an alternative Maoist approach would proceed. Would it require that most dreaded phrase, a cultural revolution?

It would, Venugopal answered without hesitation: "In most of the Maoist literature, they say the need for cultural revolution was realized in China after the actual revolution, but that in India the cultural and social revolution will have to go hand in hand, or even before that."

"Like they destroyed Confucius, India has to destroy Manu,"

Venugopal continued, referring to the lawgiver who laid down the rules of caste. "The Confucian hierarchical system, the Confucian obscurantism, had tied Chinese people to their destinies. Confucius, like Manu, wrote all the edicts, and he said inequality is right, and he said woman has to be subservient. Like Confucius, Manu also has to be destroyed, and for that we need not wait till the actual political revolution takes place."

I thought of all the interwoven old ways that would have to change for anything to move: the ideas of pollution and purity; the food restrictions of this kind of people and that kind of people; the nature of relationships at home, at work, between masters and servants; the codes of speech; the religious convictions that made hardship that much easier to bear—all the intellectual and spiritual paraphernalia of a long-unequal society. These things were now changing with the forces of the new capitalism, but slowly and organically. Indians in and around the swelling middle seemed to believe more and more that growth, and not upheaval, would resolve these injustices. Was it not dangerous and heavy-handed to impose that change ideologically, from above?

"It's dangerous if it's treated as social reengineering," Venugopal said. "It's not social reengineering. It's only removing the bad elements given by tradition. In tradition you have some good elements also. Of course, it's a very difficult task, a tough task."

"In percentage terms," I asked, "how much of the basic way of thinking needs to be kept and how much needs to be discarded?"

Venugopal thought for a moment. In Sikhs and Muslims and Christians, the figure might be different, he said, because of their egalitarian ethos. "In Hindus," he said, "I think seventy percent has to be thrown out."

To "throw out" 70 percent of the contents of the minds of 80 percent of your population: this, then, was Venugopal's stunning ambition—to purge everything that India was deep in the bones. His vision imagined a total break from the past, a rupture with an earlier Indianness in favor of new modes of being. But dreams of the new in India were haunted and tempered by the persistent, vengeful presence of the old. The new, as I had seen before, could be less new than it seemed. And in Venugopal's own story was one of the oldest patterns of all: the Brahmin sitting high on his perch, imagining how the peasants down below should live, not living that way himself but imagining and preaching all the same.

FIVE

Love

"Sir, you know Margaret? She got *married*!"

Maria came out of the kitchen to offer this tantalizing bit of gossip. She was one of a succession of part-time cooks whom I had employed in Bombay. Margaret was another, and they were friends. They were sturdy women in their late forties, both Catholics originally from Mangalore, in southern India. Maria was married with children, but Margaret had always been something of an outlier—unmarried, living with her brother, unattachment being the most terrible Indian fate.

"She got married?" I asked, lifting my eyes from the computer.

"Yeah, she got *mar-ried*! She got married to one very *rich* guy. *Ver-ry* rich!"

"She did?"

"Yeah! Now she has car and everything. She has nice flat also. She has driver also. TV also. Everything she's got. He's a very *rich* man. He's got his *own* business: cold storage or something—pork, chicken, you know, like that."

This came as a surprise. It had been six months since I last saw Margaret. She had sometimes used her burdens as an unmarried woman as a bargaining chip when seeking a raise: she was dependent on her brother, living with him and his wife; she needed to bring home a hearty wage to remain in their good graces. I asked Maria how Margaret had suddenly found a husband.

"Basically, he is an old man," she said. "And his wife expired. So he needed someone to look after him, to cook and clean and everything. Basically, he needed a maid. But he thought, What will the neighbors say if I am alone here, a single man, and there is a woman coming every day to my flat to do work? They will think bad things are happening. So he thought, Better to get a wife only. So they got married. He is from the same community; she is from the same community. He needs someone now, and she also needs company. And, also, he is a very *rich* man!"

This was, in Maria's mind, a sufficient explanation of the situation. There was a smile on her face at Margaret's good fortune, and not a small amount of envy in her voice.

And the story stuck with me, because it distilled the utter strangeness of Indian love to me even after these many years. It was a very Indian story. It was Indian in its tribalism: your wife dies, you are old and desperate for someone to take care of you, but not so desperate that you would look outside the ranks of Mangalorean Catholics. It was Indian in the man's concern that he always have access to "home food," cooked in the precise style of his mother. It was Indian in the blurred boundary between wife as love, as an end in herself, and wife as maid, as a means to other ends; Indian in its ruthless and unembarrassed pragmatism; Indian in its elevation of worry about what others will think over the promptings of fulfillment.

Margaret's story was, in short, the commonest kind of Indian love story: a love story brimming with every ingredient but love.

The Indian vision of love was, to my untrained eyes, a series of absences. It was the absence of visible affection, the absence of romantic speech, the absence of sexuality in the movies and on

television. Before I understood the ways in which my Indian relatives loved each other, I fixated on the ways in which they didn't.
It is challenging anywhere to imagine the coming together of
one's parents or uncles and aunts or grandparents. But in India
it was especially difficult, for one had to imagine a universe of
sentiments that seemed scarcely to exist in the physical world.
They, too, were young once; they, too, felt love, even lust; they,
too, knew the sadness and anxiety that come with romance—
these statements were self-evident in theory, but they were hard to
fathom in practice. And yet I had one special window into that
old world of love. It was a short narrative written by Ammamma,
my father's mother, in October 1942, titled "Our Marriage." She
had given it to my father on one of his recent visits to Bombay. It
was on ruled paper, written in a neat hand, in crisp English befit-
ting the final years of the Raj, and it conjured a world that was
unrecognizable in twenty-first-century India.

The thirty-two-page account begins in May 1942. Ammamma
awoke one morning and noticed her parents locked in discussion.
She sought to eavesdrop and found that they were talking about
her. "Having finished your matriculation, you must now enter
matrimony," her father told her matter-of-factly. She felt shy, and
her cheeks flushed. She quickly slid away. She was eighteen.

Her father had resolved to "marry her off," in the Indian phrase,
and without delay. There were no specific men or families on the
horizon. But now was the time, and he had ignited that most inexo-
rable Indian motor. He petitioned his bosses for two months of
vacation, which he would use to short-list candidates, arrange a
marriage with one of them, and see a wedding through. The family
traveled by train from the north to the deep south, Lahore to Delhi,
Delhi to Bombay, Bombay to Bangalore, Bangalore to Trichinopoly,
where their relatives were settled.

The first mention of my grandfather is sudden and jarring:
"No sooner did we reach Trichy, than my father began his quest
for a good bridegroom for his daughter. He devoted his time to

gathering each and every information, and thereby learnt that Mr. Giridharadas had come out successfully in the I.R.S.E. [Indian Railway Service of Engineers] examination securing a very high rank and that he had passed his medical examination held at Bombay." Ammamma's father was a high-ranking government servant, and he was impressed by word of a young man of promise embarking on that same road. He was also encouraged to learn that Mr. Giridharadas's father was known for his faithful renditions of Hindu religious songs.

"Nor is this all," Ammamma continues, in what is a favorite narrative device of hers. Her father obtained Mr. Giridharadas's horoscope and sent it to astrologers for counsel. Though he didn't believe in such things, his wife did: it was an act of appeasement. Ammamma lurked in the background. "I was praying to God that he should fulfill the wishes of my parents," she writes.

The story then gallops ahead in a way that is hard to imagine for someone not of that time and place. The horoscopes matched; the "biodata" of personal and familial qualifications and status were mutually impressive; possible reasons not to marry were boiling away; and so the motor roared on, as if of its own strength, propelling Ammamma and Thatha toward marriage. The two families agreed to meet in Nagpur. During the long train ride, Ammamma writes of being urged to sleep but finding herself unable. She closed her eyes and pretended but couldn't stop her mind from inventing images of this Mr. Giridharadas. She woke up from her "imaginary sleep," as she put it, washed her face several times, put on a silver *sari*, and prepared for the big moment.

On reaching Nagpur, Ammamma noticed a "tall, smart young man with good personality" on the platform. It was Mr. Giridharadas, she discovered to her delight, though she was too shy to look more than once. She and her parents went to his family's home, where they sat for coffee and snacks. She was asked to sing for her prospective in-laws. Her language in recounting the episode is the language of someone trained to see the world as

acting upon her, not the other way around. She sougl
inspiration for her singing: "I worshipped Lord Krishn
should be married to Mr. G." After singing, she attem
play her violin but was thwarted when one of its strings, taxed
by the train journey, snapped.

If law courts give a presumption of innocence until proven
guilty, Indian marriage making in those days operated according
to its own burden of proof: after some initial vetting, there was a
presumption of compatibility until proven incompatible. Western
romantics approach love offensively, actively seeking an ideal
mate. Traditional Indians worked defensively, concentrating on
whom not to marry; there was less worry about who was ideal
within the general pool of the acceptable, once the chaff had been
eliminated. Ammamma and Thatha were from well-matched families, the meeting with the families had been pleasant, and things
would now proceed because there was no reason for them not to
proceed. And Ammamma, though hardly in control of her fate,
found ways to enjoy the ride. When Thatha boarded the train
with her and her parents to install them and see them off, "Mr. G.
took the trouble of adjusting the seat, and putting up the shutters.
I also assisted him in doing so. At that time my fingers happened
to come in contact with his. I felt a thrill in me." He sat down
across from her. He chatted about Dal Lake in Kashmir and other
worldly subjects, and he wanted to hear Ammamma's views, but
words failed her.

Some days later, Thatha petitioned the railways for eight days
of leave for the marriage. A wedding date was scheduled. Clothes,
saris, silver vessels, diamond rings, and gold jewelry were ordered
from local vendors.

The wedding day—July 5, 1942—came. Ammamma rose early
for an oil bath before the rites. During the ceremony, they exchanged
garlands, and when their hands touched again, she writes, "I experienced some strange feeling vibrating through my palm." A yoke
was placed on their necks to signify the joint pulling of the cart of

household affairs and the mutual adjustment it required. They walked around the Hindu marriage fire and said their mantras. Then a "grand dinner" was held, at which the new couple was goaded to feed each other in front of their guests.

During the live music that evening, Thatha sought to chat up his new bride. He raised the question of first impressions. What had she thought when they first met? Ammamma was silent. Thatha changed tack and asked if she wanted his impressions first. She whispered, "Yes." He said pleasant things, and then Ammamma pulled off the old female trick of saying that she agreed with the sentiments he had just expressed.

Thatha asked Ammamma to return with him to Mortakka, in central India, where he was posted, and her parents came to the station to see them off. "At that moment I had mingled feelings of joy and sorrow," she writes, "joy because I was travelling with my beloved husband, sorrow because of the pang of separation from my beloved parents." But there were only bright days ahead, she wrote in conclusion: "I look forward to the pleasure of meeting my husband and keeping a happy home for him in Mortakka. Though it is only a temporary camp place, we will be happy together, for the minds and heart can build the Heaven of Happiness and loving cooperation in life."

In Ammamma's narrative, she began to refer to Thatha as "my beloved husband" minutes after their vows. She was trained to understand the patterns of a society of roles, and when the time came she played hers. It is striking today to notice how she offers only the faintest assessment of Thatha's personality or comportment. He is her husband now; he must be beloved, and she is the woman to love him. She had, from the beginning of her account, cast herself as a spectator to a drama in which she happened to be the central player. When it came to describing events around her or recounting which stations they stopped at, her telling was full of detail. But she seemed to skim over her own sentiments, either because she felt little or because she did not want to put them on paper. We have no sense of emotional complexity in her words, no sense of being torn between enthusiasm and angst, no sense of her wanting anything apart from what her parents or her new husband wanted.

There was, in her day, a straightforward idea of what a woman was and might be. Every transaction of a girl's life would have groomed her to assume this role. It was a constraining role, a narrow role, but it was a role ready-made, and from Ammamma's narrative we have the feeling that it reassured even as it reined in. If anything had changed in India since Ammamma's time, it was this old fidelity to roles.

In 1979, my father proposed marriage to my mother, and as she decided whether to follow her heart and say "yes," her fear was not about marrying him but about leaving India. Everything she knew and trusted, everyone she loved and everyone who loved her, was in India. India was the noise and chaos of family; it was love that stifled you and boxed you in and yet flooded you with care. It was people who forced you to sing at family get-togethers, who commented on your weight, your stomach conditions, the hue of your skin.

My mother feared the solitude that would envelop her in America. She knew nothing of the country, none of its mores and ways. It was a lonely and terrifying thought: two Indians adrift in the world, unconnected to home, with no one to lean on but each other. How would she fill her days at home while my father worked downtown? How would she go about cultivating new American friends, having left a society where she had inherited a web of family friends and cousins and aunts and uncles and grandparents? There were so many supports in an Indian marriage, so many people who would cushion your fall if your spouse turned out to be less wondrous than you had imagined. In America, she would be alone.

In the end, she took the gamble. And shortly after their wedding, with my father back in America and my mother still in India, waiting for a visa, he wrote her a letter that distilled how their love challenged the prevailing Indian understanding of things. Quoting a favorite song of his, he wrote of sailing "outward bound" with her, on a ship with "no crew but me and you."

Within a year, they were living in Shaker Heights, Ohio, in the depths of solitary love. It was just the two of them, as my father had promised. Twoness was the philosophy of their marriage, and this was the idea of love with which I came of age. They had none of the old Indian repression. They held hands whenever they had the chance—in the car, on walks, while watching television. They shared a small kiss in front of us when my father came home from work. Twoness meant putting their own relationship at the center of the world. Twoness also meant preserving a sphere of intimacy even after having children of their own, and not dissolving into the sacrificial banality of parenthood.

They remained ever fascinated by each other, going on regular "dates," just the two of them. They took dance lessons together, foxtrot and swing, went off to watch independent films in out-of-the-way theaters, and playfully recalled the letters they had written to each other daily during their seven-month separation after marriage. They did crossword puzzles together late into the night. They took the time for lingering Sunday-morning breakfasts soaked in jazz.

My parents' marriage stood as a contrast to what I saw in India. When I visited India as a child, I noticed that few, if any, of our relatives had my parents' kind of romance. The men in particular tended to be remote and gruff and insensitive, incapable of entering a woman's mind. Dance classes and crossword puzzles were hard to imagine. Judging by what happened in public, married life in India seemed to be a series of obligations and duties, motions to be gone through and trials to be endured. No one said "I love you" beyond the privacy of the bedroom. On the crowded streets, men walked five feet ahead of their wives. I remember my wonderment when growing up that people who treated each other so coolly by day could then cling together to make children by night.

Of course, what I saw with a child's eyes was not particular to India: the marriages I observed would not have been all that different from, say, many European marriages in the eighteenth and nineteenth centuries, when arranged alliances were the norm in a patriarchal, village-based society yet to see the urbanizing, deracinating effects of industrial affluence. And if Indian marriages lacked what I defined as love, they possessed a selflessness that was just as scarce in America.

Indians saw Westerners as overly consumed with themselves, and they practiced a love less self-involved. They didn't require constant emotional replenishment the way Americans did. They weren't told all day long that they were loved; they didn't need to be told. Love was a quiet habit. It was knowing certain things for sure and not needing them to be repeated every day. It was the elimination of the space between two beings, not the giving of space, as in the West. Love was doled out subtly and sparingly, couched in deeds more than words, expressed in sacrifice for others and in the constant involvement in each other's lives. A lover was almost like your blood: the fuel of your existence, but something that required no dwelling or philosophizing, something that simply was.

The love that Ammamma found with Thatha was wordless. He could yell and scream at the slightest provocation. She would listen meekly and wait for his storms to pass. I never saw between them a single instant of my parents' kind of affection. And yet, when arthritis cut into Ammamma's knees, Thatha knew what he had to do and did it: he cooked for her, served her, and cleaned up after her well into their eighties. It was a true expression of love that didn't need the validation of "I love you."

My mother's parents were more progressive. They called each

other "Sweetie," and there were photos from years earlier of them gazing longingly at each other. But for them, too, love was not a performance. It was quiet: Nanu's unflinching protectiveness toward Nani, his immersion in paying bills and managing accounts, his management of the burdensome outer world, his pride in the slum-rehabilitation work that she took up late in life, even as it stole her away from tending to him; and Nani's instinctual anticipation of what Nanu needed at any hour, the reflex that prompted her to pick out his clothes in the morning, to cut fruit for him before slicing her own, to remind him to take his medicine.

I remember sitting as a child on Nani and Nanu's spacious bed in Delhi—the bed being a communal hangout in many Indian households—and arguing about love. Nanu would make some assertion about Americans not understanding love and ending up divorced. Arranged marriages are better, he would insist. My mother would reply that many Indians were as unhappy in their marriages as Americans, and that the difference was simply the lack of choices for Indian women. "If it was as easy to get divorced in India as in America, do you think so-and-so and so-and-so would still be together?" my mother would ask, daring to name names. At the mention of specific terrible marriages within our acquaintanceship, my mother would win the argument, because the coldness and hostility of the so-and-sos' marriage were apparent to everyone.

I was surrounded as a child by these competing conceptions of love and marriage—and of sexuality, too. It was jarring to fly from America, in whose sexualized culture we Indian-Americans were prudes, to India, whose repression made us seem libertine. In my high school years, it was to leave a world in which everyone was dating, drinking, and having sex for a world in which my cousins of roughly my own age seemed several years younger than me, barely aware of sexuality and oblivious to adolescence itself: no one dated; the boys didn't shave their faces; the girls didn't shave their legs; everyone giggled at the slightest suggestiveness. More was going on behind the scenes in India, as I would later learn, but it was seldom acknowledged or discussed.

From time to time in my teenage years, a cousin would ask if I had a girlfriend. I usually didn't. But I felt in those moments the way migrant laborers must feel when they go to a big city or a rich foreign land, toil there as nobodies, are taunted and degraded all year long, and then return at last to their villages, where they are big by the standards of the village and must act big and play into the fantasies that others have of them—fantasies they know all too well to be false. I was my cousins' only window to a sexually, romantically liberated world, and naturally they imagined that I, as its ambassador, would know a thing or two about it.

I always felt cool in India on these visits, a Casanova flying in from the brave new world. It was a cool unavailable to me in America, where I was a nerdy Indian kid. And I offer this history to explain what I was expecting when I moved to India in 2003. I was expecting to be cool by the lights of a traditional society. I was expecting repression, hushed love, dull marriages. I was expecting a perpetuation of the past. And I couldn't have been more wrong, and couldn't have been, in the same moment, more right.

At first, there was the comfort of expectations fulfilled. The men on the street still led their wives like languorous cattle, clutching their wrists, not their hands. It was weeks before I saw a kiss delivered in public. The primary hand holding in public was man-to-man, a reflection not of homosexuality but of frustrated heterosexuality and the resort to whatever warmth and friction could be had.

The cataracts of old visions are hard to remove, and it took time to see that this prudish behavior was not the full reality. It was a surface of poses that masked simmering change underneath. Bombay was positively wild in many quarters, wilder than the places I knew in America. Among the middle and upper classes, premarital sex was becoming as rampant as in the West, with the added spark of having always to do it in places other than home, since most young people still lived with their parents. In nightclubs such as Rock Bottom and Prive, young couples mashed into each other late into the night, the women in short, dark little dresses and the men in tight jeans and bright (and frequently floral) shirts. Women who pretended at work not to drink and to be very proper would make themselves over for evening outings as unrecognizably scandalous versions of themselves, more daring in speech and deed than many women in the West. In my parents' time, only a fraction of urban teenagers had had the freedom to date (often without any physical contact), but now teenagers quite openly maintained relationships, sometimes physical and sometimes not, sometimes known to parents and sometimes not—relationships that consisted, above all, in sitting at Café Coffee Day or Barista side by side in silence, mimicking the freedoms they had seen on television, on *Friends*, *Seinfeld*, and *Sex and the City*. On Marine Drive, on Sundays, the sidewalk overflowed with young couples, including many Muslim women who had dressed in the morning in head-to-toe *burqas* to please their parents and then slipped the cover from their heads for some amorous eye gazing once out of the neighborhood. In other cases, *burqas* were actually used by non-Muslim female college students to arrange dates and slip furtively off campus, according to this news report.

GIRLS GO DATING WITH THEIR IDENTITY CONCEALED IN A BURQA

Taking a leaf out of Bollywood films, many love-struck girl students in Jamshedpur are cloaking themselves in burqas to sneak out of college to meet their boyfriends—leaving the authorities fuming!

The girls, afraid of being spotted and rebuked for bunking

classes to go on dates, usually rent the burqas—a cloak traditionally worn by Muslim women—from shopkeepers.

Hidden behind a veil from head to toe, they freely meet their
boyfriends in parks, cinema halls and other places.

There was a special rawness and intensity to these new longings, because there had been no preparation for them; they had
arrived without context. The only rule regarding romance in my
parents' days was to avoid it. There were thus none of the subtler
codes of how many dates to go on before kissing the guy, what
skirt length is appropriate for an office party, what is healthy
provocation and what is simple vulgarity, how to keep a marriage
enticing, how to resist infidelity. And so when the young started
breaking taboos, they did so with none of the restraints that controlled behavior in supposedly more permissive societies. Their
leap from repression to passion could be stunning even by liberal
Western standards.

A certain portion of the elite and of the very poor had long
known sexual openness, here as elsewhere. But now I met new
Indian yuppies who boasted, with precise gigabyte figures, of their
"porno" collections. In certain circles in Bombay, it was not unusual
to hear men speak casually of a gay orgy the night before, as they
might speak of the restaurant where they dined last night. "They're
the standard Saturday night orgy," a friend casually said one day,
referring to a regular host of such gatherings.

The taboos around marriage were also loosening. "Open marriages" were freely discussed among elite and liberated Indians,
without a trace of embarrassment, the old closetedness of such
things surrendering to the new without a hiccup. Indian women
could still be hesitant about flirting in public at a bar, with one
important exception: married women, often those who had married very early and were already bored. They wore their boredom
on their sleeve, as their husbands pattered away about the stock
market to a circle of fellow whiskey drinkers. They broadcast a

hunger to escape their narrow world, even though few would ever risk losing their servants, cooks, and company cars by following that flicker of longing to its logical end.

Further down the class ladder the sexual revolution was more of a textual revolution. India was in the grip of a mobile phone craze, and for young middle-class Indians what could not be attempted in person could now be pursued by phone. The cell phone gave the young a zone of individual identity, of private space, that they had never known. It gave those who did not have their own home, car, or bedroom a chance to have, at least, their own phone number and a collection of messages that no one else would read. Some young people, well into their twenties, still had not touched someone of the other sex, but their pockets vibrated all day long with textual innuendo, with flashes of a new kind of romance striving to establish itself.

Ashish Chettri's approach was gradualist. He was twenty-four, short, and pudgy, an assistant chef in a five-star hotel. In his middle-class world, the women did not go to bars or date or go home with men. At most, they agreed to coffees, with coffee meaning just coffee—usually with another woman brought along as a chaperone. And so Ashish's quests were made mostly via cell phone.

I asked him to show me his method. He said that he sought to take note of women who interested him when he went out in large groups of friends and friends' friends. He would obtain the phone number of an intriguing woman through his friends. He would text her anonymously for several days, perhaps beginning with a message like, "Some guy around you likes you." If he received a positive reply, he would reveal his identity, raise the temperature of provocation, and press the woman to meet him in person.

He had recently fixed his gaze on a neighbor. He sent her a message anonymously declaring his admiration, then eventually unmasked himself. "thank u for admiring me!" she wrote back.

"but u know wat i feel dnt u think dat instead of sending me msges like a thief y dnt u come up n speak 2 me openly. I mean (face 2 face) Dnt u think dat dis is a better idea? Afterall v r not strangers v r neighbours m i not right? Now the rest is upto u Ashish."

A certain subversive idea was flowering in India: the idea of romantic love, love without context and the considerations of family and tribe. The parent-child relationship had traditionally overwhelmed the husband-wife bond, with the wife recruited as an instrument for fulfilling a man's duties to tend to his parents and to procreate. Love would creep into marriage late in the game, a love built on habit and need and the accumulation of a shared past. But it was not romantic love, love that arrests the heart, love that makes life's burdens dissipate, love that shrinks the world to the vital truth staring at you from across the valley of your pillows.

A longing for twoness was now asserting itself in India. The idea itself was not unfamiliar to Indians, as Sudhir Kakar, a leading Indian psychoanalyst, and his wife, Katharina, an anthropologist, have observed: twoness has long been a repressed dream of Indian women, as Sudhir learned from years of analysis—the dream of the *jodi*, the couple alone in a world without the impositions of mothers-in-law and alcohol and abuse and the pressure to reproduce; it was the central dream of Bollywood cinema, in movies such as *Dilwale Dulhania Le Jayenge* that start out with the love of a man and a woman threatened by outside forces—like arranged marriage—but always end with love and twoness triumphant. And yet love had been shown this way in Bollywood, the Kakars have argued, in order to subvert, not mirror, the prevailing ideal of love in the society. People paid to see others' delicious love stories because they were so unlike their own.

But this was India, and there was always a layer below the layer below the layer. If a seeming prudery masked a new promiscuity, that promiscuity in turn masked something else: an enduring devotion by the young and modern to filial piety, an enduring belief that the future, however drug- and drink-laced, must be woven into the tapestry of the past. To smoke and sleep around was one thing; to sever oneself irrevocably from history, from one's elders and one's tribe, was another. And so the young Indians I knew manifested the Indian tendency to face change and its choices with a philosophy of "both-and," not "either-or."

I saw it intimately in the Indian women I dated and befriended. For them, I was a leap out of the ordinary, a man not from their world, a man without context: I had a family, but not one whose credentials and status could easily be verified; I could be judged only by my own actions. That was often an important part of the attraction; they were with me because they were progressive women, working in impressive jobs, living on their own in some cases (though in other cases with parents), willing to follow their hearts and ignore the considerations of what made sense—willing to take a gamble on a man whose virtue could not be known in advance and who had every likelihood of vanishing one day back to America. And we would be alone together, lost to the world, just the two of us, when her phone would ring and she would become a different person from another world.

It was her mother on the line. The call was never to chat or to say "I love you" but to audit. Mothers eternally feared a daughter's veering astray, and their questions resembled those of the jealous wife whose husband recently started buying her flowers. Where are you? Who are you with? Why did you go there? Who dropped you? How much did you spend? How come you stayed there? Why didn't you have lunch? The conversation would continue like this for a time, with the daughter giving irritated monosyllabic replies and the mother boring ever deeper with questions. The call ended every time with the same frustrated adjournment: "OK, OK, OK, bye, bye, bye."

There was never substance, humor, or emotion in the calls. There was only fact-checking and the psychic urge to tighten a weave ever in danger of unraveling. Even the way the phone was picked up—"*haan*," yes—evoked a discussion with no beginning and no end. A greeting would be too ceremonial: you only greet someone when you see them as their own person. But the Indian child was just an extension of the parent, and the conversation was not actually a conversation.

These phone calls sometimes angered me. Here were women so free, so open, who gave no protest when pushed into their pigeon-holes. They wanted both the world they inhabited with me and the world they shared with their mothers. They sparred with their families about trivialities, but they refused to have the broader fight once and for all, to say, "I am my own woman, and I make my own choices, and I cannot have you calling me every hour."

The woman receiving these calls would, the next morning, put on a black pantsuit and make a presentation to the board, or would direct a film, or would design a magazine page. To live in the old world was no disqualification from the new. She was cold on the surface, and hot underneath, and cold again beneath that. She was conflicted by her own many temperatures.

The brothers of these women—the men who became my friends—had their own dilemmas. They would drink and some-times drug themselves into a blur and hook up leisurely with whichever women would join them—and then spend the next night dutifully at home eating lentil soup and fried capsicum and white rice out of a metal plate with Mama and Papa and Dadi and Dada and Chachi and Chacha, making the old jokes, enduring the old questions about marriage without a hint of irritation, challeng-ing their parents at the fringes (but do I have to go to the wedding, too?) but never questioning the totality of the regime (why can't I be a lawyer and still be a good son?).

To occupy these parallel realities required a flexible mind. Many of these young men maintained two romantic compart-ments, sealed off from each other. They dated as if in New York, and then would come home one day to receive The Talk. The

Talk was when, in the new India, your parents, who knew exactly what you had been up to and had tolerated it, informed you that your fun was over and that it was now time to marry. If they were well organized, they might even suggest a specific bride.

It was often not the girl you had been dating for three years. That girl was for dating. Your folks liked her; she had a nice personality; she was pretty. But she was not "marriageable." Perhaps her father's company was not doing as well as its books suggested. Perhaps she wanted to work after marriage, and who would care for Mama and Papa? Perhaps you were not her first boyfriend, and she was, well, tainted: people talk, you know. And what surprised me was how many young playboys went along with it. Some would fight; some would win. But acquiescence was more common. A son would holler if denied his eventual right to the family car. But, after his years of recreation, he knew when duty's moment had come. Parents must be listened to; they know best. Tradition matters. A girlfriend is not a wife.

And so Indians were once again cutting a deal with modernity. Internet dating had come to India, but it had come in the form of Internet arranged marriage. On Saturday mornings, after a drunken night out, a young man might sit with his parents on either side of him, short-listing brides with mouse clicks. At bars in Bombay, a woman might wear a designer dress and might have studied in America, but you start talking and move beyond your name and the building where you live and you realize that what she is trying to assess, even with these first few sips together, is not whether you'd be fun to escape with but whether she could present you to her Nani.

I tried to explain this to my own Nani and Nanu one day. We were sitting together, and Nanu asked me if I had seen the piece on "bed buddies" in the *Times of India*. I hadn't, and it took me a moment to realize that this was an Indian censoring of "fuck buddies," friends who cleave casually together now and then solely for that purpose. Nanu cited the piece with his characteristic mix of sentiments: shock at what his country was becoming and vicarious fascination with what he might have known had he been born in a later time. Nani shook her head and said that she didn't understand women who would stoop to this. I kept a straight face, as though I didn't know such hooligans myself.

"Why do we have to become like the West?" Nani said.

"Actually, Nani, I don't think that's what's happening," I said. I decided to stand up for my Indian friends, however much they could frustrate me.

These young people, I suggested, were rebelling on the surface, sleeping around, having their bed buddies, intoxicating themselves. But, in fact, they were finding a way to reconcile their desires for such living with the old culture. They believed with equal fervor in filial piety and in promiscuity, rejecting as false the dichotomy that a Western mind would see. They were letting off steam but ultimately preserving the regime. I offered as evidence my cocaine-and-Muslim theory.

The theory goes like this. Ask this question of an upright middle-class Hindu of marriageable age: which would test your conscience more heavily, becoming an occasional user of cocaine or marrying a Muslim whom you loved? For me, the answer is simple: I would marry a Muslim, but I would hesitate to do cocaine. Most of my Indian-American friends tend to agree. But for Indians born in India, of a similar background, the choice was usually the opposite. They saw a difference between rebelliousness and rupture. Cocaine was harmful, but its harms could be kept to oneself. Marrying a Muslim would hurt others, hinder the transmission of the old ways, and complicate how your children would eat, pray, and marry. It would sever you from your parents' fate and send you "outward bound" on the "journey without ending" that my father had promised my mother, a journey that still struck terror in Indian hearts.

Nani and Nanu couldn't be sure of my observations, but they were relieved at the prospect of their being true: relieved that what they saw on television—the skin-baring music videos, the on-screen kisses, the frank talk about sex on late-night chat shows—might be an exaggeration of India's relationship with modernity, not a mirror reflection of it. The truth was that the young Indians I knew were sometimes as torn as Nani and Nanu were between the merits of the old and new.

Mallika was an investment banker, with a sharp nose and stark jawline and milky-white skin that lent her a Persian air. She dressed preppily, in polo shirts and khaki pants and thin jewelry, as if to defy the tumult beyond her gentle South Delhi world. She tied her hair into a taut ponytail. Her accent was coolly British, or the upper-crust Indian version of it.

Her family had come from little money and had risen amid the possibilities of the new economy. They now lived an upper-middle-class life, complete with overseas "tours" and fancy restaurants and spacious air-conditioned cars. But on matters of love and marriage, Mallika's parents remained of the old school: they had begun husband hunting for her some years ago, in her early twenties. They were still desperate to find someone but were now coming to face the possibility of failure in this quest. As they saw it, Mallika was on track to end up alone, and they wanted her to find healthy companionship. She disliked the men they suggested; she couldn't hold on to the boyfriends she found for herself; all the good men were being cornered. They were reminded of this last fact by the ornate cards now coming by mail every few days: invitations to the weddings of Mallika's friends. Men whom Mallika had dated, who had once professed their undying love for her, were moving on and finding themselves wives.

Mallika portrayed herself to her parents as tough and independent, a woman who didn't need a man and wouldn't accept just anyone. But Mallika wasn't entirely confident, within her own mind at least, that her parents were wrong. She had grown up in the crevice between two ways of life. Her parents' world was a coherent ecosystem, in which everything—the style of child rearing, the eating taboos, the religious beliefs—worked in concert to reinforce the old vision of love as a merger of convenience. Mallika had grown up in an age of transition, of in-betweenness, and her world was not an ecosystem in this way. The forces in Mallika's life, far from working in concert, pulled her in a hundred different directions.

Unlike her mother, Mallika had been raised to question her parents, to argue, to talk back. She was taught to cultivate herself, form her own tastes, acquire the kind of complex personality that had not been encouraged in an earlier India. Unlike her parents, who were raised in an era when marital strife was swept under the carpet, Mallika grew up watching her parents fight a slow-grinding war that had sapped their love. So she had none of the old illusions about the inevitability of things working out for the best. Like many women in the new India, she worked, in a high-stress, high-stakes job. She drank; she smoked cigarettes; she consorted with men when she wished. For the most part, her parents said nothing. They didn't press her to stop doing what she did; they just wanted her to find a husband.

And so in one way Mallika was experiencing the release, the freedom, the space for self that so many Indians were finding: her story was part of the new weightlessness in India, the untethering from others and from history. But Mallika also knew many contrary influences. Her parents took pride in her success, but they often hurt her by saying that they had made a mistake in letting her work. The argumentative streak that had resulted would make her unappealing to men, they said. Her mother showed little interest in what she did at the office; her questions were always about what *sari* she was wearing, or whether she was wearing glasses or contact lenses. (If there were to be eligible men at the wedding she was attending, contact lenses was the only acceptable answer.) Her parents let her live freely, but she felt that they could be oblivious to the inevitable consequences of free-dom. Now that marrying time had come, they wanted her to put the straitjacket back on and behave as if the preceding years of liberty had had no effect on her personality, her dreams, her taste in men.

"There have been moments when I've actually said this to my mother," Mallika told me. "I've told her that if it really mattered to her that much that I should have been married by the time I was twenty-four and by now should have at least popped out one child, then why did they expose me in the very first place?"

The tightest restraint was, of course, that she still lived with her parents. Her banker counterparts in other countries might have found this fact unbelievable. But it was so for many Indians of Mallika's background. There were sacrifices in this arrange-ment, to be sure. After hard days at work, Mallika had to suffer evening questions about potential husbands. Much of herself had to be denied: she loved meat, but at home she had to be vegetar-ian. When she was in her bedroom on the phone with friends or colleagues, her mother would barge in without a knock. "What should I make for dinner?" she would whine, as though her daugh-ter's call could not possibly be of significance. But the family gave security in India, even now, even to the rebellious, and Mallika was happy to depend on its advantages. She lived off her father, in a house for which she paid no rent, buying designer purses and shoes with his money. One day she would transfer seamlessly from his care into the care of a man of similar means, who would continue to finance her life, such that her considerable salary would be "pocket money," as Indians called it, money for her own amusement.

The closest that Mallika ever came to marriage was a rela-tionship in her early twenties with a man called Ashok. She was young and infected by the dream of twoness spreading among her generation. He came from a different world, which excited her. He lived with his parents in the distant outskirts of Delhi.

His family was of humble means, but he was smart and had climbed on merit into leading schools and a lucrative job. He was driven. He had targets in mind. He was a man on the make.

They fell in love, and with their love they sought to overcome the differences of class and culture that were so feared by earlier generations of Indians. There were plenty of irritations. She was put off by the blandness of his dress. She looked down on his family for rarely dining in restaurants, as her family did, and for failing to belong to one of the prestigious British-era clubs. She wondered why Ashok had no desire to read the newspaper, to educate himself about the world beyond his work. But Mallika was flush with the idea of romantic love, and their differences, which to an earlier generation would have seemed fatal, could now be interpreted as proof of their promise as a couple. Context had once been everything, and to love a man without context was in these new times to offer the deepest imaginable commitment.

Mallika craved a marriage unlike those of her parents and grandparents, one built on a love that didn't make sense: a man without impressive origins, whose family did not speak English as hers did and did not come with the money or connections or affectations of Delhi polite society, a man who had his own energy and momentum and would get there walking alongside her, not five feet ahead. He, in turn, was attracted to a new kind of woman: a woman who would enthrall him, not just cook and breed, who would be less malleable than his parents might like, but who would, correspondingly, be more stimulating to him, who would challenge his thinking, share his ambitions, question him, and go passionately to bed with him.

For a time, it worked. They spent a glorious year and a half together. But in a society that is slow to change, they underestimated the lingering power of context. The two of them were willing to overlook differences; Mallika's parents were willing to overlook them, too. But Ashok's parents never accepted Mallika.

She was from a better background economically, but that came with a spirit of independence with which they never made peace. Under pressure from his parents, Mallika suspects, Ashok phoned her one day and ended everything.

Like her upbringing itself, the relationship filled her with contrary lessons. One reading of it was that love without context just doesn't work; that what works for the Americans and the French doesn't work in India; that she had better choose a man who matched her point by point on the "biodata"—education, occupation, salary, parents' background. An alternative reading was that Ashok simply didn't love her enough; that if you are taking the risk of twoness, of cutting your own romantic path, it had better be with someone who adores you and possesses the courage to blow all the naysayers away. Still another reading, neither traditionalist nor romantic, drawn more from present-day Western thinking, was that a woman should never reduce herself to needing a man, as Mallika had, that she should indulge herself, live for herself, have children alone—that she should exist not for a dozen, not for two, but for one.

Mallika read all of these lessons into her situation, whatever their contradictions. In the Indian way, she was tolerant of the rival ideas that swirled within her. Since the breakup, she had acted on all of these lessons—sometimes coherently, sometimes with confusion. She had stopped extending serious romantic consideration to anyone from a wholly different world, and she had banished the thought of marrying a foreigner. She knew now that, in all likelihood, she would marry an upper-middle-class professional from South Delhi with prosperous parents and a good income of his own. "I think I was more of the Romeo-and-Juliet style when I was twenty-three, not when I'm twenty-seven," she said one day, "because I've realized that it's not only love that makes marriage work."

But she had not jettisoned the dream of twoness, either. She seemed in some ways still to be grasping for pure love, and now with a certain amount of experience to her name. She expected men who approached her not only to possess grand ambitions and a desire to share the future with her; she also wanted to know vividly how they felt about her; she desired small bits of proof from time to time that this was a man who would march together with her despite the thousand Indian obstructions. She had recently become involved with a Singaporean of Indian origin who had been an intern at her bank. He had gone back to Singapore and broken up with his girlfriend in the hope of starting a relationship with Mallika. He sent her loving text messages every day. Mallika was falling for him; she told me so. But she wouldn't tell him. It was as if she wanted to elicit as much evidence as she could that he was not Ashok, that he didn't just love her in a vacuum but would continue to love her even in the face of complications. When she boasted about his affection for her, a good part of her pride seemed to lie in the fact that she was testing him, being mean and unfair to him, and that he wanted her still.

"He openly declares the fact that he's madly in love with me, and that I'm one of the best things that has ever happened in his life, and how I'm superior to any woman that he has ever known or dealt with," she said. Sometimes, she said, she happily acquiesced in these declarations, though she provided few in return. Sometimes she snapped and attacked him with all of her buried fears and frustrations: "This is not working. This is not what I wanted in my life. Fucking piece of shit. Fucking bastard. You're to blame for everything."

And every time she attacked him, he would say something like, "I don't know how it's going to work out, I don't know what's going to happen, but I have this very strong leap of faith that you and I will work out, that somehow it's going to work out, that I'm going to marry you."

When I asked if she thought that she would marry him, she said nothing and just serenely nodded.

And yet she also subscribed to that third reading of her plight, to the idea that she should abandon the husband chase and be a woman all her own—a lover, a temptress, a corporate dynamo, not merely an aspiring wife. But she pursued this idea in a most Indian way: flirting with rebellion, building an image of herself as daring, but never following through, never taking it so far as to threaten her security.

She gave herself a sense of adventure, of escape, by forming friendships with older men she encountered at work, men who became mentors to her, some of whom she fantasized about and some of whom fantasized about her. Nothing happened physically with these men, Mallika said, but she called them her "sugar daddies," and they gave her a way to rebel in the mind, to be daring in theory, to break out of the smallness of Delhi life—but to do so without hurting family bonds, without damaging her chances of settling down someday with a suitable, high-earning man.

One sugar daddy was a European diplomat in his forties. They had come to know each other some years earlier, when he lived in Delhi and she was his intern. Now he was in the Middle East, from which he regularly sent her expensive gifts and messages about her hair and about making love to her. Mallika described the relationship as "nurturing on several levels." He explained Middle Eastern politics to her, sent her articles to read, gave her the intellectual stimulation that the men around her in Delhi could not. She had had a similar relationship with a successful senior partner at one of her clients' firms; she described herself as being "his favorite little girl."

These relationships allowed Mallika to feel free without having to make the hard choices that true freedom required. "In my mind," she told me, "I live out instances of sitting at a beautiful nice little roadside café in Paris, or going and sitting before a massive Rothko painting." She added, "I don't even want to live that life, but I want to get that taste. I want to live that one moment, and that's it. I want to see what everything's all about."

Within Mallika there battled contending visions of love and womanhood. There was the desire to be loved romantically, to be wooed by a man who would give and possibly lose everything for you. There was the desire for love that was pragmatic, that would not always exhilarate, perhaps, but that would pay the bills and offend no one and be unlikely to fail. There was the desire for stimulation, for receiving expensive gifts and naughty messages, for being told on the phone by a man that he wants to take you. And there was the desire for self-love, for completing yourself before seeking to complete another, for wanting a child without a husband, with a hardness and wholeness born of the fear of not turning into your mother.

Observing the young women around me in today's India, living with this grueling inner war, I found myself wondering whether they were happier than Ammamma in 1942. Their freedoms were incomparably greater. They had acquired a complexity of sentiments so absent from her generation. They were regarded increasingly as equal partners in relationships. They were rebelling against the old habit of passively waiting for others to arrange their lives. They were hunting for men in their own right. But the border between old and new was never cleanly drawn in India, and in many cases the freedoms of these women had come at the cost of great confusion. The old had not completely vanished; the new had not fully settled in. These women lingered in the badlands in between, liberated and anxious, no longer certain of what they were supposed to be.

Twoness was a dangerous dream. It put the couple at the center of the world and shoved the joint family into second place. It made room for affection, passion, sweet nothings. It breathed yet another form of freedom into the lives of young Indians seeking independence in their work and private lives. But as love was reimagined, as personal fulfillment moved to the center of things, couples inevitably began to expect more of each other. Indians who fell in love, who chose each other, could not be as resigned as their parents and grandparents had been about their partners; indeed, they were not resigned about much of anything these days. In this society of roles, roles were losing their status: they were little more than gentle suggestions now. And a prime place to witness this turning was at the Bandra Family Court in the suburbs of Bombay, because along with these new expectations of love had come a rising tendency to divorce.

The court stood on a leafy stretch of road, in a district being overtaken by software companies and big banks. It was humming with activity when I arrived: lawyers wearing their traditional black-and-white costumes, speaking breathily into their cell phones, as their clients sat nervously and ashamedly, adjusting to the loss of privacy that a court case brings.

India was in the thralls of a divorce boom, if there can be such a thing. In Bombay, the annual number of divorce petitions had more than doubled since 1990 to surpass four thousand, discomfiting many older Indians but reflecting the priorities of a younger generation. I had several friends in their twenties and thirties who had been married for a few years, then ran into a case of infidelity or just unexpected tedium and decided to part ways. (It was usually couples who chose each other that suffered this fate, rather than those in arranged marriages.) And it was not a problem limited to urban sophisticates. The founders of SecondShaadi.com, a matrimonial Web site specializing in remarriage, were shocked to discover that most users came from beyond the five leading metropolises, and fully one-third from beyond the twenty largest cities.

And yet divorce remained shrouded in secrecy. It was, like sex in an earlier India, something that admittedly did occur every now and then, but was seldom a topic of conversation. I wanted to understand what was behind the rise in divorces, and why it had come at the very time when Indians were embracing romantic love. My idea was to spend a week in divorce court watching cases, but the Family Court was off-limits to outsiders. Yet this was India, where the possible is often impossible and the impossible often possible, and I had been told by a judge on the phone to visit him in person to seek permission.

I found him in his chambers. He was sitting behind his desk, tall and slender, handsome, instantly affable. I explained my interest in divorce cases, and he permitted me to sit in the court, so long as I disguised the litigants' names. Then he retreated into his inner office to prepare for the day.

In the hallway outside his chambers, a diverse crowd of rich, poor, and middle class had begun to gather. (The rich women could be distinguished by their identity-masking designer sunglasses.) I entered the courtroom and sat just below the judge's bench, at the far end of a long table used by the litigants. A fan whirred gently overhead; a January breeze blew in from the open grated windows. Lawyers came and went from the courtroom, bowing according to custom as they entered, filling several rows of chairs behind the front row, where they would wait all day for their case to be heard. Light green folders were everywhere— stacked high on the judge's desk, piled on the litigants' table, stuffed into shelves on the wall: cases, hundreds of cases, of families in dispute. In this court, as in so many Indian government agencies, the computer was regarded as an interesting technology of the future.

The judge made his entrance from the chambers and the hearings began. India has a tendency to swallow any alien concept and make it its own, and divorce proceedings were no exception. The solemn reality of divorce had come from abroad, but in this courtroom divorce became just another part of the Indian carnival. The cases were handled almost simultaneously: a few minutes for this case, then someone had to go find a document, then another case for a brief time, then the original case resumed, then some haggling over schedule among various lawyers and the judge. The feeling of chaos never lifted. The general language of the courtroom was a confident, ever-shifting admixture of English, Hindi, and Marathi, and the judge had the wondrous Indian talent for knowing how to apportion the quantity of words from each language depending on who stood before him.

Unlike in American courts, the cases were conducted informally, without much fuss about procedure or the letter of the law. The husbands and wives sometimes spoke to the judge directly, without their lawyers' filtration. The judge got one spouse's story, then the other's, but kept going back and forth between them, asking him why he had hit her, asking her why she had betrayed him, offering from-the-hip grandfatherly advice. Every few minutes, a breach occurred that in America would have led to a mistrial. In one instance, when a lawyer began to cross-examine a witness and revealed a remarkable lack of talent, the judge scolded him in front of everyone for not knowing the law and not knowing how to cross-examine. And then he began to cross-examine the woman himself.

In one of the first cases that day, a woman testified that her husband spent undue amounts of time in an apartment not their own. But it was not a lover whom he was charged with visiting. It was his parents. They all lived in a two-story house, with the parents on the ground floor and the couple above them—a traditional-modern hybrid arrangement gaining popularity in India. Every night, when the man got home, he would go to his parents' level, unwind there, talk about his day, and only later find his way upstairs. When he made major financial decisions, he consulted his parents and siblings, not his wife. She wanted, in the new romantic style, to be at his core, with family on the periphery. But he seemed to embody earlier habits, with his wife as merely one node in a web of obligations.

In a later case, a waifish street vendor of *pani puri* appeared to fight a custody battle. It was often assumed that the divorce boom was an elite phenomenon, but I had heard from experts that it was not so, and now here was a street vendor proving the point. He had been in a divorce suit with his wife, who had died with the case unresolved. He was now suing her parents for the custody of his children, meekly answering the judge's questions.

Then a wealthy-seeming couple came before the judge. I gathered their story partly in the courtroom and then over lunch with the husband, who elaborated on his version. He had married his wife many years earlier. She was eighteen, came from a poor family, and was already divorced. His family was educated and of a higher class, and they staunchly opposed his choice. He ignored them and married her anyway.

He was a tall, well-built man, with a bald head and a jaw-lining beard. We were sitting in the courthouse canteen. After the wedding, he said, he had helped to turn his wife into the sophisti-cate she now was. He had paid for her education and had watched with pride as she gained important positions at leading compa-nies and then became the CEO of a venerable Bombay club. He, meanwhile, was the CEO of an Indian-European joint-venture company, and his role came with a house, a car and driver, and free education for their children. But over the years they had slowly traded places, the husband said: she, born with little, became more glamorous and consumed with money and success. He began to tire of luxury and some years ago resigned from his job, surrendered his perquisites, and started riding the local bus and even a bicycle again. Something of the Brahmin ascetic came over him. This didn't go down well with his wife; in his nar-ration, he failed to meet her lofty requirements as soon as he was the CEO of nothing.

Tensions grew, and when she had finally had enough of him, he said, she strangled their marriage in a most Indian way: she stopped serving him food. They officially separated, but he con-tinued to live in the apartment, which, owing to the complexities of the Bombay real-estate market, was taking a long while to sell. This was the obstruction keeping them from a divorce. So they lived on in their misery, he taking the bus and riding his bicycle around town, she continuing to pursue the aspirational existence that had once attracted her to him and that now had driven them apart.

Then there was the saga of Rajesh and Preeti. They lived in a slum in Chembur, a distant suburb of the city. Rajesh was a paunchy, mustachioed man in his late thirties. He wore a red open-collared shirt, and the heels on his shoes had become detached and flapped around wherever he went. He seemed assertively bored even though it was he who had filed for divorce; when his eyes weren't shut, he tended to stare at the ground or into the distance. Preeti wore an embroidered *sari* and had a nervous habit of rolling her fingers over her necklace of gold beads.

Rajesh told his story first. He spoke in Marathi, with the judge very loosely translating his testimony into English, in which the official record was kept. (One cost of the carnival environment was the inevitable imprecision of these translations, which in a less flexible legal culture might have struck people as a threat to the integrity of cases.) Rajesh testified that, roughly a decade ago, he had noticed his wife becoming friends with a neighbor in the slum who was also named Rajesh. Rajesh Number Two was a bachelor. Preeti felt sorry for him, living all alone. She used to send food to him and look out for him. The couple's daughter, rattled by her behavior, told Rajesh Number One about Rajesh Number Two.

"I used to find them in one room of the house in privacy," he said, in the judge's summary translation. "I used to knock at the door, and thereafter Rajesh used to leave the room embarrassed. I used to get angry, and I used to tell Preeti not to entertain him or else our marriage would break."

Preeti's story was very different. She testified that she had been a good woman, and good in the Indian way: she and Rajesh Number One had had an arranged marriage; she had given him a daughter and then a son within two years; she attended to him dutifully. But she had learned not long into their marriage that her husband had a woman on the side called Roopa. And when she confronted him, he didn't take it well: "He assaulted me and threatened that he would leave me if I asked about it," she told the judge. "He told me that he would not leave her."

One night, wondering about her husband's whereabouts, she went over to Roopa's home. She knocked on the door and, sure enough, her husband came out. She appealed to Roopa to let go of her husband, but in vain: "She told me that she had friendly relations since prior to our marriage and that I was a latecomer." Preeti also said that her husband beat her on the spot. Later, upon returning from the hospital after giving birth to their son, she discovered that Rajesh had been sleeping at Roopa's during her pregnancy. Their marriage was effectively over.

"My husband then spent no nights with me," she said in the judge's somewhat stilted translation. "I had no occasion to have sex with my husband thereafter." It was around this point in her testimony that Preeti began to cry.

Mothers have a special place in India's legal system as witnesses and mediators, as when the Ambani brothers had turned to their mother to divide their multibillion-dollar empire. So it went in divorce court. Rajesh Number One's mother eventually came before the judge, wearing a hot-pink *sari*, which she had draped over her head. She wore a red *bindi* larger than her eyeball. She testified in blunt terms that Preeti used to finish the housework and then sit outside the house chatting with Rajesh Number Two. When asked about her own son's behavior, she answered that Rajesh Number One and Roopa have "cordial relations," as the judge put it, and nothing more. At one point, as the mother-in-law spoke, Preeti shot a glance at her as if to question her account. The mother began to scream at her with all the feudal derision that an Indian elder could summon, as if the courtroom setting and the judge meant nothing to her: it was the traditional belief that nothing in the world, not even the law, could cut into the relationships of a family.

Suspicions of infidelity, and infidelity itself, had long been rampant in the slums. What was novel was that Rajesh had chosen to go to court instead of just moving in with the other woman; what was new was that the wife now had a forum in which she could speak out against an allegedly abusive man in some safety (at least while in court). And yet the old ideas of wifely duty, of endless adjustment, of making it work at any price were still with Preeti. Although she thought him unfaithful and abusive, she had come to contest his petition for divorce. She wanted to remain his wife.

Back in his chambers, the judge explained to me the evolving law of divorce. In cases like that of Rajesh and Preeti, where the parties differed on the desired result, the person seeking divorce had to prove his or her case on grounds such as adultery, mental disorder, leprosy, or venereal disease. Until the 1970s, this was the only way to get a divorce, mutually agreed upon or not. The requirement served as a heavy deterrent to women, in particular. But in the 1970s India, moving in the direction of the West, began to grant divorces by mutual consent. So long as both parties agreed and could negotiate a settlement, you didn't need to justify your parting to a judge. Today, most cases were filed in this way.

Over the next several days, the judge used breaks in the proceedings to talk me through one aspect or another of the divorce world. He was mournful about the shift in values that he saw. As I got to know him, I saw that his own marriage stood in stark defiance of the prevailing trend. It seemed to be a beautiful marriage. His wife, who also had a government job, would hang around the office in the mornings, sipping tea with him, chatting with his staff; she returned on some days in the afternoon to repeat the tea ritual, before they went home together. She was a strong woman, a blend of the Indian old and new. As I asked the judge my questions, she never hesitated to answer them before him or to cut him off when she disagreed. There seemed to be chemistry and equality between them.

Threading my conversations with the judge was a theme that came up often with Indians of his generation: a sense that dissolution and fragmentation were the bitter price of modernity, that the old virtues were crumbling. But as we spoke late one afternoon, the judge offered a more nuanced view of things.

The fraying of the joint family, with its arranged marriages and communal living, was commonly considered the culprit for the rise in divorce. But the judge argued that the traditional family system was not as flawless as Indians liked to imagine, that it "protected mediocrity," in his words. He described an uncle who lived in the traditional way. He had five sons, all of whom lived with the family after marriage. Two of the sons worked hard, and, thanks to the communal economics of joint families, their success permitted the three other brothers to shirk. Family closeness subsidized their laziness. In nuclear households, the wives of those lazy brothers might have walked out or pressured their husbands into action, but in the joint-family system they didn't depend on their husbands, and so they coasted along. The portfolio effect kept things whole and peaceful, but in the judge's telling it also limited the pressure on the good-for-nothing brothers to stir.

The traditional system, with its fixed roles and arranged alliances, also suppressed the talents of the young, the judge said. "They don't invent themselves," he said, "because they're not allowed. They are not permitted to think." They are preprogrammed with activities, with schooling, with marriage. Even today, he said, a trace snidely, many men in their twenties ask their parents to arrange a marriage to a suitable woman because "they don't have the strength and responsibility to go find one." Arranged marriage, as he told it, was part of the traditional obsession with security. The young would gravitate to secure spouses found by their parents, and to secure jobs that didn't ruffle feathers.

"How come so many doctors have doctors for children?" the judge said. "They push them in that direction. They want clones, at whatever cost." A moment later, speaking of the traditional form of child rearing, he added, "Everything is curtailed, very ruthlessly curtailed."

The judge had mourned the rising divorce rate when we first met, as everyone did. But now, in deeper discussion, he seemed to cast divorce almost as another facet of the Indian awakening, a bitter side effect of the liberation of spirit that was coming.

He urged me to speak to the court's marriage counselors, who worked in the trenches of divorce. In a corner room on the sixth floor of the courthouse, I met with a dozen counselors, all women. At first, they rattled off familiar truisms: divorce was rising because women were earning more money, because laws were changing, because taboos were eroding. They noted that, among the poor, it was usually the husband who filed for divorce, with women's filings increasing with social class.

But as they spoke, it became plain that there was more to the rising divorce rate than these shifting social trends. There was, as in the stories of Ravindra and Mukesh and the Naxalites, a new and different conception of life and the self and the good that was pushing in. The young now approached love in the way they approached success and consumption and the future itself: with an underlying assumption of abundance. They expected more out of love than earlier generations did and were willing to fight to secure it, but when it failed they were equally at ease in walking away. It was one strike and you're out. They rejected the moral vocabulary of an older generation: patience, tolerance, adjustment.

"The present generation doesn't really understand love," one of the counselors, a woman in her twenties named Kasturi, told me. "Marriage is based on love, and the concept of love over the years has changed." She spoke of her parents' generation: "People used to be more committed—the whole concept of finding one person and working things out with that person and compromising and making certain adjustments. But now it's like we see someone and like them, and we'll see if things work out or not. If things don't work out, we'll break up and move on. Maybe to a certain extent, the present generation is confusing love with attraction."

Another counselor, an elderly Parsi woman named Freny, saw the dissolving marriages as symptoms of a deeper change in how young people were socialized. A child raised in the traditional Indian universe learned to sacrifice from day one, to live in shared spaces, to wait for others to eat before eating herself. This was good training for marriage. But such training was no longer available to many young people in the cities, who now had their own rooms, their own phones, their own spheres of privacy.

"Earlier, it was more 'we,'" Freny said. "It was for the sake of the family. It was for the sake of the children. There was a lot of giving and sacrifice. But now they say, 'I'm an individual. I have my needs.'"

Love, in the traditional Indian way, had little to do with individuals. It was a merger of families with similar backgrounds and attitudes. But in an India drenched in foreign influences— Hollywood in the theaters, teenagers named Sunita who called themselves "Sarah" and answered phones for Citibank—more and more couples were marrying each other for each other, out of personal enthrallment rather than a sense of family duty, setting out into the world largely on their own. And it was this new conception, with the couple at the core, that made marriage both more exciting and more precarious than before.

In the earlier vision of marriage, a person derived emotional sustenance from a dozen people. In the new marriages, without the supports of parental approval and regular family contact, everything was wagered on the feelings that crackled between the two.

The pleasure and joy and consolation that those dozen people once provided were now expected to come from one human being. It was sometimes more than one human being could give.

"Historically, the fulcrum of the Indian family has been the parents-sons unit rather than the couple, which was subordinated to the former," Sudhir Kakar, the psychoanalyst, told me a short time after my week in the court. He added, "The couple is now taking center stage and is under great pressure, not only from the normal expectations that the partner fulfill all emotional needs but also from the persistence of the former ideology, which leads to conflicts of loyalty, especially in a man who is torn between his wife on the one hand and his parents and siblings on the other."

As I left the sixth floor to return to the courtroom, I noticed a poster on the wall bearing this acrostic:

Mutual understanding
Adjustment with each other
Responsibility
Reassurance to each other
Importance to family
Acceptance
Get together of two families
Emotional bonding

There was only so much that I could gather from the courtroom and my conversations with the judge and the counselors. I wanted to hear from the litigants themselves, and I asked the counselors if this could be arranged. In the West, merely to harbor that wish would be an impertinence. (These people are getting divorced! Why would they want to talk to you?) And yet in India, where people are rarely asked to share what they feel and relish opportunities to do so, and where a sense of sacrifice was not yet wholly gone, I received several acceptances.

Satish was thirty-two and Heena, thirty. They had married

after a ten-year courtship that began in college. He worked in the media and she for a leading Indian bank. They worked incessantly the whole week, then partied feverishly on the weekends: the emergent way for the Westernized yuppie class. They lived alone. They referred to themselves as DINKs, an American moniker for couples with a double income and no kids.

Like many young divorcing couples in India now, Satish and Heena had dated before marriage, which made their breakup confounding: it wasn't that they didn't know what they were getting. But as they told it, their history led them to make less of an effort after marriage than they might otherwise have made. They spent too little quality time with each other, and virtually no time with anyone else. Two years before they married, Satish had developed an alcohol problem. But they were buried in work and buried in each other, and they ignored it. There were no relatives around to detect the problem or offer solutions. The drinking grew worse. One day, Satish became drunk and agitated and he hit Heena's father. Heena at once walked out.

"I was totally influenced by alcohol, and everything went haywire, and her love diminished into hatred," Satish said, sitting next to her in a side room of the courthouse. "There have always been problems," he added a moment later, "but today women have started working. Today they feel that, if I am working, I have some kind of self-respect, and I am not going to be treated like a doormat. Our parents would have compromised. My mother would have carried the relationship on and tried to pacify my dad."

Heena now joined in: "Continuing the relationship only for the heck of the family and society, coming back to the house and fighting like dogs—it doesn't make any sense." And yet she seemed to lament the shift in the society: "At the end of the day, two hearts break. Two hearts began with a dream in mind, and when it ends, everything gets shattered."

"Neither of us is happy living apart," Satish said, "but we cannot live together."

A short time later, the counselors introduced me to Ajit. He was a trim and robust man in his sixties, with a square of a Hitler mustache in the center of his face. He had flown for the Indian Air Force, dropping bombs over East Pakistan in 1971, in the war from which Bangladesh was born. Ajit returned from the hostilities a swaggering hero, and he married a woman in show business. She had had a good amount of sex before marriage, he said, and had problems with drinking and depression. But he loved her, and they plodded on. They settled and started a family. Then her erratic behavior began to affect their son's education and Ajit's career in the military. After five years of marriage, his wife suddenly left him and moved away with their son. They were officially divorced in 1983.

Five years later, he was married again, to a woman in Bombay. All was well until she hit menopause. A turn in her hormones bent her personality, he claimed: "She totally changed and wanted complete independence." She began to sleep in a separate bedroom. As Ajit saw it, he was patient and willing to adjust, but she had taken things too far. Even without full intimacy, he said, as if repeating what he had once told her, "you can stroke your husband's back or ask, 'How are you?' or shake hands."

They separated, and Ajit moved to Pune, a three-hour drive from Bombay. At this point the story took a turn for the bizarre. He said that he had "adopted" a Muslim family, in what sounded at first like a charitable endeavor. But the reason for doing so, he said, was that a friend had advised him that, despite his age, he would go crazy without sex. And so he lived now with this Muslim family, giving the woman what she needed, getting what he needed in return.

It was not clear to me why he was in court. Then he explained that his estranged second wife had suggested they divorce eight years earlier, but he had resisted. His mother had suffered gravely after his first breakup. He wanted to wait for her death to get the second one. She had recently passed, relieving him of his burden, and so now here he was.

Like Ajit, Chitra came to me alone. She was thirty-one and worked as a trainer for a cell phone company in India. She was a Brahmin from the south, educated as a homeopathic doctor. Nine years earlier, she had fallen for an unlikely partner: a street vendor of Chinese food from a different region and another caste, a "Chinesewallah," in her parents' phrase. They scoffed at him; they begged her to reconsider. But new winds were blowing, and Chitra loved her Chinesewallah, and that seemed enough. They lived for a short time with his family, in the traditional way, and then set out on their own. They cobbled together money for a small apartment outside Bombay.

At one point, his business began to falter. She was pregnant at the time, and for a traditional woman this would have been insupportable: her work was to breed, and his to feed, and he was not doing his part. But this was a new kind of marriage, a marriage of equals, and Chitra wasn't upset. Not to worry, she told him: her job as a teacher could support them, and she didn't mind buying fewer dresses or having only one pair of shoes. She loved him; that was what mattered. But, as her husband's stresses grew, he felt inferior beside his upper-caste, better-educated, higher-paid wife. When they argued, he would tell her, "You're earning too much, so you're talking too much."

"Somehow along the way I became a more dominant figure in the household; somehow I became a braver figure in his eyes," she told me. "His depression of not being able to earn was made worse by the fact that I earned more."

In my mind, twoness had always been an uncomplicated virtue, something inherently fuller and richer than the old pragmatic love. But in Chitra's story was another way of judging the merits of twoness, a way that challenged my American visions. Living on their own, there was none of the din of the big Indian family to distract the two of them from their fights. There were no prying relatives to conduct household shuttle diplomacy, to urge them against angry instinct into reconciliation. They didn't have the feeling of injuring a dozen people's lives whenever they disagreed. They had paid a great price to be together, but they were unprepared and ill-equipped for the work that came with freedom. Their lives had been gambled on how they felt about each other minute to minute; nothing else bound them.

Their fights continued. One day, as they watched television, her husband rose to fix himself a drink. It bothered Chitra, and she decided to tell him. Money was tight, she said, and drinking was a luxury they could no longer afford.

Her intervention jolted him. He stopped making his drink, slipped on a T-shirt, removed some money from a drawer, and made for the door. "I said, 'If you want to go, go. But don't come back,'" Chitra recalled. "And I regret my words, because he never did. He hugged and kissed me, he kissed my daughter, and he never came back."

She wondered for a time what had befallen him. She visited hospitals looking for amnesiacs and accident victims; she searched morgues for the freshly dead. She found nothing and eventually came to accept what had happened. "The fact that he doesn't want to face us makes him somebody I don't want to know," she said. "If after seven years of courting, seven years of marriage, this man can just walk off, then he was never mine."

It had been two years now since he left, and she had come to the court to formalize the reality with a divorce. "This could happen only in this current generation," she said. "In our parents' era, I couldn't imagine something like this, because they were more family-oriented, and women were more docile. To some extent, women have shown men that we don't need protection."

She was ready to lead a new life, she said. She had thrown away his things, thrown away their wedding photos, sold the house full of their memories, and moved into another. But it was still not easy to be a single mother in India. Male neighbors and colleagues preyed on divorced women, because they were a coveted Indian catch: sexually experienced but unattached. A close family friend, a man whom Chitra thought of like a brother, made a move on her soon after her husband left, spiking her drink in her own house. Acquaintances have come to her and pityingly offered her grocery money in exchange for sex. They see her as a ruined woman, for whom any scrap of love must be better than the present barrenness.

What pains her most is when her daughter's school holds a special evening event and mails tickets to her home. Three tickets invariably arrive, for her daughter, her husband, and her. It still comes as a shock, Chitra said, every time she has to throw one of the tickets away.

SIX

Freedom

The Shatabdi Express from Delhi to Ludhiana was not like other Indian trains. The seats all faced forward, as in the West; they were not arranged in the usual forward-backward family clusters. The breakfast of croissants and *chai* was served on individual trays and eaten individually. There was none of the communal eating and singing and "what village are you from" encountered on other journeys. There were no vendors or beggars or eunuch dancers angling for money at every stop. This was a new train designed to entice business travelers away from low-cost airlines, and it seemed to bring not only a new standard of service but also new ideas about order and space and the very nature of human relations.

We arrived presently in Ludhiana, deep in the Punjab. On the road into town from the station, idle clothes vendors reclined below a bridge fanning themselves in the June heat; one of them was beating his clothes with a broom to release the trapped dust. Tea sellers boiled their supply on hot coals. A boy with a Nike "Just Do It" T-shirt punched his fist over and over into a ball of dough, which was to be kneaded and pulled into smaller balls and baked into *chapatis*.

But in Ludhiana, as in every prosperous part of India, these images were like postcards from the past. Commerce was moving indoors now, shielding itself behind walls of glass, bathing itself in air-conditioning, for those who could afford it. Unlike the citizens of Bombay and Delhi, who could feel sadness at the remaking of their history-laden cities, there was little in the physical land-scape of Ludhiana that would inspire preservation, little that spoke of a great old civilization. And so the city was being made over by a florescence of jeans stores and car dealerships and shop-ping malls.

Ludhiana was well known in India for having fallen in love with consumption. McDonald's on its own was said to account for 10 to 15 percent of all restaurant sales in the city. Ludhiana was also reported to have the highest per capita ownership of Mer-cedes sedans in India. A local businessman had made headlines by paying more than $30,000 for the easily memorized vanity cell phone number 97800-00000. ("I am happy to get a number like this," he said after the auction, according to a local press account. "I borrowed money from friends and relatives to buy this number. I will repay them later.") The streets were lined with the brands and slogans repeated at every mall around the world. Only the signs affixed as afterthoughts to every stall door in the toilet of one of the malls spoke of how new this all felt to a place that was, until lately, a farmers' settlement: "Used toilet paper should be flushed"; "Do not mess the toilet seat"; "Remember you are not the only person using the Facility."

Ludhiana, an overgrown town that longed to become a big city, was making every effort to groom itself for the dizzying new world.

I was traveling with a friend, Neha, who had invited me to meet her father's brothers in Ludhiana. We had stopped in a mall to buy them gifts. I had been advised to refer to the Dubey brothers, with whom we'd be staying, as Upstairs Chacha and Downstairs Chacha. "Chacha" was a term for uncle, simply enough; the Upstairs and Downstairs thing was more complicated. All I knew was that the two brothers lived with their respective families on different floors of the same house. Downstairs Chacha belonged to the old world of Punjab, an aimless and loving man, occupied with the chaotic goings-on of his own home. Upstairs Chacha was, fittingly, a man on his way up, ambitious and determined, the kind of man to whom the businesslike Shatabdi train might appeal; he had built an oasis of order and quiet and selfhood on the second floor, buffered by a staircase from that other notion of home.

It was Upstairs Chacha who came to get us from the mall. As we drove, I explained my interest in understanding the story of his family. As our eyes met in the rearview mirror, he seemed gruff and gangsterlike, his dangling gold watch loose enough to admit a second wrist. He asked Neha, who lived in Delhi, perfunctory questions about her parents, who lived in London, and then resumed his silence. Before long, we had entered a sprawling neighborhood of narrow streets and, in the middle of one of them, protected by a white gate that was never locked, the Dubey household stood.

The house, like so many houses in Ludhiana, was constructed to resemble a village dwelling. Most of its square footage was given to an open courtyard—the kind that in the village would host a cow. The low white walls were village walls, incapable of keeping people out and designed instead to keep animals in: an intruder who scaled the wall would come upon several unlocked screen doors. In the courtyard, managed by Downstairs Chacha's family, two motorcycles served as racks for drying laundry. The vinyl was peeling from two chairs and the golden upholstery on a sofa was turning a chocolate brown. A plastic patio chair, missing one arm, was still in service. The paint on the wall was cracking and, as the layers of white wore away, the green of an earlier era was reasserting itself. Two trays with uneaten food had been placed in a corner for a stray dog that the family tended but didn't own. The dog was absent when I came, and the food had attracted a swarm of bulbous, black flies.

Ever since the two brothers had separated to pursue their different lifestyles, Upstairs-Downstairs diplomacy had become complicated: visitors had to carefully divide their time and attention with each side. We had driven over with Upstairs Chacha. Now we spent a few minutes in the Downstairs sitting room making polite conversation. Neha offered tidbits of family news; I spoke to Downstairs Chacha's son Rohan, who was built like a rugby player, with hair parted down the middle, macho and suspicious and full of questions for me. He began to offer his own thesis about the transformations afoot in India today. My original lens in India had focused on scenes of liberation, of opening; it was only with time that I had come to appreciate the strains involved in that evolution. Rohan went straight to the strains. Respect is declining, he said. More and more families are breaking; more and more children are deserting their parents (as he had not done). The rich are getting richer and the poor poorer. He even suggested, in what had begun as a polite little chat, that a revolution was coming, referring to the Maoists.

"India will become America," he said. Thinking of the new malls we had seen and the crowds of enthusiastic Ludhianans, I asked if that was a good or bad thing. "*Kharab cheez hain,*" he said—a rotten thing.

At this moment Neha, with an awkwardness that would emerge every time we had to switch floors of the house, asked if I wanted to go Upstairs. I attempted to say "yes" without seeming enthusiastic about it; I would improve with practice. And then we climbed the stairs.

A firm wooden door, wide and unbreachable, guarded Upstairs, where a more aspirational form of living flourished. In the living room was a comfortable sofa facing a television, which, unlike Downstairs, where the box droned on all day, was turned on only for particular programs. There was a big dining table at which the Upstairs family ate, instead of removing their shoes and piling onto the bed, as they did Downstairs. To the right, behind glass walls, was a second living room with its own air conditioner (as the master bedroom also possessed), for special occasions. Each of the three bedrooms was decorated in its own style, with vaguely African-seeming prints hung on the walls. Behind a glass display case in the living room, over the television, was exhibited the business card of an important man the family had once met.

The defining sound Upstairs was of servant summonses. Every few minutes someone would scream "Prakash!" or "Reena!" and then a meek voice would cry "Yes, Aunty!" and the servant in question would come running. Prakash, twelve years old, wearing soiled orange shorts, scampered around the house at high speed; when called upon to fetch some vessel from the kitchen cabinets, he would kick off his shoes, hoist himself onto the countertop, grab the item, and drop just as swiftly back down. Reena was fourteen and somewhat less servile, used more for cooking than for menial labors, poised halfway between a servant and a daughter, which in any case were not always distinct roles in India.

With our arrival, the servants received a new task: Neha had bought the board game Monopoly as a gift for Upstairs (its acquisitive theme being more in line with the ethos of that floor), and Gunjan, Upstairs Chacha's school-age daughter, seeing a shortage of players, asked the servants to join us. We sat on a bed, all of us, and after a short time Downstairs Chacha walked in. (The Downstairs people sometimes came up, but the Upstairs people rarely went down.) We were introduced, and he joined in the game. He had no idea how to play, and Prakash, a novice himself but quick and shrewd, became his adviser.

At a certain point in the game, Downstairs Chacha realized that he was going down in flames and he began to lose interest.

He looked like the full-blooded Punjabi that he was, with his strong Pashtun nose that projected forward from the bridge before remembering to drop downward, his thick mustache, and the long white tunic that he always wore unbuttoned. He was the kind of man who could not let a joke of his pass without, by a round of eye contacts, gathering the room's approval. He leaned over to me and tried to whisper, at a volume far louder than a whisper, a long word that I did not understand. I couldn't decipher whether he was speaking Hindi or Punjabi or English. He repeated the word several times, and then I realized that it was really three English words compacted into one: "whiskeychickenmutton," he said, over and over. It took me a further minute to realize that this was a proposition, and a proposition of a rather delicate nature.

The Dubeys were Brahmins and proud of it. Like many Brahmins today, they maintained a public squeamishness toward meat and alcohol. I had thought of bringing them a bottle of whiskey as a gift, but Neha had testily warned me against doing so. But now I was having the word "whiskeychickenmutton" loudly whispered in my ear, and, looking uneasily at Neha across the Monopoly board, I meekly nodded my interest in such things. Downstairs Chacha made the gesture of drinking a shot in one swig. Glancing nervously around the Upstairs home, he asked if I engaged in the deed he had just demonstrated. I nodded again, not realizing the small conflagration that would follow.

Although my purpose was to understand the family's two branches, I was considered by the Upstairs household to be primarily its guest. I had come from the big city; I would have high tastes and elaborate requirements; it was assumed that the Downstairs branch couldn't handle me, with their one-armed chairs and cracking paint and sagging sofas. And so Upstairs Chacha, without asking anyone, had taken ownership of my schedule and made our dinner plans. The Upstairs family, along with Neha and me, was going to eat at the home of Upstairs Chacha's sister, known to all as Bua. The Downstairs family was not invited. But a few minutes before we left, Downstairs Chacha came Upstairs again, wearing a white *kurta* and *pajama*. He mentioned quietly to Upstairs Chacha something about whiskeychickenmutton. Upstairs Chacha replied that we were going to Bua's for dinner. Downstairs Chacha was upset. He had bought and prepared meat. He proposed that I be allowed to stay behind and the rest of them go. This was flatly refused, and with no say I was hustled out of the door.

There had been a misunderstanding with Bua. She thought that we were coming for a drink (for a soft drink, that is), not for dinner. And so, on top of the absurdity of Downstairs Chacha's making an illicit meal for us that we could not eat, Bua now summoned her driver from the street to come in and become, temporarily, her cook. We sat in a sofa-ringed sitting room under fluorescent tube lights and listened to Punjabi folk music on a stereo as we waited for a meal to be generated. When the food came after an hour or so, I ate lightly, keeping space for a possible second meal. But this was taken as an insult. "Was my food too spicy?" Bua asked. "Next time I can make it less spicy. You know, it's not my regular cook." My insistence that, no, the food was delicious led inevitably to forced seconds and stomach cramps.

We returned home at 10:30. A paralyzing fatigue had crept into me after our early morning train, and I was fading quickly, with barely enough energy to ascend the stairs. There was no question of eating another meal, I told Neha, who agreed.

And now Downstairs Chacha, by this time drunk, stumbled into the courtyard, his right foot crossing over his left, then his left foot over his right, babbling. He welcomed me with special effusiveness and asked if I was ready to eat. I told him apologetically that I was tired. Neha, whispering urgently to me in English, told me to run. This seemed a most impertinent thing to do in the middle of a conversation. I brushed her advice aside and said that I would graciously explain the situation and then go.

Big mistake. Downstairs Chacha could not understand why I didn't want his whiskeychickenmutton. He tried giving me a handshake and then used that grasp to seek, in vain, to pull me into his son's bedroom. I resisted, which intensified his resolve. He grabbed my right arm, digging his nails into my bicep rather painfully and dragging me, this time successfully, into the room. Sitting there were Rohan, Rohan's wife, Purnima, who was playing with their infant son, and Downstairs Chacha's wife. The television was on but no one was really watching.

I was made to sit next to Downstairs Chacha, who began what seemed to be an attempt to explain the culture of Punjab to me. He explained that Punjabi wives were thin when young and gigantic when old. "She was like this when we got married," he said of his wife, holding up his index finger. "Now she's like this," he said, puffing out his cheeks and spreading his arms sideways. I avoided the temptation to look for her reaction. Then he began to explain something called *izzat,* honor, which would be the most important word I learned in Punjab, with its connotations of honor and respect and dignity; it was the word that explained so much in northern India—the hospitality, the repression of women, the endemic violence, all of which could be defended by invoking one's honor. "In Punjab, we serve guests like God," Downstairs Chacha said. "In Punjab, we get meat and whiskey for our guests." And so, to preserve his honor, he began to press food on me. Eat something. I can't. That's OK, but at least please eat something. I really can't. No, no, that is OK, but you must at least eat something. And so forth, until I had no idea where to run.

It was now that I saw the wisdom in Neha's initial advice, which she was continuing to repeat. So I got up in the middle of the conversation and left, denying my own urge to apologize and explain, knowing that any opening I gave them would be interpreted as a false signal of hunger. And as I climbed the stairs into that gentler world, I began to understand what had prompted Upstairs Chacha all those years before to build a second story and a new life above the only life he had known.

The Dubeys' property began with what was Downstairs, a single-story horseshoe of rooms arrayed around a courtyard. It had been constructed when the brothers' parents, who were prosperous and important people in the northern city where they lived, saw the city go to Pakistan at independence. They moved to Amritsar and then again to Ludhiana, and there built a house. Their sons married and brought their wives into the home, remaining with their parents in the Indian way.

They lived with the traditional Indian family dynamics, in a noisy household filled with compromises, meddling, and unspoken, overwhelming love. A brother might live for some years in one bedroom, then switch rooms when his brother had a baby, then move again to another room when a cousin came to stay for a year. The brothers worked in their father's business, selling hosiery in a local shop, and their wives shared a kitchen. There is a lovely word in Hindi for families like these: *behisaab*, without accounts. They pooled their money and shared their expenses, and no one took note of who earned what, who worked when, who purchased what food, whose liabilities were whose. It was family Marxism: from each according to his ability, to each according to his needs.

The bed was the locus of life in those single-story days. There was no dining table in the house. To be with people, you sat on a bed, with the television on, sort of watching it, sort of making conversation, but mostly just being around one another. On the bed dinner was eaten, children were conceived, newspapers were read, letters were written, rituals were performed, arguments were waged, marriages were arranged. And a kind of love flourished on these beds that was unlike the family love I had grown up with. It was ambient love, love that was not about your feelings and thoughts and psychology. It was love that hung gently in the air, a simple awareness of the presence of those around you, a love that felt no need to proclaim itself.

You, the individual, were not important as an individual but rather as an organ in a greater organism. Children were raised in common, each child receiving a little love from everyone and a lot of love from no one in particular. An excess of personal attention was thought to corrode character. Every daily transaction— the way food was slapped onto your plate; the way you were told to sit here, sit there, slide forward, move back, drink water, don't drink water; the way no one asked a child's opinion of major family decisions—would have reinforced the sense of one's own smallness in the larger tribe.

No one could say with precision when relations in the Dubey family soured or why. Downstairs Chacha claimed that it was because his wife, raised in a village, tended to entertain often, showering guests with food and attention; he said that Upstairs Chachi ("Chachi" being the word for aunt), born in a city and thus less generous, did not like her house functioning like a hotel. But the truth was that the Dubeys' separation was really Upstairs Chacha's decision. It was partly that Downstairs Chacha broke the Brahmin ways every night with his tumbler of whiskey, which Upstairs Chacha didn't want his young daughter to see. It was partly that Upstairs Chacha's wife craved freedom and didn't want to consult her sister-in-law and mother-in-law, who lived with the brothers, every time she went to the market to buy vegetables. Upstairs Chacha began to feel that living *behisaab* subsidized his brother's sloth, as the Family Court judge had suggested to me about his own family. Upstairs Chacha noticed that his brother did not work as hard as he did, did not have his burning ambition. He began to want more for his daughter than his brother wanted for his children. He began to think of the future, of progress, of where India was headed and how he might secure a place in the new order. He began to dream of things—a car, a television, short-sleeved shirts from Van Heusen, a gold watch to dangle loosely from his wrist, a cell phone with loud, status-enhancing ringtones.

And as he relayed to me in a series of conversations, he began to see in his own family what he had not seen before, and what an Indian was not supposed to see or acknowledge: the resentment and backbiting and petty inwardness that sometimes lurked beneath the calm surface of that ambient love. He began to sense that real love was impossible when spread so thin. He felt that silent prompting for release that so many Indians were now feeling and pursuing in their own ways.

Upstairs Chacha decided on a separation. He would leave the family business and set out on his own as a contractor, building roads and parks and such; he would eventually seek to become part of the state-level Congress Party political organization. And—much as Ravindra did when he came into money, much as Mukesh Ambani did when he separated from his brother—Upstairs Chacha resolved to carve out a physical space for himself in the world, a home of his own. Families across India were fragmenting in this way, in the villages and cities alike. But in India, where the old always has the upper hand and the new always stands on the defensive, Upstairs Chacha also decided that he wanted to keep just enough of the old ways. Like Mallika, he wanted to split the difference with modernity.

Without announcing his intentions to the whole family, he asked some of the laborers who worked for him to do a project in his own house. He had them build three stand-alone bedrooms on the roof. His daughter, Gunjan, had just been born, and he was able to explain it to his brother in terms of needing space for the new infant. The three of them began to sleep Upstairs, but they had no kitchen or bathroom of their own, and so the basic rhythms of communal living continued. It would have been possible for the Downstairs branch to tell themselves at this point that it was only a question of space, that life's essential patterns would remain unchanged.

Then, in 2001, Upstairs Chacha built his own kitchen and bathroom above his brother's. A rupture had been torn. The two families began to move in separate orbits in daily life, although they came together for important events—weddings, funerals, visits to the ancestral village. A few years later, he added the living room Upstairs, which was followed by the second, glass-encased one, which was followed in turn by a veranda where the family could sit in the evenings, overlooking Ludhiana's lanes.

I asked Upstairs Chacha one day if he considered the household he had cleaved to be a "joint family" in the Indian sense or two nuclear families.

"It's not full joint," he said after ruminating for a moment, "but semi-joint."

Over time, the Dubey household began to seem like a body debilitated by a stroke, the skin sagging and movements slowing and expressions dulling on one half, with the vitality of the other half thrown into stark relief. The Upstairs world began to fill with stuff: a color television, air conditioners in two rooms, a washing machine, a car down below in the garage, a computer, an Internet connection. Downstairs, the walls were decaying, the ceiling was erupting in welts from moisture, and there were so many flies that it was actually difficult to have thoughts about anything other than the flies when you were there. Upstairs, there were no flies because the floor was scrubbed afresh every morning, with the servant boy slipping and sliding across it after the cleaning as a kind of quality control.

A certain decorative fatalism reigned Downstairs, such that whatever happened to the house became accepted as a divine intention. In the toilet Downstairs, a bad flush tank left remnants of earlier defecations floating in the bowl. On the floor beside Downstairs Chacha's bed, dozens of used matches from his smoking were scattered, waiting to become populous enough to reach the cleaning quorum. An old bottle of ginseng and an old can of shaving cream stood in the windowsill. Upstairs, by contrast, a new attentiveness ruled. Every detail of the house was considered and tended. The toothbrushes were arrayed in a toothbrush holder. The beds were made every morning. There was even gray tubing, installed by Upstairs Chacha, around the power lines that ran along the street, inches from the veranda. It was the only such tubing on the street, and it suggested a protectiveness and sensitivity to risk, an insistence on living in spite of the gods, that had come with the new aspirations Upstairs.

But theirs was more than a physical divergence. The greater drift was in the two households' senses of time and of their place in its flow. Among the deepest differences between industrial and agrarian societies was in perceptions of time. In agrarian society, time was cyclical. It was to be endured, not extracted for profit. Time was the seat of life; one lived through it and didn't expect much from it. Conversations involved the trading of banalities and gossip; they helped the time to pass. Your relatives fulfilled a role that in the linear modern world would be taken over by anti-depressants and insurance policies and alcohol: they palliated, protected, and occasionally intoxicated you. With the advent of modern industrial societies, time began to be felt as a linear thing. The idea of progress dawned. A man was supposed to be today where he had not reached yesterday, and tomorrow where he had not reached today. There came the idea of conquest and perpetual forward motion. Time was to be consumed, not endured, to be seized and not suffered.

Upstairs, this linearity prevailed. You slept in your bed, of course, but then you got out of it and dressed yourself and moved on with your life; a bed was not for lingering. Time was to be managed wisely and schedules to be packed. Gunjan was constantly running—from school to a tutoring session to the temple to a roller-skating competition. Downstairs, the family took things day by day. They, too, had work to get done, but I never got the sense that they had committed to be in any particular place at any particular time. Upstairs, the future was methodically planned and built: just as Upstairs Chacha had constructed the three bedrooms, then the bathroom and kitchen, then the living rooms, so, too, had he planned his political career: he determined that he would remain in his current role as a local Congress Party secretary for four years, then run to be a municipal councillor, and then five years later run for a seat in Punjab's state legislature. Downstairs, the family didn't save for the future, didn't strategize about the crockery business they now ran, and were blissfully unaware of their plans for tomorrow, let alone for twenty years from now.

Upstairs Chacha had once told me, seeking to distill his philosophy, "Money makes a man perfect. If a man has money, all his relatives give him *izzat*. If he has no money, he gets no *izzat*. Before, you didn't need money to have *izzat*. Before, it used to come from love."

"Today, there is no *bhai-bhai, behen-behen*," he added, no brotherly or sisterly love.

The morning after the whiskeychickenmutton affair, there were reparations to be made.

After a cup of tea Upstairs, I went down with Neha, wondering about the fallout from our episode the night before. We found Downstairs Chacha in his bed, half-watching a singing-contest show on television. He lit up at seeing us and motioned for us to cast away our shoes and join him in bed. He called me "Mr. Nund" in his thick Punjabi accent and shook my hand heartily, as he would every time he saw me thereafter, including sometimes upon returning to his company after a two-minute bathroom break. His greeting suggested an unspoken truce.

Yet the talk turned at once to the night before. Now sober, Downstairs Chacha wanted to articulate in words what earlier only his firm hands could express. To treat guests well in Punjab required a man to serve them, he said, and, if at all possible, to serve them whiskeychickenmutton. Nothing spoke more eloquently of love and respect for one's guests. He hadn't meant to upset me. He was trying to show me love. I expressed my gratitude and protested my helplessness and apologized for the confusion.

We ate fried *parathas* Downstairs, evening out the balance of Upstairs-Downstairs ingestion, and then Downstairs Chacha took me on the back of his motorcycle to see his shop. It was called Sai Crockery House, recently renamed to reflect the family's new enthusiasm for Sai Baba, the bearded *guru* they had taken to following. Chacha proudly handed me a business card, which described the shop's offerings this way: "Deals In: All types of Crokery. Spl in: Cello, Bluplast, Treo, Acarylic, Mellamine."

He sat at his desk, with Ramu—who was a house servant when Downstairs Chacha was in the house and a shop assistant when he was in the shop—at his side. He began to speak of the family history: the Dubeys' origins in what was now Pakistan, their time in Amritsar and Ludhiana, the building of their house. He said that he was proud of his two younger brothers, who had studied to earn master's degrees. This was quickly followed by the assertion that he had not had the chance to study himself because it had been his duty, as the eldest brother, to fund their studies by entering the workforce. He spoke of his marriage to a woman from the villages. Some years into their marriage, she had returned to her village to see her family. She had fallen ill quite suddenly and been unable to reach a hospital in time, and she had died. According to the village custom, he married her younger sister as a kind of replacement. His first two children were from the first wife and his youngest son from her sister.

These were Indian family stories of the traditional kind: stories of sacrifice and duty and of human interchangeability: if I can't have my wife, at least I can have her sister; if I can't study myself, then at least my brothers can study. But they were, in Downstairs Chacha's telling, stories that came from a beautiful, vanishing past.

"The world has changed," he said. "The love that once existed between brothers, between parents and children, doesn't exist anymore. Before, when an elder brother said something, a younger brother listened. Today, brothers barely even acknowledge each other. This world that's coming, it's not a world for men without money. A man with money has brothers, a wife, parents. A man without money has no one. No money, no family."

"If you go to a rich man's home," he said, "he won't speak to you like I am. He won't give you much time, the way I am sitting with you and telling you so many things. He will tell his servant to make you food, and then he'll go to work. But a middle-class man will give you full *izzat*. In Punjab we serve our guests ten different vegetables until they cannot eat anymore. We give them meat and whiskey, and they say, 'My, how well you have taken care of us!' "

It was difficult not to see this as a criticism of his own brother, who was usually at work while Downstairs Chacha lingered at home, who did have his servants do things for guests that Downstairs Chacha did himself, and who, almost like a Westerner, did not insist on stuffing me with food, offering just once. I asked Downstairs Chacha if he was referring to his own family in disparaging the new mores.

"Our own family? No," he said firmly. "I see it in other people's houses; I see it in the world. In Ludhiana there are families where one brother is a millionaire and the other doesn't even have bread. I've seen it in our own neighborhood." This, again, seemed to describe his own situation with his brother, but Downstairs Chacha's idea of *izzat* perhaps kept him from seeing or admitting the feelings that were in plain view: his brother may have been dishonorable to him, but his own honor required him not to say so.

As our conversation continued, Downstairs Chacha's talk of

loss and his nostalgia for a receding way of life spread into other domains. It was not just the family that was coming apart but so many of his old certainties.

Children were not listening to their parents anymore, he complained. And arranged marriage was giving way to the love kind, in which couples dwelled on each other and neglected their wider duties. And women were ceasing to wear their baggy Patiala pants and all-covering *kurtas*. And children were increasingly raised only by their own parents, not by the entire tribe.

Perhaps most ominously for a graying Brahmin, the hierarchy of masters and servants was dissolving, he said. In the old days, a servant, usually from the lower castes, could not walk into the master's bedroom. He could not eat from the same dishes. He couldn't touch the master. Now, Downstairs Chacha said, with palpable frustration in his voice, the serving classes were becoming rich. Low-caste people in the villages had moved overseas, remitted money back home, and built houses bigger than his own house. India was now full of upstart Ravindras. "There is no longer any difference between big and small men," Downstairs Chacha said. He turned to his servant at this point to solicit his opinion, and the servant obediently agreed.

The Dubeys were Brahmins, and he was proud of that. But even being Brahmin was not what it used to be. Nothing in the village used to happen without a Brahmin's involvement, he said. Today the Brahmin stands on the sidelines. And it was perhaps the Brahmin's own fault, he was willing to admit. He offered his own meat eating and drinking as an example of Brahminical unraveling. He said that he had no choice. This was how the society worked now, and because he needed friends and contacts in the society, he had to play by their rules. "Without connections, none of your work gets done," he said. "In Ludhiana, if you need something done by a powerful man, it won't happen without meat eating and drinking."

He seemed aware of his own hypocrisy in saying this, and he

pivoted to a funny, distracting story. There was a Hindu priest who kept pressuring his son to give up meat and alcohol. The son made him a deal: you have whiskey and chicken with me tonight, and I will give them up tomorrow. So they ate, and they drank, and the next day the priest went to his son with a 500-rupee note and said, "Go get a bottle and a chicken and let's enjoy!"

He insisted that the story was true, and in the story, as in all that he had said, was a vision of the world fully the opposite of his brother's: the world as seen from Downstairs looking up. The loss of his brother to the cult of ambition; the rebellious, self-consumed young; the skin-baring women; the withering of filial piety; the precariousness of his position as a master; the hypocrisy of his Brahminism. When I had first sensed these movements in India, they had struck me as signs of rebirth and renewal, of a thaw in the millennial freeze. They were all part of the coming of modernity to India, of a future that was urban, youthful, atomized, free. But the stories of the Maoists, of Mallika, of the couples seeking divorce gave quiet reminders of how much had to be lost in India for anything to be gained.

And now it was possible to understand the gentle, familiar humiliation that my refusal of Downstairs Chacha's meat and drink had caused. It was to him just another sign of the passing of a world premised on his idea of *izzat* and of the coming of a world that seemed to make space and make time for everyone but him.

Later that day, I was to meet Neha's cousin Karan, the son of Bua, from dinner the night before. Like so many Punjabis, he had migrated overseas for work: he was a security screener at the airport in Melbourne, Australia. He happened to be in town on a visit, and Neha had insisted that I meet him. He was, despite his mere twenty-some years, an important man in the Dubey clan, and so there was only one space suitable for our meeting: Upstairs, of course, and in the air-conditioned special sitting room. Everyone spoke reverentially about Karan as we waited for him to come over: "He is very smart, that boy. Very wise, that boy. He will tell you all things. Whatever you want to know, you ask to him only."

He walked in presently, with an air of detached cool that instantly set him apart from the others. He wore a black T-shirt and jeans. He had the appearance of a rebel whom his relatives had learned to love, a rebel whom they might have scorned if they did not envy him so much.

We sat on the sectional sofa, and he began by telling me about Australia. He had gone there for money, having memorized five thousand English idiomatic expressions from a book before he left, in order to ingratiate himself with the locals. He had worked as a taxi driver and then in security to make a living. But he had regrets about leaving India, he said: "If you want to earn some money, it is OK if you go to foreign country. But the thing is, if you have capacity, you can also earn in India. India is now on fire. I don't think that for the sake of some money we should pledge our soul and mind to those people."

He found the Australians very alien to him, with very different ideas about life. "Foreigners, they live for themselves, and Indians, they live for everybody," he said. "Foreigners know that their childhood is going to be spent in a crèche, and their old age is going to be spent in an old-age home. But this doesn't happen in India. Here the childhood is spent in the lap of the mother, and the old age is spent in the house."

I began to steel myself for another paean to the old culture. He disparaged how "Australian people go to nightclubs, they fetch liquor, they smoke, they move in with their girlfriends." He said everything there was "too open." He claimed never to have committed any of these sins himself, despite his ultra-cool demeanor.

"I have not been grown up in that way," he said. "I have been grown up in a very conservative way, in a very myopic way.

I am not too myopic like the Muslim people of Saudi Arabia. Even in America or in Australia, you will find Muslim people wearing *burqas*. I am not so much conservative, but I am still conservative."

Here I was sitting with yet another eulogizer of the old ways, but this time it was a man in jeans and a T-shirt who had moved away from India, had ceased to live with his widowed mother, as tradition demanded, had seemingly abandoned these old ways he described. I put it to him: wasn't he proof that in India it was now possible for the young to break with the past and chart their own way? And now his instinctive flexing of Indian pride, having been accomplished, dissolved into an honest and surprising airing of views.

He began to describe the India of his childhood, whose remnants remained, as a place where the young could not dream. "Only in India can you still force your kids," he said, speaking of the survivalism that dominated the choice of professions in small towns. "The major problem is that in India the people who are doctors or officers or engineers, they are respected the most, and they only want their kids to be doctor or engineer because these positions are well-respected by society. Why don't these people allow their kids to be political science lecturers or English lecturers or Hindi lecturers or Sanskrit lecturers? Because they are not earning good money. But in foreign countries you can't force anybody. If someone has the potential to be a doctor, but he says no and he wants to be a lecturer, the government there or the parents can't force them. But here you can force."

This forcing was achieved by guilt-tripping so intense that Karan referred to it as abuse. "They say, 'I did this thing for you, I did that thing for you, I did this thing for you, I did that thing for you.' They start chanting everything they have given over the last twenty years, and after that the kid emotionally starts listening to them, and once the kid starts listening to them, he starts following them."

"It's guilt," he went on. "Kids are not allowed to do anything. In India, the parents never allow their kids to think differently. We can't live independently in India."

He was reminding me of an idea that a former Indian politician had suggested to me some time earlier: you can only understand India's ills, the politician had said, by going beyond corruption and deprivation and overpopulation and investigating what is done to the minds of Indian children in their first years: the way they are barked at to shut up, to stop asking questions, to accept and adjust, and, as they age, the way that guilt-tripping moves into the center of the parent-child relationship.

Karan now made a peculiar distinction that explained his own earlier defense of India and subsequent criticism of it, and explained his own reason for emigrating: India was the best country, but foreigners were the best people. "They are matchless," he said of foreigners, using the word more than once.

"The most beautiful thing which I like about the foreigners," he said, "is there is no hypocrisy or stereotype imagination in those countries. For example, no one needs to be married at a particular age. If you see this girl," he said, gesturing toward Neha, "at this age, if she would have been in India, she would have been forced to marry, with gunpowder. But she was born in Britain, so nobody can force her. This is the most important, most beautiful thing I love about them. You can't force anybody. Why these idiot people are forcing us, I never understand."

"Basically, the thing is that in India there is no law and order," he continued. "So everybody wants to live collectively. They have five or six sons, and they feel that, if any nasty thing happens to me, my family will help me. But in foreign countries, you depend only on the government." In India, he said, "the family is the state."

There seemed to be a contradiction in his vision of how children should be raised: for his own children, did he favor the freedom that made foreigners "matchless," or did he fear his children becoming too open like the Australians?

He said he wanted freedom for his children. "It doesn't mean that I will supply them with drugs; it doesn't mean that I will give them some extra money to become womanizers," he said. "But I will allow them to find themselves on their own, find their own educational path. I was forced to do so many things: don't do this, do this. I will never let my children go through that."

I asked Karan to make his ideas more concrete, to apply his philosophies to the Dubeys themselves.

He swatted away the question with a look of boredom on his face. "For me, only one person lives in this house, and that is my grandmother, and after that I don't have any interest," he said, with a strange tartness. "I am an independent man," he explained. "I have got my own norms of working, my own style of working. You are a writer; you write and you think in different ways. You play with the words. And I am also, I suppose, a writer. I think in a different way. At one point you clash with your relatives and then you find that, instead of fighting or arguing with each other, it is easier just to say hello, have a cup of tea, and move on."

He tried to keep his distance from all of his relatives, he said, "because Indians are too much nosy. Here people have too much time. They look around, they poke into each other's lives. I am an independent man in the way I want to live, the way I want to dress up, the way I want to think, the way I want to do business. It doesn't mean that I want to become a womanizer or drink wine or go to nightclubs—going against the norms of society. I am completely following the norms of Indian society."

And then he offered a theory of the Indian family that was perhaps the only thing that he and Downstairs Chacha would agree on. "Basically, we love too much," he said of Indians. "This is our problem. We have too much of affection, and because of that our love becomes binding love."

After talking for a while, Karan said that he wanted to show me a bit of Ludhiana. We went down and into his car. He turned the music on loud and drove to a shopping market a short distance away. On the way we passed the signage of a land newly enthralled with "personality development" and "skill upgradation" and other forms of self-perfection: Dr. Goyal's Orthodontic Clinic, a weight-reduction center offering "unlimited weight loss" for 2,999 rupees, a middle-class finishing school called the Siddhartha Academy of Competitions.

The shopping market was packed with cars. It felt like an island of Westernness in the Punjabi ocean: a new pharmacy, a step up from the "chemists" of old, with orderly aisles and bright lights and air-conditioning; a music store blasting loud beats; a Barista espresso bar. And it occurred to me, after speaking to Karan, that it was becoming possible to emigrate from India for a few hours at a time without having to leave it, by coming to spaces like these, with a watered-down version of the openness and choice and freedom that Karan had discovered so far away.

We walked into the espresso bar. I asked Karan what he wanted. He opened the menu and was overwhelmed by the terminology of iced lattes and hazelnut mochas and Brrrista Frappes. Perhaps his life in Australia was simpler than I had imagined. He looked up at the server and, smiling, switched to Hindi: "You're an Indian and I'm an Indian. I just want an Indian cold coffee, so give me whatever that is." The server smiled and said that he knew just what Karan wanted, not to worry. And in that moment Karan, the Dubeys' proud rebel, the foreigner returned, the man who didn't need his family anymore, seemed relieved to be back home.

The Dubeys were every Indian family, and they were certainly mine. The conflicts between love and freedom from the constraints of love, between communality and the longing for space, that tore them apart could seem like just another instance of tradition battling modernity in the convulsive present. But there was an eternal quality to these different longings.

Whenever my parents visited India, something in my mother

always came alive and something in my father always died. Love would gush around them. They were asked at every meal what they most desired. They were hugged, kissed, argued with, guilt-tripped, coddled, nagged.

The older she grew, the more my mother basked in it all. With my sister and me living far from home, she felt America to be colder and lonelier than it had felt to her before. Everything was orderly and proper and scheduled. No one popped in unannounced to have tea with you, she would often say, as if that single fact said it all. There were, of course, things that she didn't like in India: the enduring male chauvinism, the dearth of privacy that came with the love and attention she relished, what she called the perpetually "dug-up" streets. But none of that mattered in the end. When she landed once a year in Delhi, she awakened. She had all the freedom and space for self that she needed in America. When she returned to India, she most craved not *azadi* but *pyaar*, not freedom but love, the concepts that divided the Upstairs-Downstairs Dubey family.

My father favored freedom. He was an eternally patient man, almost incapable of anger with his children, no matter the crime. Only when he visited India, where he was born, did his patience dry away. When it was taking ten people ten times longer than necessary to make a decision that could be made by one person, exasperation filled his eyes. When no one was straightforward about what they actually wanted to eat or where they actually wanted to go, all trying to please the others, with the result of a suboptimal outcome for everyone, he became frustrated. When we had to meet relatives whom we did not like but had to meet because it would "look bad" if we didn't, I could sense him saying to himself, "Look bad to whom?"

I came to India built in the mold of my father. I was an American kid, used to my space and freedom of action, and I remember the strange sensation of stepping into my Indian relatives' world in my childhood visits. It was a visceral, physical feeling. I knew at once that there was no chance of being alone, of reading quietly in a corner somewhere, of having a heart-to-heart discussion with my sister or one of my parents. I felt possessive of my parents on those trips: when I had something to tell them, my own parents, I could not get a few moments alone. I didn't like being asked in front of half a dozen people whether I still had diarrhea. I didn't like public debate on whether my latest haircut was too short. I didn't like that everyone talked and no one listened during dinnertime arguments, and that the only way to get into the conversation was to interrupt.

And yet I grew up with the idea that it was our relatives back in the motherland who genuinely understood family and sacrifice and love. Some of our Indian relatives implied in whatever ways they could that we in America were self-absorbed and materialistic. *Americans let aging parents die alone in nursing homes! They call their parents by their first names! They take money for helping with chores!* And it did not matter if these claims were true. Their repetition created a hierarchy of filial piety in my mind in which the big, noisy Indian family was the real kind of family, and our own kind of family in America, intensely loving in its own way, but smaller and less sacrificial, a confederation of strong individuals, was somehow a dilution.

Coming to India as an adult had, in many ways, allowed me to peel away the misperceptions of my youth. But, when it came to family, I now saw a certain wisdom in my childhood discomfort with the Indian family. Family was always put forward as India's great strength. But what I saw on my travels was that family was also the beginning of the Indian tragedy, the force that had, perhaps more than any other, prevented so many Indians from becoming the fullest possible expressions of themselves. What had most frustrated me as a child was, I now realized, the inwardness of the family. There was little interest in the neighborhood, the community, the country, the world. What consumed its members hour after hour was one another. Why are you wearing this? Why are you eating that? Why didn't she invite her? What will she think if he doesn't do that? The Indian family could be a cesspool of its own petty resentments. It was obsessed with itself. It wasted so much energy on itself. It stewed in its own juices. It struggled to think of what could be more important than what this one would think if you didn't go to that one's wedding.

It was no accident that a new generation consumed with things to do—with courses to take, businesses to found, cars to acquire, homes to build—was turning away from these preoccupations. There was a new conception of life available to them, a conception focused on the vital self and its fulfillment and cultivation. There was a geographic diffusion of family networks as people attempted to profit from the new economy. The complex debt transaction underpinning Indian family life—that you forget yourself and sacrifice everything for me now, until my debt to you compels me to forget myself and sacrifice everything for you—began to feel inefficient to Indians. It seemed easier simply to seek what you desired.

And yet my years in India began to change me in turn. Every time I stepped into my grandparents' home, with its glasses of chilled *nimbu paani* and homemade food and curious questions, my stress and anxieties would melt away. It was not that the stresses had been cured or their underlying causes addressed. It was simply the vibration and madness that numbed one's sensitivity to oneself, just as painkillers pushed a headache to the background of consciousness without actually curing it. It was a different kind of family love. It was an attentiveness to ten people's needs, without a focus on any one person. It required what the psychoanalyst Alan Roland has called a "radar conscience," a perpetual mental sweeping of one's clan to detect opportunities for aid and sacrifice and intervention. I began to realize that I belonged to history, that I was the product of generations of dreams and illusions and successes and failures, and that to know that past more fully was to know more fully the person within. I began to understand *pyaar* and not just *azadi*.

And now, in a humble two-story house in Ludhiana that began its life as a single story, I had found an Indian family moving in the very opposite way.

On the second evening, I had no choice. As dusk cloaked Ludhiana, Downstairs Chacha reminded me that it was whiskeychickenmutton night. Shortly after eight, Neha, Downstairs Chacha, and I sat on his bed. (Neha, who as a woman was not invited to any gathering involving alcohol, was allowed in this case because she was my friend.)

Downstairs Chacha brought in a tray with metal bowls of chicken in a thick brown gravy and mutton in a thick brown gravy, along with a salad of raw cucumbers, tomatoes, and onions thinly sliced. A bottle of whiskey emerged from a metal cabinet: I drank it with soda, Downstairs Chacha with water and ice.

The talk turned, as it so often did with him, especially when he was drinking, to love. He boasted for many minutes that, of all the relatives in the family, people loved him the most. Neha's mother disliked his drinking and meat eating, for example, but she loved him anyway because he was honest and straight. Neha's father refused to drink but made an exception when he was with Downstairs Chacha.

The talk of love led him to marriage. True love between husband and wife blossomed only in one's fifties, he said. Until then, a couple was focused on the children, on the preservation of the race. You fought over their clothes, their education, the food, the household finances. And then in your fifties, as the children began to lead their own lives, you realized that it was only the two of you for the remainder of your lives, and you reached a new level of marital intimacy. But this story was immediately counterbalanced by another that suggested the limits of such intimacy. It was a story about another kind of love, his love for his brother. Once, early in Downstairs Chacha's first marriage, Upstairs Chacha had come home in the middle of the night and requested that his sister-in-law make him some food. She refused, citing the hour. Downstairs Chacha claimed to have grabbed his wife by her hair and spun her around and around in circles to force her to accede to his brother's request. He made the motions now as if swinging a bag of groceries rather than a human body.

I could not keep up with Downstairs Chacha's eating and drinking. When I resisted his offers of more whiskey and more meat, he insisted. This, too, was about love. So I made up a story about having a serious ailment that forbade the eating of these very things. He asked what the ailment was. I invented a heart condition, which was a bit much but, I imagined, would end the pressure. And I was in luck: for heart trouble, Downstairs Chacha informed me, whiskey was said to be the perfect cure.

I kept drinking.

When the session ended, we spilled out into the courtyard. Downstairs Chacha's son, Rohan, was stumbling around drunk, looking on as his wife and baby played together. He tried to intervene in the play every now and then, but his drunken motions seemed to scare his wife. She had the tired look of a woman who knows that she will have to brave this alone. Downstairs Chacha was also stumbling. He went to the freezer to get Popsicles and was now shoving them into everyone's mouth. He gave one to his aging mother, who was acutely diabetic and definitely not supposed to eat Popsicles. Someone noted this doctor's instruction as she began to bite toothlessly into the orange ice. Downstairs Chacha retorted, with great confidence, that Punjabis had been eating ice cream for centuries and that nothing had ever befallen them as a result.

As I walked toward the staircase, Rohan looked at me with a drunken glaze over his eyes and muttered without further explanation, "Upstairs, they sleep with the doors shut. Down-stairs, we sleep with the doors open."

Neha was supposed to return to Delhi early the following morn-ing, and I was to remain in Ludhiana. But the night before Rohan had pressured her to stay, by offering this incentive: first thing in the morning, he would drive her and me two hours out of Ludhi-ana to his mother's "native place"—her *pind*, as it was called in Punjab—and we could see the Punjabi rural life for ourselves. It was a Monday, and Neha had obligations at work in Delhi, but she had always wanted to see the village and so agreed to post-pone her journey.

And then some combination of miscommunication, laziness, poor planning, deception, a funeral, politics, and honor culture got in the way.

Rohan had told Neha to be ready to go at eight a.m. She set an alarm and in the morning went Downstairs to rouse Rohan. He waved her off. He had no memory of promising to take her to any village. He intended to continue sleeping.

We let some hours pass. Both levels of the household gradually arose, bathed, sipped tea, breakfasted. We kept asking Rohan and the others when we could leave for the village, what was keeping us, what was the problem, our urban impatience simmering. At first, the problem was said to be this: the car was gone. Upstairs Chacha, who had left the house on some business, had taken it with him. We discussed and analyzed this fact for a while. Then it was discovered to be untrue, because the car was, in fact, right outside the house. Now the problem was said to be the absence of the keys. We had the car, but we had no keys, and Upstairs Cha-cha, who owned the car and usually kept the keys, was gone. The keys' absence, too, was soon revealed to be false; Upstairs Chacha had left the keys at home. At this point, with the car in front of the house and the keys in our possession, a much deeper problem presented itself: the car belonged to the Upstairses, not the Downstairses, and if Rohan, a son of Downstairs, wanted to take it to the village, he had to do more than just inform Upstairs Chacha or seek his permission; he had to give him a first right of refusal on the voyage; he had to ask him if he wanted to come along. Only when he said "no" to the invitation, as Rohan expected him to say, would it be appropriate for the three of us to proceed.

This was, at least, what I gathered from my observations. Neha and I now began a new strategy of individual conversations with family members, trying to address the root problem. In these one-to-one exchanges, every man of the house and aspiring man of the house, his chest puffed out with Punjabi machismo, pledged that he would take us right away, done deal, no problem at all. Rohan said that he would take us shortly. Downstairs Chacha, who was not yet intoxicated at this hour, claimed that he, too, could drive. Upstairs Chacha returned from his work and said that it would be only a short while longer. And yet each man, individually determined, became collectively paralyzed, lost in a flurry of petty arguments and telephone calls and logistical obstructions. There was a consensus on departure in principle, but a mysterious force that kept anyone from actually going. Those who have spent time in a big Indian household will know this force. It was the force that defined how Indian marriages traditionally operated, how Indian children were traditionally raised, how Indian choices were traditionally made. Where so many were in charge, no one was truly in charge. Where power was so diffused, no one needed—or was able—to take responsibility for the whole situation.

In those hours I began to realize that *izzat*, honor, was an aesthetic idea more than a moral idea. It was a way of carrying yourself, the bluster of claiming to go to any length for your relatives, to serve guests as much food and whiskey as they could consume, to love and be loved more than others loved and were loved. But while it purported to be fundamentally about others, it was really about oneself: about one's own marvelous virtue and the elaborate public demonstration of it. The same person who honored you by preparing meat, or inviting you to sleep in his house, had little conception of what it meant to make a promise to you, to keep his word, to empathize. Neha had forgone a train ticket and angered her boss in order to visit the *pind*. Amid all the talk of honor, this seemed to bother no one.

At this point, Upstairs Chacha was our roadblock. He had returned to the house, but still there had been no movement toward leaving, and now we learned why. He had decided, when presented with the idea of a village expedition, that he wanted to drive us himself instead of letting Rohan do so, but he had one more thing to do before he could leave. A young man in the neighborhood, in his twenties, had died some days earlier of what was euphemistically described to friends as a "heart attack," and Upstairs Chacha had to attend the funeral. Of course, everyone knew that the boy had died of an overdose of heroin, which the Dubeys casually called "smack." (The word had become an important part of the Punjabi-English lexicon as the old family values dissolved and more and more young people turned to the consolation of drugs.)

Upstairs Chacha left the house again. We waited. He returned an hour or so later, and we were warned not to touch him because he had been to a funeral. He bathed and put on his gold watch. *Parathas* were fried. (You will notice that, just when you think the mysterious family force has abated and everyone is ready to go, a meal will invariably be served.) As we gathered to eat, Upstairs on this occasion, it was revealed that there had been a change of plans. Now every single member of the household, except Purnima and the baby, wanted to go to the village. We would need a second car. There was talk of hiring a taxi. But this, too, was problematic, because it would cut the family in two and diminish the large-group road-trip gaiety that was half the motivation for going.

It would require a conversation the following day with Upstairs Chachi to deconstruct why it had taken so much effort to leave. It had to do with the special idiosyncrasies of the semi-joint family, she said. Such a family was two families when it came to small, quotidian affairs, and it was one family for the big and sad and ceremonial things in life. Neha and I had made the error of treating a visit to the family village as a small event, part of everyday life; that was our urban tick-the-box mentality. We found someone who would take us, we fixed a time with him, and we were ready to go at the appointed hour. What we did not understand was that going to the village could be interpreted, at least by some, as a big event. The native place, as I had learned in my early days in India, was the place to which any Indian, no matter where she lived, traced her identity. When we went to the village, food would be made for us, cheeks would be pinched, gifts would be given. *Izzat* would be performed in every imaginable way.

So the confusion had been over whether this was a small event, to be dealt with at the level of the small group, or a big event, requiring a consensus and a ceremonious group expedition. As time wore on, the latter vision had won out. I gathered that handling situations of precisely this kind was an essential art of living in a semi-joint family: to understand just how much self-direction, invention, initiative—how much freedom—you could get away with, while making sure never to offend the tribe, making sure to preserve the illusion that everyone sinks or swims together, that no one will be left behind.

We debated and debated, and we waited. Morning had by now bled into midafternoon. In the end, we did not use Upstairs Chacha's car at all. Although the Dubeys had chosen to live on two different floors, to pursue two different visions of the good life, something about driving in two different vehicles offended their sense of family unity. They rented a cavernous Toyota Innova van. We piled in, eight of us and a driver. Neha, Gunjan, and I were in the far back. The two couples, the Upstairses and Downstairses, sat on the bench seat in front of us, which was really designed for three. But they were Indian, and residents of a semi-joint family, and they knew what to do. The two Chachas slid back deep into the seat. The two Chachis slid their bottoms forward in the Indian way, to create space for the more important male bottoms. Normally, the extent of one's bottom-sliding obligation correlates inversely with age. But, perhaps because money was coming to outrank age as a marker of status, Upstairs Chachi pushed her younger bottom only slightly forward and Downstairs Chachi kept her older bottom so far ahead as to be almost off the seat.

We drove dozens of miles out of Ludhiana, through acres of lush paddy, until we reached the *pind*. We entered a tiny village home and sat in a circle while *parathas* were fried for us. A cow hovered a few feet behind me. Silent, smiling nods and stories were exchanged: in the Indian way, people were asked more about others not present than about themselves. Then it was decided that we should have a tour. We strolled through the fields, visited a local shrine, saw gaunt Bihari farmhands traveling across the plains. We came upon a new-age farmer whose tractor had a stereo, and some spontaneous *bhangra* dancing ensued. Then, as we prepared to leave, a battle erupted over whether village relatives should be allowed to send Gunjan home with a cash gift: it was customary for family elders to give to the young, but it was strange for villagers to send money to the city. At dusk we drove home, returned the van, and split again into our Upstairs and Downstairs worlds.

On my last day in Ludhiana, Sunil, Downstairs Chacha's youngest child, agreed to take me to his temple.

I had not been able to figure him out. He was twenty-two, tall, scrawny, handsome, with gel-spiked hair and a perpetual slouch that kept his shoulders ahead of his stomach. He wore tight short-sleeved T-shirts over baggy cargo pants. He was more modish than the rest of the family but also had a shyness and piety to him. On the night of our whiskeychickenmutton session, he had declined to join us. He kept to himself in the sitting room next door, arranging things in a cabinet where he housed his religious paraphernalia—candles, incense, framed pictures of Sai Baba.

Sunil, like so many in Ludhiana, was a Sai Baba fanatic. Shirdi Sai Baba, as he was formally known, was an influential Indian *guru* and ascetic who lived in the late nineteenth and early twentieth centuries—not to be confused with the less ascetic latter-day Sai Baba, Afro-topped and with a professed ability to conjure watches and rings out of thin air. Shirdi Sai Baba had drawn on Hindu and Islamic tenets, combining the former's stress on renunciation and self-actualization with the latter's emphasis on the universality of a single God. In recent years there had been a massive Sai Baba revival in Punjab. The entire Dubey clan had jumped on the bandwagon, though, like most devotees, without abandoning their Hindu commitments. They were, in this as in all matters, "semi-." But no one in the family was more devoted than Sunil, who had taken to spending much of his time on a construction site outside Ludhiana where a vast temple complex in Sai Baba's honor was rising. I asked him if he would take me there, curious as I was about the source of his new piety.

As soon as we got into Upstairs Chacha's Hyundai hatchback, Sunil queued up his Sai Baba CD. Sweet, *ghazal*-like songs streamed out of the speakers at full volume, lilting music with heavy Punjabi drums, cyclical and emotive. The lyrics praised Sai Baba's ecumenical nature, his equal embrace of Hindus and Muslims and Sikhs, his command to love all beings. I noticed, meanwhile, that Sunil's driving style and his spiritual inclination were in high tension. He drove, for all his gentle piety, like any other combustible Punjabi man, weaving in and out of the lanes, constantly veering into the oncoming flow of cars to circumvent a slowpoke, swerving and jerking this way and that, accelerating to within two inches of the car in front to make a point, then braking just before a collision. Inner peace seemed perhaps to be a longing more than a present-day condition for Sunil.

We arrived at the complex, which was a vast construction site in the middle of open fields. We walked into a tiny temporary shrine where Sai Baba worship was to be performed until the real temple was completed. Then we sat under a tent, with a thick haze of flies hovering above us, and Sunil told me of his journey into belief.

He had been, contrary to his appearance (but consistent with his driving style), a typically testosterone-charged Punjabi boy. He spent his evenings outside the home, eating meat with abandon, in contravention of Brahmin ways, roaming the streets with his friends and getting into fights anytime he could find one. Whenever a friend got into a dispute, Sunil could reliably be enlisted as backup. He showed me the dozen or so scars on his arm from fights, which, by the scars' appearance, were more than neighborhood tussles.

"The fights that were happening—the end would have been terrible," he said. "I thought this is how my name will get known."

Then, two years earlier, Sunil was sitting at a friend's house one day when his eyes drifted up to a photograph of Sai Baba on the wall. He claimed to have been transfixed at once. He could feel Sai Baba speaking to him through the photo, summoning him into the fold. He behaved from that moment on like a man possessed. A few days later, he arranged to have a large photograph of Sai Baba sent from Jammu and Kashmir, where this particular style of poster was printed. He started conducting a twenty-five-minute prayer session every evening. He deserted his friends from the neighborhood, changing his cell phone number to deflect their calls.

He was drawn to the fact that Sai Baba was a real *fakir*, an ascetic who walked barefoot, and not one of the new-age *gurus* who was driven around in a car, he said. This distinction between the barefooted and chauffeured *guru* was important to him, and he repeated it several times. It was part of his rebellion against Ludhiana, which was now obsessed with cars.

He had never thought highly of his own Hindu religion, which he considered weak and effete. He told me a story about going to get a haircut some years ago. The barber was Muslim, and when Sunil went to his shop one day, the barber turned down his business. It was prayer time, he said, and prayers came first. The moment stayed with him. He remembered admiring the vigor of the barber's faith, how it shut out other competing duties, how it rendered a complex world simple. "A Hindu would have put money first," he said. Muslims, he concluded, were strong in their faith and devoted to a larger cause, while in Hindus a dormancy and passivity had set in over centuries of foreign conquest and domination: a retreat into a private piety that left the outer world to others.

And that story explained his attraction to the strangely evangelical nature of the Sai Baba faith. It could seem, with the saffron-clad *guru* and the cluttered, idol-filled temple, to be merely an offshoot of Hindu tradition. But it was, in fact, a more energetic, zealous movement, adamant about bringing others around to its universal truth, much in the way of the Abrahamic faiths, and in direct contrast with the Hindu tradition, which did not promote evangelism. Sunil actively worked to spread Sai Baba devotion, going door-to-door in his neighborhood to speak to people about the *guru*. He bought posters with his own money, embellished them with glitter and framed them, and then gave them to people whom he was particularly eager to convert. It struck me as a strangely un-Hindu thing to do, with its focus on bringing change to a world believed by Hindus to be illusory, rather than on refining the self from within.

"He has surrendered to Baba," said an old man sitting next to us, listening to Sunil's narration. He fanned away the flies with a straw fan.

"For us, this is everything," added the old man's grandson,

sitting beside him. He was one of the new friends that Sunil had made.

"Without Sai Baba, it is impossible to be happy," Sunil joined in. "There will come a time when the whole world will worship him."

I asked if they genuinely believed, as Hindus did not, that there was only one path to truth—their path. And the answer was one that I did not associate with Hindus. Yes, they agreed, and the old man looked at me and told me that I, too, would believe one day. He couldn't make me, but I wouldn't be able to resist Sai Baba himself, he said, pointing to the nearby shrine.

Sunil said that he had stopped listening to all forms of music besides his Sai Baba songs. He believed that Hindus had been pulled in too many different directions before. He craved purity and completeness in his faith. He reminded me of fundamentalist Christians and Muslims I've known, with a practice very unlike the traditional Hindu's. He and his friends came every Sunday to offer *seva*, service. They washed dishes and served food to guests, which a traditional Brahmin might well dismiss as degrading and unclean.

It seemed that this was another kind of rebellion against Downstairs Chacha's world. It was a rebellion against the nothingness that Sunil saw all around him: the drifting father with beautiful but fading notions of honor and pride; the drunk, pot-bellied brother fated to turn into their father; the silent, depressive sister-in-law. It was not Upstairs Chacha's rebellion, with the dream of a house and a car and two air conditioners, and it was in many ways a rebellion against such materialism, too. But it was possible to see how the work of Sai Baba, the construction of this new temple, the door-to-door spiritual sales, the task of ordering posters and glittering them and framing them and giving them away—how all this motion and activity would have created a sense of linearity and purpose that was, in its own small way, a path out.

As the sun went down, Sunil drove me home. But when we arrived, he told me to go in without him. He said he wanted to sit alone in the car for a time longer, listening to his Sai Baba songs.

Some months passed before I returned to Ludhiana to see the Dubeys. Neha was going to pay her relatives another visit, and she asked if I would like to join her. The occasion was that a favorite cousin of hers, Deepti, Downstairs Chacha's daughter, was visiting from England.

When I entered the house, saying my hellos Downstairs first, then migrating Upstairs, where my bags inevitably had to go, they treated me like a long-lost son. There were hugs, inquiries about my fortunes since we had last met, some guilt-tripping about my failure to keep in contact. We were family now, it seemed.

Upstairs, Neha and Deepti were in the early stages of cooking pasta for the family. Deepti was slightly plump, with puffy cheeks and a pretty, unmistakably Punjabi face. Her accent, I noticed, was almost Italian in its vain attempt to average out Punjabi cadences with her new British ones. We greeted each other, and I joined in the cooking. We worked diligently, blending tomatoes, eggplants, mushrooms, and bell peppers into a sauce, and throwing in several Indian spices. But even this pandering did not distract the Upstairses from the foreignness of the resulting meal. They sat around chewing their way through our creation, but with none of the praise that Punjabis normally gave when something special has been made.

I was informed shortly after arriving that the family's focus right then was on a party being thrown the next night. It was in Deepti's honor, to celebrate her return from Ing-Land, as they pronounced it in the Punjab. Invitations had been issued, food was being ordered, and, most important, Deepti was in need of a new outfit. That evening we went shopping in the bazaar, where Deepti's taste was gradually revealed to be a fantasy of Western styles rather than a careful emulation of them: T-shirts worn under waistcoats, frills on cuffs, sequins everywhere.

I did not know at the time how contested such clothing could be. Deepti told me later that she had returned to India, for just the second time since leaving, on the condition that she be allowed to wear such things. She had even called before leaving to verify the promise. On her previous trip, she had been told to keep her loose English ways in England and had been forced to revert to Punjabi *salwar kameezes*. She seemed on our shopping trip to be exploiting her new freedom to the fullest, wearing a red T-shirt and an improbably tight vest that made her already large breasts even larger, even more prominent, even more a part of the conversation than they would otherwise have been.

It was a remarkable about-face for a woman who had grown up in the traditional way of a good Punjabi girl—in silence. Men spoke freely in Ludhiana, but I had had difficulty getting women, here as elsewhere in India, to tell an unfamiliar man their stories. I realized over time that this situation was beyond my power to rectify. Women were bred in this environment behind a virtual veil; so many were encouraged not to think, not to question, not to know themselves and certainly not to express what they knew. They were dispensers of silent smiles and of ceaseless inquiries into whether you had eaten. Anything more than that would have exceeded the permissible quantity of personhood. Some women could not even name a favorite television show, so blank had their minds become in a world with no use for their minds.

Deepti grew up in this world, playing by its rules. She was shy, barely able to put her thoughts into words. She was not allowed to leave home unsupervised—another facet of her father's idea of *izzat*. As a child, she left Ludhiana only once. She agreed unquestioningly to an arranged marriage fixed by her parents. She was miserable from the beginning. But she had grown up and caught wind of the new ideas then spreading, and something inside her revolted—just as so many Indians were revolting in so many disparate ways. Deepti did what once seemed unthinkable: she divorced the man, and she announced to her family that she was moving to England to work and study and make a life of her own. She had wanted to leave Ludhiana since childhood.

She spoke no English when she moved to England, and she was innocent like a girl. She was lucky to be hired as a beauty therapist at a boutique in London within days of arriving. She enrolled, meanwhile, in a part-time MBA course. She lived at first with Neha's family; when the stress of the crowd got to her again, she moved into her own place, a cheap and dingy room in a larger apartment whose other tenants were "druggists," as she called them, meaning drug dealers. In England she learned to be hard, she said. At first, she used to cry for every little slight at work, every client poached from her by a rival stylist. She gradually began to stand up for herself and to fight back. She became less reverential of seniority and more capable of disagreement. "I always used to say 'yes' to people," she said. "I have learned over there to say 'no,' too."

She had not had a close male friend in Ludhiana. The only men she was allowed to socialize with were within her family. In England, she decided to venture as far away from that past as possible: she not only found a boyfriend and not only moved in with him, but also managed to find one who was a Pakistani Muslim. Her parents did not know, and it was assumed that they would go into simultaneous cardiac arrest if they ever found out. She liked Saif because he was honest with her. When their female flatmate came to him one day wrapped in a bath towel and sought to kiss him, he immediately called Deepti and told her. He was up front about having been intimate with women before Deepti. She didn't love him, she said, but she liked him, and she was lonely and wanted someone to share her days with.

It felt strange to her to be home again. She had left this clois-tered world and acquired new visions. But her parents and her brother Rohan saw her as they had always seen her. They kept trying to shove her back into her hole. Rohan was harassing her, telling her which male former classmates could come to the party and which couldn't. Think about our reputation, he said; there was *izzat* to bear in mind.

"I always thought this world is not for me," Deepti told me one day. "I cannot live here."

The party for Deepti was to be in a private room on the second floor of a restaurant called Basant. The "pure veg" snacks and dinner and the nonalcoholic drinks for the two dozen guests, along with the DJ, had come to 2,700 rupees, less than $60. Deepti instructed the DJ to play only Punjabi songs; even Bollywood music, Indian but not of this particular region, would inspire no one, she feared. The songs throbbed with that gypsy sound, nostalgic and exuberant at the same time, major- and minor-toned, the folk music of farmers spruced up now with electronic hip-hop beats but with a certain lyrical grounding in the farms all the same.

The party was a segregated affair, with two circles of dancing, one of women and one of men. The men seemed more than shy; they appeared to be entirely incapable of contemplating what it would involve to dance with a woman who was not their mother. It seemed likely that they would follow the traditional pattern of having no contact with a woman until the day when they would gain the legal right to force themselves on one. As one often observed at large gatherings of Indian males, they tended to make lusty eyes at one another instead. A man named Hemant, not long after being introduced to me for the first time, dragged me across the room and into the male dancing circle. He stood before me and began to pump his hips and thrust his hands into the air, with every expectation that I do the same, which very, very tepidly I did.

Hemant would later reassure me about his intentions by sending Deepti this late-night text message: "U r so sweet. U look gorgeous. U should try Hollywood for modelling. U will be next generation superstar."

In this way, too, Deepti was finding it hard to be home. These men were her age, had been her peers, but they now seemed to her to be boys. They had perfectly decent, perfectly boring small-town jobs—managing a supermarket, working in a bank. They wouldn't dance with her, even when she tried on occasion to merge the circles. They didn't drink. They were coy and maladroit. When one of these men liked a woman but was rejected, he would invariably invent rumors about her purity, so that no one else would want to have her.

In some ways, they seemed to her to be regressing. The boys she grew up with, like the men in her family, were finding more and more solace in religion. One of them tied a woman's scarf on the headrest of the front passenger seat of his car, to pay tribute to the goddess Mata Rani. When driving with others, he would insist on keeping the seat empty for the goddess, asking friends to sit in the back. The ringtones on her friends' cell phones were often devotional songs now. They were weak and fearful and dull. It was Deepti who had left them behind, but she was so far outnumbered by the stagnant that she felt left behind in her own way, with no one from her former world able to understand her new one.

Her first trip home a few years earlier had unfolded differently. She had jumped right back into her old life. When someone needed tea, her radar picked up the need immediately, and she dashed into the kitchen. When male school friends called, she told them that she could not meet. She still knew how to be the good Punjabi daughter, and she was happy to play the role. This time, she had set a new tone by wearing whatever she liked, and the rest had followed from there. No one asked her to make tea anymore. She met her friends at will. She had thrown a party and danced and let herself go.

Downstairs, they seemed to feel Deepti slipping out of their hands. Rohan was unable to bear the idea of a woman less docile and dutiful than his own silent wife, and Deepti's return had made him tense and resentful. Downstairs Chacha, who was especially fond of his daughter, found that he was getting less and less time with her. Feeling that she was pulling away, he pulled away, too.

He kept to himself during most of her visit, spending many evenings drinking whiskey alone on his bed and sobbing.

Late one night, as I prepared to go to bed, a blaring female scream ripped through the house. Several people rushed Downstairs to the site of the scream to see what had happened. Rohan and Sunil had gotten into an argument, which was not typical of Sunil but very typical of Rohan. Things had escalated, and Rohan had smashed his fist into a mirror and shattered it. He was drunk, and it was his wife, clutching their baby, who had screamed in fear, then pulled her husband away from the violence that she feared was looming.

After some minutes, the crisis was over, and everyone started to return to their beds. Upstairs Chacha and Neha made their way toward the stairs. And with them was Deepti, the daughter of Downstairs Chacha. She had slept Downstairs on her first visit, but this time around she had wordlessly changed her allegiance. She slept Upstairs now, ate Upstairs, treated Upstairs Chacha and his wife like her own parents. It was as if she had sensed which way history was moving and had wanted to place herself on the right side.

Deepti climbed the stairs and tucked herself into bed and left the world Downstairs to drift as best it could into the new country being made.

Midnight

What are Papa and I doing here?"

These words, instant-messaged by my mother from the outskirts of Washington, D.C., whizzed through the deep ocean cables and came to me in the village where I was living, in the country that she left. I had departed Bombay for a time to live in a tiny hamlet called Verla in the former Portuguese colony of Goa. Jungle surrounded the small studio that I had rented; the air had that thick, humid Indian quality that my mother has pined for since the day she took off from Bombay. My sister, Rukmini, who lived in California at the time, had recently announced that she was considering a work opportunity in India; now it seemed that India, my mother's India, the place from which she had only reluctantly gone, was enticing both of her children. India was the talk of the world and was where the magazines declared the future to be, leaping from history and making itself new.

If the whole world was descending on India, then what was she doing in America?

It is a milestone in any nation's life when to leave becomes a choice, not a necessity. India was now passing that marker, and how blessed to live in a land you needn't quit to become your fullest possible self. But for those already gone, who left when leaving could still feel necessary, the turning that I had witnessed in India brought new feelings of displacement—the loss not so much of place as of time, the inevitable wondering about what might have been had they remained.

My mother sometimes wondered aloud about going back home. Now that it was possible to make a living there, now that it stood at the edge of things, she seemed to feel more acutely the losses she had borne: of family connections, community, the confidence of being among her own tribe. One can only speculate as to how things would have turned out had the ocean of change come to India a generation earlier. But because it came between my parents' generation and mine, the premise of our family history was gradually pulled out from beneath us. We were American citizens now, my family, and proudly so. But we had to accept that we were Americans because of a choice prompted by truths that history had undone.

For many in my parents' generation, it was too late to change their minds. A new India could only be marveled at from afar and on occasional visits: there were now mortgages taken, friendships made, careers built in other places. And they, too, had changed. India, however new, was still more corrupt, more bureaucratic, more interfering than they were accustomed to. So they lived with a nebulous sense of place, unable to claim one country or another as fully their own. But we, their children, our lives still forming, had greater possibilities to reimagine our belonging. Thousands of India's stepchildren felt its change of spirit as I had, felt the gravitational force of condensed hope. And we came.

India was confounding at first. But it was plain to those who returned that we lived in new times, that Indianness was no longer something better to deny. We tried to reinvent ourselves, as our parents had, but in reverse. Some of us studied Hindi; others learned yoga. Some visited the Ganges to find themselves; others tried days-long Vipassana meditations. Many who shunned Indian clothes in their youth began wearing *kurtas* and *chappals*, *saris* and *churidars*. There was, of course, a sad reality in this: we had waited for our heritage to become cool to the world before we were willing to drape its colors and textures on our own backs.

We learned how to make friends in India, and that it requires befriending families. We learned to love: men found fondness for the elusive Indian woman; women surprised themselves in succumbing to chauvinistic, mother-spoiled men. We forged dual-use accents: we spoke in foreign accents by default, but when it came to arguing with accountants or ordering takeout kebabs we went singsong Indian. We gravitated to work specially suited to us, becoming part of a new worldwide fusion class: people positioned to mediate among the multiple societies that claim them. We built boutiques that fuse Indian fabrics with Western cuts, founded companies that trained Indians to work in Western companies, became dealmakers in investment firms that spoke equally to Wall Street and Dalal Street, mixed albums that combined throbbing *tabla* with Western melodies.

Our parents' generation still participated in India from afar. They sent money, advised charities, guided hedge-fund dollars into the Bombay Stock Exchange, attended émigré conferences. But many were too implicated in India to return: to reverse their journey threatened somehow to invalidate the years spent away. Our generation, bearing less of the past's baggage, was freer to embrace the India now coming. I had grown up defining myself by the soil under my feet, not by the blood in my veins. The soil I shared with everyone else; the blood made me unbearably different. Before I loved India, I loathed it. But the more India called to me, the more that feeling began to seem like a relic from a buried past.

And India now called not only to us, its far-scattered seeds. Its sharpest call was to its own, to those who had remained and may once have felt outsmarted by those who left. It summoned them now to seize hold of their destinies. And so they were becoming the unlikely, long-lost cousins of my parents in America: restless, ambitious, with dreams vivid only to themselves. In leaving India, my parents had beaten the odds in a bad system. What had changed since they left was a systemic lifting of the odds for those who stayed. From languorous villages to pulsating cities, Indians were making difficult new choices, rising to the occasion of history, coming into their own in a thousand ways. And it was addictive, this improbable rush of hope, these many answers of the call.

I will never be able to relay the fullness of what it was to live in India in that dawn. The world turns slowly; nations, heroes, visions of regeneration come and go. To history we are ever chained, and the new is seldom as new as it seems. But there are moments, sprinkled stingily among the centuries, when fate breaks, when souls open, when the shoreline of the past falls irretrievably into the distance. Nehru spoke eloquently in that midnight in 1947 of the instant when "the soul of a nation, long suppressed, finds utterance." But it took two more generations to bring utterance not just to that collective soul but also to the millions of souls within, one by one by one.

That idea first came to me in the dusty lanes of Umred. It came in meeting Ravindra and in hearing in his voice not just ambition, not just hope, but also a sublime kind of freedom: a freedom from the definitions of the past, of his tribe, of rank; a freedom to make himself new. And I wondered how he judged the freedom that he had found in relation to the freedom that Gandhi and Nehru had won in 1947. For the world, and for many well-born Indians, those men were paramount heroes: they had given India voice; they had ushered an improbable country—vast, fractured, argumentative—into being. But farther away from the leading cities, that independence seemed to matter less. In places such as Umred, the British had been a faint presence; the Indians, once they took over, improved little. The landlords, the humiliations, the smallness of life—it all lived on. What was coming to India now was a sense of awakening, much as it had in 1947. But this time it felt less theoretical; this time it felt like another kind of independence—an independence of the soul, not just of the nation.

"If these kinds of things are happening and continue to happen in the future, India will become a real independent country," Ravindra said when I put the idea to him one day.

"Today, we are independent, no problem," he went on. "We do not have anybody's kingdom over us. But still we are not that much free; we are not living a completely free life today. We need financial freedom, which we do not have now. So when young people come ahead, the new generation will come ahead, and they will start to live in the way we're talking about, India will really become independent, and we will really become a superpower. We will not depend on anybody else. We will live the life of our own dreams."

To live the life of one's own dreams: this, then, was a second independence for Ravindra, the coming of a new midnight. That first midnight had expelled an empire, had resolved the political question of whether Indians could govern themselves, had shown the world, in the person of Gandhi, a specially Indian way of melting oppression. And yet so much of the Indian stasis—so much of what challenged the life that Ravindra sought—was not of British provenance and would not just leave when the colonizers sailed away. The family relations of guilt, the never-questioned rituals, the intricate taxonomy of castes and sub-subcastes, the rural cruelty, the poverty—these facts would require their own thousand Gandhis: a diffuse army of activists and entrepreneurs and philosophers and farmers, toiling across the land, cutting these other fetters, stretching the Indian idea of the possible, making it more than lyrical to speak of a life of one's dreams.

That first midnight had anchored Indians in place. They had lived for so long with smaller allegiances—to the tribe, the caste, the faith. Gandhi, returned from South Africa, and Nehru, returned from Britain, saw a wholeness in India that many Indians did not see for themselves, and through the force of their actions they made that wholeness a reality. This second midnight was, by contrast, about the dissolution of place, about returning to another kind of fragmentation. It was a revolution of quiet refusals to know one's place—geographic place, place in time, place in the tribe. It celebrated the lightness of being without roots, the possibility of reinvention, the dignity of anonymity. It brought a kind of independence that 1947 had not brought: that of not depending on others for the discovery of what you might become.

It could be argued that these ideas were alien intrusions, colonial in their own way. But the reality was that this vision of the self had hovered in India in the decades leading to independence, though it had never quite been realized. In their various ways, Gandhi, the first Hindu nationalists, Swami Vivekananda, the poet Rabindranath Tagore, and others all spoke of a link between a society strong on the outside and a society of strong and whole selves, free not only from their British masters but also from the many bindings within.

"Not the English; it is we who are responsible for all our degradation," Vivekananda had said. "Our aristocratic ancestors went on treading the common masses of our country underfoot till they became helpless, till under this torment the poor, poor people nearly forgot that they were human beings. They have been compelled to be merely hewers of wood and drawers of water for centuries, so that they are made to believe that they are born as slaves."

And Tagore, in 1911, extolled what we think to be the modern idea of individuality: "It is only when he comes to feel the glory of his individuality that man tries to reach greatness even though it means suffering. And it is only when they reach greatness that union among men becomes a reality. Union in poverty, union in subjection, union in compulsion—all these are no more than patched-up unions." The individuality of which he wrote inevitably brought separateness and fragmentation, he conceded. But these were to be embraced: "There are no distinctions amongst sleeping men; but as soon as they wake up the identity of each shows itself in various ways. All development means the unfolding of diversity in unity. There is no diversity in the seed. In the bud all the petals are closely fused into one; it is only when they are differentiated from each other that the bud unfolds into a flower. The flower reaches fulfillment only when each of the petals fulfils itself in a different direction in a distinctive way."

It was this vision, long deferred, that had now found a place in India. And it was the modern vision of the human condition: not only of Ravindra's India but of all those who believed in the making of themselves, who were willing to bear the lonely suffering to which Tagore referred in order to gain the glory of selfhood and the possibility of greatness.

This was the bargain that bound my family's story in America to the stories of so many Indians I had encountered. I grew up in homes with few traces of our ancestors, except for some jewelry and silverware and shawls and such. There were no crests, no artifacts, no heirloom furniture, no pictures on the wall of anyone older than my grandparents, no maps of our homeland, no uniforms of wars in which our forebears had fought, no reminders of their triumphs and defeats—no living embodiment of being more than what we were there and then. We lived in houses purchased on the open market, not inherited from ancestors. We were taught values mixed in my parents' head, drawn from the many cultural wells around us. And this placelessness had become, over the course of my lifetime, the way of the world; in India it had upended the old certainties.

Ravindra put it well. "Instead of you should know your place," he told me, "you have to imagine your place. That's what I believe."

In the ninth grade, when he still lived in Bhiwapur, Ravindra was lying outdoors one night when he stared up and noticed for the first time a plane slicing through the sky. What extraordinary freedom it was: he imagined the passengers, miles above the ground, unfastened to their native places, going in their different ways, with projects to complete and people to meet. How different their lives were from his. Ravindra knew that if he walked the wrong way for five minutes, he might have gone too far, might have entered a *mohalla* not his own, might have invited a shouted lesson about his place. When you fly, the earth can seem so small, but in Bhiwapur, on the ground, it could seem unconquerably vast. Ravindra remembered thinking to himself, "Some day will be there when I will be in this kind of flight."

It took about as many years as he had lived at that time for the vision to take flesh. But in the end it had. His flight to Hong Kong, where he would manage the Indian roller-skating team, was the first of his life. A man of gadgets now, he made sure to document this historic occasion. He recorded long stretches of video from their departure from India to their stopover in Singapore to their arrival in Hong Kong. He had given me the clips on my last visit to Umred. Some months later I watched them, in the hope of seeing how Ravindra had first confronted the outside world.

I suppose that I expected him to be his usual social self, telling stories, inspiring, motivating. But in the clips he was utterly silent as the others talked and joked. After takeoff, he filmed nothing of the plane's interior life, nothing of the colleagues beside him. He kept the camera trained to the window and, through it, to the passing green farmland from which he had once looked up in aspiration. He panned back and forth from the wing to the loose weave of clouds to the ground below. He had come a long way. He would be in the air only for some hours, but life for him now contained all the motive possibility of the airplane. His view of the world, whether airborne or not, was now the view of the flying man, not of the place-bound village boy.

At the end of my third visit to Umred, a short time after he had returned from Hong Kong, I had asked Ravindra if we could visit Bhiwapur and the house in which he grew up. We had spoken of making the hour's journey before, when his parents still lived there, but we had never gone. Now they had moved to Umred to live with him, and the house was occupied by some of their relatives. He agreed to take me.

We passed through a warren of lanes too narrow for the small hatchback car and reached the house, which was as Ravindra had described it: a house for landless laborers, with no land for tilling, an outdoor latrine, a small well in front. We entered the first room, and I was invited to sit on a *charpoy*. Images of Hindu gods were everywhere. The calendar on the wall was two years out of date. But there was a new phone in the house. Ravindra picked it up curiously and asked his cousin if it worked. The cousin, though no more than six, already knew enough about the world, about the requirement that people like them pay in advance for calls, to say, "There's no money on it."

Badminton rackets, sweaters, and a lone jacket hung near the front door, above an abandoned tape deck whose metallic surface had browned over the years. The wooden ceiling beams were inscribed with the birth and death dates of ancestors. The sitting area led into a dark, narrow corridor, which led in turn into a cramped kitchen. The room was lit by two bulbs, hanging on thin wires from the ceiling. A collection of pans stood in one corner, next to a small wood-fire stove. There was an ornate Hindu shrine in his mother's cooking space, which had perhaps soothed her hours.

The house fascinated me. I found my mind seeking to put Ravindra back in this setting, to ask how he had risen from this. I peppered him with questions about the house and the past. And for the first time, he grew impatient. With a jocular air on the surface and irritation simmering underneath, he pressed to leave. There was nothing to see here, he said many times; it was only a village house. I had traced the arc of his life, but in reverse: he began in a *mohalla* in Bhiwapur, and had fought to reach Umred, then Nagpur, then Bombay, and, through it, the outer world. I was born in that outer world and had come to Bombay, then

Nagpur, then Umred, and, finally, Bhiwapur. Now, standing in his old house, asking my questions, I was challenging the premise of Ravindra's life: that destiny is in the mind, that the past can be escaped, that you must imagine, not know, your place.

As a boy, he never imagined that he would leave Bhiwapur. My parents never imagined that they would leave India. I never imagined that I would leave America to return to what had become another India. But history bends and swerves and sometimes swivels fully around. Visions of new terrain and new beginnings possessed us in our different ways. We imagined and reimagined our places. And so I sensed when returning to India that I was not undoing my parents' journey, but in some way fulfilling it. Like them, I was chasing the frontier of the future. Which just happened, in my case, to be the frontier of my own past.

ACKNOWLEDGMENTS

There are two ways to imagine the making of a book. The first pictures a solitary figure, hunched over his desk, silencing all other voices so that his own might speak: the writer as a monk with words. The second sees writing as a social act: social because the writer has no words without everything written before, without the people who catalyze his ideas, without the stories that others tell him, without the roots that give him his own story. There is some truth in the first vision; many days of the past many years were spent in that way. But if these years taught me anything, it is that a book cannot be written alone.

I came to Bombay knowing almost nobody and left with a family. So many ideas in this work were born not in interviews I did or books I read but in late-night conversations with my friends. We found ourselves in a dizzying Indian moment, and together we sought to understand it: Prashant Agrawal, Shweta Bagai, Sheetal Baliga, Beenu Bawa, Anu Duggal, Scott Eells, Nasha Fitter, Fabio Fonseca, Amar Goel, Komal Goel, Rohan Gopaldas, Christie Johnston, Aurélie Khattau, Nikhil Khattau, Haani Khorakiwala, Priya Kishore, Anjalee Kohli, Ravi Krishnan, Anshuma Lal, Kunal

Mehta, Salma Merchant, Nitin Nayar, Shuchi Pandya, Deepak Rajegowda, Jérôme Rouch-Sirech, Bandana Tewari, Divya Thakur, Raj Yerasi.

Urmila Jain made sure that I had food, a cell phone, and a hug when I first touched down. The endlessly creative Morarji family provided me with beautiful spaces for writing, first in Bombay and then in Goa, where I wrote most of this book in the tree house of my gracious friends Kim Morarji and Di Cooper. Raul Rai and Simran Lal generously shared their sun-soaked Bombay apartment with me. The Deora family—Milind, Mukul, Hema, and Murli—helped me to get my bearings when I began as a correspondent and made sure that I met everyone in town.

Others helped me on my journey in ways too various to count: Gautam Adhikari, Ravi Agarwal, Luis Ernesto Araujo, Tom Ashbrook, K.B., Dominic Barton, Eric Bellman, Mahesh Bhatt, Alain de Botton, Elizabeth Bowie, Jennifer Brea, Daniela Cammack, Fiona Caulfield, Sudeep Chakravarti, Brahma Chellaney, Deepak Chopra, Stephen Cohen, Adam Cooper, Shobhaa Dé, Santosh Desai, Meenal Devani, Siddharth Dube, Andrea Echavarria, Antonio E'Costa, A.G., M.G., Adheet Gogate, David Grewal, Ramachandra Guha, Pooja Haldea, Dan Honig, Marline Israel, Nick Israel, Narendra Jadhav, Yogesh Kamdar, Sandeep Kapila, Kaavya Kasturirangan, Tarun Khanna, Naina Lal Kidwai, Rashid Kidwai, Shambhu Kumaran, Jhumpa Lahiri, Ellis Levine, Hillel Levine, Christopher Lydon, Kishore Mahbubani, David Malone, David McCraw, Jamal Mecklai, Pravina Mecklai, Sonny Mehta, Tanya Mendonsa, C. Raja Mohan, Tory Newmyer, Nandan Nilekani, Joe Nocera, Anuvab Pal, Ranjit Pandit, the Pandyas, Priyanka Pathak, Nandini Piramal and the Piramal family, Jairam Ramesh, Arundhati Roy, Michael Rubenstein, Dipti Salgaocar, Raj Salgaocar, Chiki Sarkar, Rajiv Sawhney, Jonathan Segal, Suhel Seth, Siddharth Dhanvant Shanghvi, Jayant Sinha, Ranu Sinha, Sree Sreenivasan, Ramesh Srinivasan, Chiara Superti, Ekta Thakur, Rajesh Thind, Ashish Tuteja, Loulou Van Damme, Ashutosh Varshney, Karishma

Vaswani, Ravi Venkatesan, Ireena Vittal, the Wagles, Omar Wasow, Nora Young.

It would be most un-Indian not to honor my *gurus*, my teachers. At Sidwell Friends, Susan Banker, Dan Entwisle, Bryan Garman, Mark Reford, and Neal Tonken nourished an early romance with ideas and words. At the University of Michigan, Carl Cohen transcended the role of professor to become a friend and infected me with his love of creative argument. Mills Thornton taught me that history is nothing but the story of colliding perceptions. And Theodore Zeldin, more than any other teacher, made me a writer: after I read *An Intimate History of Humanity* and came to know him, it became clear to me that my life's work would be to study other people. In India, Sudhir Kakar was my teacher first through books and then through friendship with him and his wife, Katha; few people think as searchingly about the character of modern India. At Harvard, Michael Sandel and Henry Louis Gates Jr. are thinkers who live to teach, and they make learning a thrill. Amartya Sen, who doesn't just construct ideas about helping others but lives those ideas every day, has been a constant guide and friend, reading parts of the book, sharing long meals, and ever egging me on.

It is no small favor to read a friend's manuscript in full, and so I will probably be mowing some lawns for a long time to come. I was indulged in this regard by my parents, my sister, and my Priya, about whom more later, but also by the wonderful John Blaxall, Deepa Narayan, and Jennifer Page. They edited, corrected, and suggested, and they made the work immeasurably better. Of course, I bear responsibility for the mistakes that remain.

I am deeply indebted to those who opened their lives to me for this book. It is an act of generosity that words cannot repay. In some cases, for obvious reasons, I changed the names and circumstances of particular people. Their stories, though, are entirely true. And a word on language: in certain cases, like Ravindra's, the subject speaks in the hybrid dialect of Hinglish. I have generally printed the words exactly as they were uttered in order to preserve voice, sometimes at clarity's expense. But on select occasions, where a word or phrase made a quotation hard to understand, I have translated a bit, nudging the language a little away from the Hindi pole of the Hinglish spectrum and toward the English end.

I have had extraordinary colleagues at *The New York Times* and the *International Herald Tribune*. Jill Abramson started me in journalism as a seventeen-year-old intern at the *Times*. On my first day, she mentioned casually that I should write articles, not just hang around; I haven't stopped since. Her support has made this path possible. At the *Trib*, Walter Wells took a risk on me that I'll never forget. Len Apcar, Jeanne Moore, and Alison Smale have edited me with wisdom, curiosity, and grace; they have made me a better writer week by week. My *Times* editors Marc Charney, Dave Smith, and Sam Tanenhaus are true fellow travelers, with a gift not just for working with what I have written but also for coaching and teaching and making me reach higher. I am indebted as well to Keith Bradsher, Susan Chira, Roger Cohen, Amelia Gentleman, Larry Ingrassia, Philip McClellan, Tim O'Brien, Jane Perlez, Somini Sengupta, Patrick Smith, Nick Stout, Heather Timmons, and Sheryl WuDunn.

Book writing takes some hand-holding, and I found myself surrounded by hands. Shashi Tharoor lent early enthusiasm and introduced me to my agent, Steve Wasserman, who has book pulp in his veins. We first met when this was a book about democracy, and he has seen it through its turns with patience and good cheer. He steered me to Paul Golob at Times Books, who has been a careful editor and generous cultivator of a young writer. I am also grateful to Alex Ward at the *Times* and to the marketing and publicity team at Henry Holt and Company. Michelle Daniel was a very meticulous and extra-mile-going copy editor. Simran Preet Gill and Sneha Singh, in Bombay, have served as skillful research assistants. And from the beginning to the end, Vrinda Condillac has been the fairy godmother of this book. She refined my thoughts, told me when to scrap them, and edited the resulting work with her flair for narrative energy.

Like so many Indians today, this book is bound to no one place. It was written in Bombay, Goa, Maryland, Massachusetts, and Colombia. In this new world, it is people, not places, that anchor you. I am blessed with my anchors. Priya is the only person in the world who has heard most of this book out loud. She wanted the words to sing, and so she listened to *India Calling* even before she read it, edited it, told me where to rewrite it, gave me new paths forward. She knows the stories deep within me, even when I forget, and inspires me to be a better writer and a better man. And then there are my oldest anchors: my Nanu and Nani, my Ammamma and late Thatha, my cousins and uncles and aunts, who make me feel proud to be Indian, who have taught me what it means to possess a past. And Mama and Papa and Rukmini: this one is for you. What words are there? You have given me life, and you give it again and again, through the darkness and the light. You are my music. Without you, I would not be.

INDEX

accents, 83, 124, 247
  dual-use, 247
Aden, 92–93
advertising, 47, 84–85, 131, 132, 134
agriculture, 214
  cooperative, 155
Ahmedabad, 10–12
air-conditioning, 203, 213
airlines and airports, 4, 130–32, 252
Aiyar, Swaminathan, 151
  "Swaminomics," 151
alcohol, 5, 175, 197, 200, 207–9, 211, 216, 217, 219, 228, 229, 231
All India Radio, 16
aloo parathas, 4
Ambani, Anil, 101
Ambani, Dhirubhai, 87, 91–96, 100–101, 111
Ambani, Mukesh, 93, 95–117, 120, 145, 154, 194
ambition, 38–76, 120, 204, 248

Ammamma, 123–24, 161–65, 167, 185
Amsterdam, 16
Andhra Pradesh, 138, 139
Anglophiles, 77–87, 103, 114, 115
anti-imperialism, 123
arranged marriage, 17, 63, 70, 147, 161–65, 167, 168, 176, 190–91, 193–94, 216, 240
  Internet, 176
Assam, 90
astrology, 162
Australia, 219, 220, 221
automobiles, 57, 102, 125, 128, 230, 233
  industry, 23–24, 203
  taxis, 26, 44–45, 46, 131–32, 232

Bachchan, Amitabh, 28
baingan ka bharta, 3
Bakhtavar, 20
Bandra Family Court, 186–92, 196, 198

ABOUT THE AUTHOR

ANAND GIRIDHARADAS writes the "Currents" column for
the *International Herald Tribune* and *The New York Times*
online. A native of Cleveland, Ohio, and a graduate of the
University of Michigan, he worked in Bombay as a management consultant until 2005, when he began reporting
from that city for the *Herald Tribune* and the *Times*. He
now lives in Cambridge, Massachusetts.

To learn more and to join an online conversation, visit the
author's Web site at http://anand.ly.